Options for Britain II
Cross Cutting Policy Issues
Changes and Challenges

WILEY-BLACKWELL

Options for Britain II

Cross Cutting Policy Issues – Changes and Challenges

Edited by
Varun Uberoi
Adam Coutts
Ian McLean
David Halpern

Wiley-Blackwell
In association with *The Political Quarterly*

This edition first published 2010

© 2008 The Political Quarterly Publishing Co. Ltd except for editorial material
Chapters © 2008 by the chapter author

Blackwell Publishing was acquired by John Wiley & Sons in February 2007. Blackwell's publishing programme has been merged with Wiley's global Scientific, Technical and Medical business to form Wiley-Blackwell.

Registered Office
John Wiley & Sons Ltd, The Atrium, Southern Gate, Chichester, West Sussex, PO19 8SQ, United Kingdom

Editorial Offices
350 Main Street, Malden, MA 02148-5020, USA
9600 Garsington Road, Oxford, OX4 2DQ, UK
The Atrium, Southern Gate, Chichester, West Sussex, PO19 8SQ, UK

For details of our global editorial offices, for customer services, and for information about how to apply for permission to reuse the copyright material in this book please see our website at www.wiley.com/wiley-blackwell.

The rights of Varun Uberoi, Adam Coutts, Ian McLean and David Halpern to be identified as the authors of the editorial material in this work has been asserted in accordance with the Copyright, Designs and Patents Act 1988.

Wiley also publishes its books in a variety of electronic formats. Some content that appears in print may not be available in electronic books.

Designations used by companies to distinguish their products are often claimed as trademarks. All brand names and product names used in this book are trade names, service marks, trademarks or registered trademarks of their respective owners. The publisher is not associated with any product or vendor mentioned in this book. This publication is designed to provide accurate and authoritative information in regard to the subject matter covered. It is sold on the understanding that the publisher is not engaged in rendering professional services. If professional advice or other expert assistance is required, the services of a competent professional should be sought.

Library of Congress Cataloging-in-Publication Data
Library of Congress Cataloging-in-Publication Data is available for this work.

ISBN 978-1-4443-3395-4

A catalogue record for this book is available from the British Library.

Set in 10.5/12pt Palatino by Anne Joshua & Associates, Oxford
Printed in the UK by the Charlesworth Group

Contents

Notes on Contributors

Fran Bennett is Senior Research Fellow at the Department of Social Policy and Social Work and also works in a self-employed capacity on social policy issues, especially gender, social security and poverty.

Jo Blanden is a lecturer in the Economics Department at the University of Surrey and a Research Associate in the Education and Skills Programme of the Centre for Economic Performance, London School of Economics.

Adam Coutts is Consultant at the Department of Politics and International Relations, University of Oxford.

Patrick Diamond is Group Director, Strategy at the Equality and Human Rights Commission. He writes here in a personal capacity.

Matthew Flinders is Professor of Parliamentary Government and Governance at the University of Sheffield.

Scott L Greer is Assistant Professor of Health Management and Policy at the University of Michigan School of Public Health and Senior Research Fellow at LSE Health.

David Halpern is Director of Research, Institute for Government.

Christopher Hood is Gladstone Professor of Government and a Fellow of All Souls College.

Alan Hughes is Director of the Centre for Business Research and Margaret Thatcher Professor of Enterprise Studies at the Judge Business School Cambridge.

Paul Johnson is Research Fellow, Institute for Fiscal Studies.

Peter Kenway is director of the New Policy Institute, an independent London-based think tank.

Roger Liddle is Vice Chair of the progressive international think tank Policy Network and was formerly adviser on European policy to Tony Blair, UK Prime Minister and then José Manuel Barroso, President of the European Commission.

Helen Margetts is Professor of Society and the Internet in the Oxford Internet Institute, University of Oxford and Professorial Fellow at Mansfield College, University of Oxford.

Iain McLean is Professor of Politics at the Department of Politics and International Relations, University of Oxford.

Shamit Saggar is Professor of Political Science: University of Sussex, Visiting Professor of Public Policy: University of Toronto; and former Senior Policy Advisor: Prime Minister's Strategy Unit, Cabinet Office.

Varun Uberoi is Post Doctoral Research Fellow at the Department of Politics and International Relations, University of Oxford.

Michael Woolcock is Professor of Social Science and Development Policy, and Research Director of the Brooks World Poverty Institute, at the University of Manchester.

Introduction

ADAM COUTTS and VARUN UBEROI

In 1993 a group of academics and policy experts gathered at Nuffield College Oxford for a conference on British public policy. The government had been in power since 1979, despite its electoral victory in 1992 it was far from popular and the economic climate was bleak. It was an opportune moment for an independent assessment of how the government had done, what the major challenges in a range of policy areas were and what options existed to address them. This assessment culminated in *Options For Britain—A Strategic Policy Review* (Halpern et al., 1996) whose authors were all experts in individual policy areas. Examining thirteen of the most prominent areas of policy, *Options* provided one of the most thorough overviews of social, economic and constitutional policy in the 1990s and was influential amongst policy-makers. Indeed, whilst some of the original *Options* editorial team stayed in academia, some went on to serve in No. 10 and much of what was discussed in *Options* became accepted wisdom.

By 2005, some of the original *Options* team began to think about repeating the process partly because the government and its opposition would always struggle to give an impartial account of the government's record. A non-partisan assessment of what had happened, what had worked, what challenges remain and how they might be addressed was seen as crucial to informing democratic debate. However, as time went by there was also a pervasive sense of déjà vu. The government had been in power for a protracted period, its opinion poll ratings were low and the economic downturn that we are now living through began to emerge. The time once again was ripe for an independent assessment of how the government had done in a range of policy areas, what the current challenges are, and what options the current or an incoming government might have to tackle them. Funded by the ESRC, Gatsby, the Fell Fund and Nuffield College, an editorial team assembled in late 2007, some of whom led the original *Options* process and some of whom were new. The result is *Options for a New Britain* (Uberoi et al., 2009) which reviews fifteen different policy areas. Like its previous incarnation, the volume is unusually broad with chapters on traditional areas of policy like health, crime, housing and education. However, there are also chapters on policy areas that underpin public policy as a whole such as the economy and the constitution as well as new areas of policy like climate change and extremism.

Yet despite this breadth there was a feeling amongst the editors that more attention should be paid to cross-cutting issues and, of course, all, or at least most, areas of policy are cross-cutting to some extent. Improving public health, after all, is related to various issues of inequality (Appelby and

Published by Blackwell Publishing Ltd, 9600 Garsington Road, Oxford OX4 2DQ, UK and 350 Main Street, Malden, MA 02148, USA

Coutts, 2009) and reducing some types of crime necessitates social inclusion strategies (Hough and Roberts, 2009). Many areas of policy seem then to cut across one another, yet some issues are in their very nature cross-cutting, such as measuring public sector performance, our approach to the EU, regulation and so on. Such issues are also less frequently discussed. Yet examining them is necessary to gain a clear understanding of how public policy has developed under New Labour, and thus that is what we will do in this special issue.

In light of the current necessity to reduce public service spending, we begin with Christopher Hood's analysis of how to measure and manage public service performance. He traces the development of performance measurement and 'management by numbers' which featured notably in the changing politics of public services in Britain after 1997. Given that the next few years may be dominated by fiscal squeeze and or an ideological mood stressing the need for lower taxes and a smaller state, Hood proposes there may be corresponding pressure for fewer performance indicators (PIs), and particular pressure on those PIs that are the most expensive to collect, such as the university RAE ratings. He notes that the emphasis of PIs would need to move towards input-reduction targets, with increased weight on productivity indicators. After all, given that a number of empirical studies have found that increasing resources does not necessarily improve service outcomes, it may be that input reductions need not necessarily be at the expense of service quality or quantity.

From the details of measuring public sector performance we move to Matthew Flinder's discussion of the role of the state. The state has historically been viewed in a narrow way, as either the source of many problems or as the answer to them. But Flinders charts the rise of a new more nuanced debate about when and why to involve the private and voluntary sector in delivering state services. Indeed, while some argue that the future of the state is likely to be 'post-bureaucratic', Flinders suggests otherwise and argues that whilst its structure will change in years to come, it is more likely to grow than diminish.

Turning to social protection policies, Peter Kenway focuses on the Labour government's poverty-reduction policies on children. He describes how these policies have followed the route of insisting that work is the best form of welfare. Hence the national minimum wage (which most commentators believe has worked, in a modest way) and tax credits (not so successful because of administrative costs and glitches). Kenway regards Labour's 'Sure Start' programme (subsidised child-care centres for under-fives) as successful and notes that commentators across the political spectrum welcome the principle of means-tested anti-poverty measures. The main problem now seems to be the stubborn persistence of in-work poverty and poor job quality for those at the bottom end of the labour market. The recent focus on means-tested benefits leads directly to Kenway's most uncomfortable observation: that those emerging from poverty face an effective marginal tax rate above 70 per cent. For those receiving Housing Benefit or Council Tax Benefit, this rate can be as high as 95 per cent.

Jo Blanden goes on to show that social mobility has become a priority for all the main political parties. Indeed she shows that both the idea of social mobility itself and how best to measure it is increasingly contested with sociologists preferring one approach, economists another and politicians (perhaps unsurprisingly) preferring an approach that maximises what they have achieved and minimises what they have yet to. But focusing on relative social mobility and data derived from two cohort studies from 1958 and 1970, she argues that relative social mobility has decreased and alludes to some of the potentially unpopular policies that may have to be contemplated to address this, such as making the best schools available to the poorest children.

Paul Johnson's data neatly follow on from Blanden's. In his review of tax policy he argues that the majority of redistributive changes under New Labour arose from changes in benefits not taxes. He shows why a coherent narrative on Labour's tax policy is incredibly difficult to provide (even for a former treasury mandarin like himself), by pointing to the long-term inconsistencies in this policy area. One such example is what he calls the 'economically illiterate' introduction of the 10p starting tax rate in 1997 which was then controversially reformed in 2007. Another is the reduction of VAT on domestic fuel which he describes as something 'which presumably those within government who take environmental issues seriously now regret'.

Fran Bennett's and Shamit Saggar's respective chapters both focus more explicitly on equalities related issues. The former focuses on the utility of a gendered approach to social protection policy. She shows how originally 'women were supposed to achieve social security through their husbands', but as times have changed so must policies. However, she shows how the government continues to perceive social protection policies through the traditional lens of a 'unitary household', despite a growth in family breakdown and economic independence of women. She argues for a conception of the household that gauges need and earnings through assessing individuals. Other policy innovations include ones that encourage gender role sharing and greater financial autonomy for all adult members of contemporary households. Shamit Saggar's chapter focuses on how regulation can and is being reconceived to deliver equality related outcomes. Saggar first shows how equality related objectives and regulation are interlinked and then substantiates this with reference to the actions of certain regulators. The article concludes with an interesting discussion about how the Equalities and Human Rights Commission might usefully pursue equalities objectives in the private sector like equal pay, the retention, recruitment and promotion of minorities by working with 'leader firms . . . whilst bearing down on laggard firms by highlighting poor performance'.

Scott Greer focuses upon the organisation and delivery of healthcare in Britain. He examines the healthcare systems of each of the devolved regions focusing on the structural inertia that inhabits each, the similar contextual and compositional constraints that all face but also the very divergent policy-making journeys of the regions. He argues that an incoming government should be wary of the damage that may be caused by a complete overhaul of healthcare systems and less tempted to introduce organisational fixes that have demonstrably failed throughout the regions. He states that the quality, effectiveness, transparency and accountability of the NHS and healthcare are more likely to arise from encouraging a climate of professionalism and improved management than would be achieved by structural reorganisation of the system.

Turning to enterprise and innovation policies in the UK, Alan Hughes examines the role and significance of small- and medium-sized enterprises to the UK economy and how the government has tried to stimulate an increase in entrepreneurial activity and innovation via a range of policies under the ten-year science and innovation investment framework targeted at UK universities and the sciences in general. Hughes examines one particular aspect of the innovation agenda which has become the focus of government policy over the last ten years: the relationship between businesses and universities and how this can influence and facilitate entrepreneurial and innovative activity. Hughes describes how these networks and links can be enhanced by a variety of policy initiatives designed to increase the rate at which ideas created from scientific university research can be commercialised. He outlines and proposes a number of questions concerning the challenges facing the UK in terms of increasing research and development expenditures and, given the likely fiscal constraints, considers how resources can be effectively targeted to improve innovation but also science and technology in general.

Helen Margetts considers citizens' information seeking behaviour and how the internet has been utilised and can be enhanced to improve the flows of information between government and citizens. She traces the rise of the internet from being a 'virtual library with no cataloguing system' to the major social innovation it is today. Margetts examines how e-government has developed and adapted to this new socio-electronic context and increasingly sophisticated information seeking behaviours as well as how the internet is used by government agencies to collect, store and use information about its citizens. She also describes the series of costly information technology blunders that have beset the UK government's adoption of internet-based technologies to deliver public services such as that of the Passport Agency in 1999, the Child Support Agency in 2003 and the Revenue and Customs loss of 25 million people's personal details in 2007. She states that government agencies are not fully utilising the potential of the internet to improve service delivery and disseminate vital information about services. A number of 'e-options' are proposed that could be adopted to harness this potential in order to enhance the provision and flow of information, whilst also increasing and improving the interaction between government and its citizens.

4

The final two chapters offer an analysis of Britain's relationship with our European neighbours and our global partners. Patrick Diamond and Roger Liddle describe how Britain's relations might develop over the coming years, offering three scenarios and policy paths for our relations with Europe. The implications of these are discussed for issues such as the EU budget, enlargement, foreign policy and defence. As they note, these scenarios are, of course, highly dependent upon a range of factors both internal and external to Britain, although as they comment, whoever is elected at the next general election, they are likely to maintain a weak pro-European consensus. Michael Woolcock presents an account of the recent trends in poverty and inequality in developing countries and how the UK government has responded to these challenges over the last decade. He notes that the government's record on development and poverty alleviation issues has improved over the last ten years with the UK often being at the forefront of international efforts to reduce global poverty. Woolcock argues that effective poverty reduction strategies should aim to support responses to both technical and adaptive development problems. As he notes, concentrating on technical problems alone will not 'make poverty history'.

Conclusion

There are a number of important lessons that arise from the broader and longer term assessments generated by the *Options* process and its outputs. First, the continuities across political administrations are generally larger than the changes—which is an important issue to remember as an election nears. Second, the big problems of each generation generally come to be addressed, though not in the rhetorical time-frames of political campaigns. Bok's classic work on the performance of governments is relevant here—that the performance of governments and public services have generally improved markedly over recent decades at the same time as it has become ever more fashionable to bemoan them. Finally, it is clear that the current political and policy moments have yet to come to an end. There is particular uncertainty how the long march to 'solidaristic individualism' in public opinion that has shaped the last few decades will interact with the challenges of the current recession. Indeed there is also a pervasive feeling that 'government cannot do it alone'. As President Obama echoed in his inauguration speech, we are moving towards an era of personal responsibility, that our social and economic behaviour must change if we are to successfully deal with the challenges that lie ahead.

References

Appelby, J. and Coutts, A. (2009) 'NHS, health and well-being'. In V. Uberoi, A. Coutts, I. McLean and D. Halpern (eds), *Options for a New Britain*. Basingstoke: Palgrave Macmillan.

Halpern, D., Wood, S., Cameron, G. and White, S. (1996) *Options for Britain—A Strategic Policy Review*. Aldershot: Ashgate.

Hough, M. and Roberts, J. V. (2009) 'Crime and criminal justice: exploring the policy options'. In V. Uberoi, A. Coutts, I. McLean and D. Halpern (eds), *Options for a New Britain*. Basingstoke: Palgrave Macmillan.

Uberoi, V., Coutts, A., McLean, I. and Halpern, D. (2009) *Options for a New Britain*. Basingstoke: Palgrave Macmillan.

Options for Britain: Measuring and Managing Public Services Performance

CHRISTOPHER HOOD

What happened over ten years of travel

PERFORMANCE measurement and 'management by numbers' featured notably in the changing politics of public services in Britain after 1997. Measured performance indicators (PIs) can be used in various ways—notably as targets, benchmarks or league tables, or as background intelligence to aid improvement or policy intervention[1]—but targets and league tables were the most politically salient applications. Endless recitations of target successes—for instance on health waiting times—became a familiar political weapon in the armoury of government ministers, while opposition parties and the media focused on failures and fiddles and all the ills they chose to attribute to a 'target culture'. Indeed, 'targets' as such became an election issue for the first time in 2005, with the opposition Conservatives (who had introduced performance targets for executive agencies and the NHS in the 1990s) pledging to abolish public service 'targets' and do away with the Prime Minister's Delivery Unit in the first week if they won government.

Against that background, three features of the post-1997 history can be noted. One is the context in which those performance measures and associated management systems for public services developed. That comprised a mixture of dramatically rising spending on public services after 1999, accompanied by a marked distrust on the part of politicians and Whitehall bureaucrats of the capacity of professionals to manage public services efficiently or effectively without strong controls from ministers, regulators, auditors and central agencies.[2] So a rhetoric of decentralisation was coupled with more centralised control, and the performance numbers were there for two related reasons. One was to give the managers at the centre more leverage over professionals and the other was to reassure voters that extra tax funding was producing demonstrable improvements in the quality and quantity of public service activity, in contrast to the stereotype of Labour public spending increases in the past. That applied particularly to those services that mattered most to voters.

Second, there was a marked disparity among the different countries of the UK in the development of management-by-numbers performance systems. Of course for the minority of major public services that are run on a UK-wide basis—principally defence and security, foreign affairs, social security and (most) taxation—there is no such disparity, but none of those services have been leading areas in the politics of management-by-numbers systems. Outside of those services there is scarcely any common UK or British position,

Published by Blackwell Publishing Ltd, 9600 Garsington Road, Oxford OX4 2DQ, UK and 350 Main Street, Malden, MA 02148, USA

particularly in the traditionally most electorally salient areas of public policy, namely health and education.[3] After devolution in 1999, official school league tables were done away with in the early 2000s in Scotland, Wales and Northern Ireland, leaving only England operating and developing such a system (notably with the 'contextual value-added' rankings introduced in 2006).[4] The English use of performance indicators for high-stakes composite league tables for health trusts and local authorities was likewise not emulated in any of the other British countries. What has been called the 'targets and terror' system (that is, targets with strong incentives attached) that was used particularly for managing the English NHS in the mid-2000s was much less a feature of the other British countries, whose targets were generally more relaxed and for which 'terror' exercised by central progress-chasing units was less in evidence.[5] Indeed, England seems to be an international outlier in the extent to which targets and official ranking systems were taken in the 2000s, probably because of the combined effect of its scale, political centralisation and majoritarian political system.[6]

Third, the development of public management by numbers is something that pre-dates the Labour government elected in 1997, though that government certainly developed and stretched the approach in various ways. We can perhaps speak of a long-term political 'mood' for performance measurement and management by numbers, analogous to what some called the 'planning mood' of the 1960s. After all, the Conservatives had introduced performance tables for local authorities in the early 1980s and for university research from 1986, had introduced school exam league tables across the UK from the early 1990s, and had set performance targets for the then-new central executive agencies and for the NHS in the 1990s. What the Labour government added (beginning with its literacy and numeracy targets of 1997 and the first public service agreements in 1998) was

- a set of performance targets across all government departments and not just executive agencies—these targets took the form of public service agreements (PSAs) linked to departmental budgets, and represented an ambitious attempt to increase the coherence and transparency of central budgeting and policy-making;[7]
- new central units (notably the Standards and Effectiveness Unit set up in the Department of Education in 1997, and later the Prime Minister's Delivery Unit and the NHS Modernisation Agency, both set up in 2001), for monitoring those targets and encouraging delivery organisations to meet them; and
- a set of composite measures allowing English local authorities and health trusts to be ranked and rated on Michelin-star-type scales from the early 2000s, with significant 'P45'[8] consequences for managers and chief executives.

A definitive history of those developments has yet to be written.[9] No doubt advances in IT (despite much-discussed public sector IT failures) have made public management by numbers easier than it was a generation ago, but at least three social factors seem to have been behind that development as well. One is the long-term growth of a performance measurement movement that spanned the worlds of consultancy, academia and central agencies in government and was devoted to developing the practice of performance management by numbers. Another is the appeal to some public managers of rating and control systems that at least appear to involve more transparent steering processes than the control of public bureaucracies by the traditional double-bind method (which consists of holding contradictory but often implicit goals in tension and blaming managers who succeed on one goal for their failure to achieve an equal and opposite one).[10] A third, but itself perhaps contradictory, factor is the apparent attraction to politicians presented by management-by-numbers systems. Such systems have potential politician-appeal both in providing indicators of demonstrable achievement for voters as mentioned earlier and in providing apparently technocratic systems that nevertheless lend themselves to subtle political finessing on the choice of indicators and weightings to fit political needs.

Present discontents: problems and shortcomings

The development of the system for public management by numbers that has been sketched out above can be evaluated both in terms of party-political advantage and in terms of public service effectiveness in a more neutral sense. Any overall judgement will of course depend on the relative weighting to be assigned to those two criteria. But the system as it has developed over the last decade or so seems problematic on both criteria.

Viewed as a political strategy, it is not obvious that targets and ranking systems had any appreciable electoral payoff for the incumbent political party. At local government level, research on the English case has shown that poor performance in the official comprehensive performance assessment (CPA) rating systems was indeed associated with electoral losses by incumbents, but also finds there was no corresponding electoral reward for top-level performance—meaning that incumbent politicians (as opposed to bureaucrats) had no apparent electoral incentive to achieve more than mediocre results.[11] It is much harder to assess electoral payoffs of measured performance results at national level, but it remains to be demonstrated that the targets contributed greatly to Labour's electoral success in 2005. Changes in voter support for the government in the two most salient target public services (health and education) tended to be indistinguishable from voter assessments of the government's general economic competence.[12] And though the government had slightly more voter support in health (where it hit its key waiting time targets for A&E and elective operations) than in education (where it substantially missed its key literacy and numeracy SATs targets for 11 year olds),[13] there is no perceptible difference in the changes in voter support in these two domains. Nor is there any evidence that Labour did substantially better in changes in vote share in England, where targets and terror were most emphasised, than in the other two countries of Great Britain that had much softer target systems, mostly without the 'P45' element. Of course that doesn't amount to knockout evidence that targets had no electoral impact; but if they did, any such impact is very hard to show. The benefits flowing to managers, bureaucrats and the performance measurement industry more generally are far easier to demonstrate.

One obvious political-psychological mechanism that might well have come into play here is that of negativity bias—the often-observed human tendency to pay more attention to negative than positive information.[14] In the media, target successes tended to receive much less attention than the fiddles and failures, and indeed the most notable impact of targets on the 2005 election campaign was a Channel 4 *Question Time* TV programme six days before the election (29 April) in which the Prime Minister was embarrassingly confronted by an irate mother complaining about the way many GP surgeries in England were gaming the 24/48 hour access target (on the time taken to see a nurse or GP) by refusing to book appointments more than 48 hours in advance. That episode forced Tony Blair to promise to address the 'idiotic' way the 48-hour target was affecting patients[15] and indeed political enthusiasm for targets was already cooling by that time.

Viewed in a more neutral sense, as a way of improving the quality and quantity of public service provision, the management-by-numbers system that has developed over the past decade or so is far from problem-free either. In general, quality of public services is much harder to measure than quantity of certain types of outputs, which presents various well-known problems, but beyond that at least three significant shortcomings of the system can be identified.

First, the system of public management by numbers that developed since 1997 does not lend itself to effective learning about the results of different public service policies and initiatives. In fact, it might almost have been designed to place the maximum obstacles in the way of such learning, for two reasons. One is the instability of the measurement systems and consequently truncated runs of data caused by high churn rates in targets and never-ending alterations in the composite measures used to evaluate local authorities and health trusts. That instability was driven partly because of the perceived need to keep changing the indicators to deter gaming behaviour by managers and providers and counter the problem of Goodhart's Law (the proposition, originally developed for measures of the money supply, that any statistics used for administrative purposes will lose their validity over time).[16] It was also partly driven by changing political considerations like the need to stealthily bury targets that had been embarrassingly failed (such as those over school truancy or smoking during pregnancy). The result is that, in an age much given to the rhetoric of 'evidence-based policy', it becomes at best no easier than before to ascertain 'what works' by quantitative before-and-after analysis over time.[17] The other basic roadblock to effective learning from the performance numbers is the lack of comparability among the countries of the UK on some of the key performance indicators (such as waiting times for healthcare, differently computed in Scotland and England[18]), which makes it hard for the different public services policies across the countries of the UK to be used as a Montesquieu-type laboratory for trying out different approaches, and therefore cannot live up to the rhetoric of devolution of a decade ago.

Second, there is no coherent theory of value or public intervention that underpins the system that has grown up. As with so much else in government, the system developed in an *ad hoc*, pragmatic way, with no careful evaluation of the costs and benefits of different kinds of performance indicator regimes, no attention whatsoever to the well-documented history of target systems, and no attempt even in the more cerebral parts of government to fashion anything approaching a workable theory of when it is better to use subjective rather than administrative data as performance indicators, or of the circumstances in which it is better to use performance indicators as targets, rankings or background intelligence.[19] Some performance measures had high 'P45' consequences for managers, but the incentives were haphazard and there is no evidence that departments were systematically punished for poor performance on PSAs by lower budgetary allocations. Moreover, even fifty years after the advent of modern cost-benefit analysis, cost-benefit analysis was almost never carefully applied to the expansion of performance indicator regimes.[20] But the collection of quantitative performance information about public services is far from costless. The creation of such data uses up resources in money and time that could be put to other purposes, and though the direct, compliance and opportunity costs of such systems are almost never officially calculated, they can be considerable. An example is the officially estimated £45m that it cost universities to comply with the 2007–8 Research Assessment Exercise and the time spent on the process by the 1,500-plus members of the 82 panels involved, most of them research-active academics who could be engaged on teaching and research—a key consideration in the later attempt by the Treasury to replace the peer assessment system with a 'lighter-touch' metrics system.

When public money is tight, these sorts of direct costs can matter: it is worth remembering that various official statistical series were one of the first things to fall victim to the 'Geddes Axe' in 1922 and the same thing happened in the less dramatic fiscal squeeze of the late 1970s and 1980s. But it is the hidden or indirect costs of data-gathering over performance indicators that tend to be the most controversial, and at the time of writing the most salient example concerns the costs of testing the performance of school students, with numerous educational specialists alarmed at what they perceive as the negative social effect of frequent high-stakes testing in narrowing the curriculum, 'teaching to the test', and high stress on the students concerned.[21] Those hidden costs, arising from the 'observer paradox' (that observation changes the nature of what is being observed), can be viewed as having a negative effect on the quality of the overall performance, induced by the very tools intended to improve service quality and quantity. For the performance measurement industry, it tends to be an article of faith that any performance numbers justify their costs in providing the basis for better management of public services. But that view is not taken in the private business sector or even by government ministers and departments when they refuse to provide replies to parliamentary questions on the basis of what they deem to be the disproportionate costs involved in gathering the data.

Third, and perhaps more intractably, these developments in public management by numbers have to be set in a context of low public trust in official numbers generally and widespread perception of 'shonkiness' in public service performance data more particularly.[22] In spite—or could it be because?—of its emphasis on public management by numbers relative to the other European countries, the UK (the numbers are not broken down among England, Scotland, Wales and Northern Ireland) had the lowest level of public trust in its official statistics of all the EU countries in 2007, according to Eurobarometer data.[23] And according to ONS survey data in 2005, hospital waiting time data were the least trusted of all sorts of official statistics at that time.[24] That is perhaps linked to the strong negativity bias about performance targets in the national media that has already been mentioned. It is probably not accidental that Soviet analogies were frequently used to characterise the performance management system, and that stories of fiddling and gaming gained widespread publicity, even though the extent of 'gaming' in the numbers is disputed and inherently hard to ascertain.

The official response to this culture of distrust and negativity over official statistics has been to increase the formal independence of the statistical apparatus, culminating in the creation of a UK-wide Statistics Board in 2008 under the chairmanship of a retired senior civil servant and with the mission of guaranteeing the integrity of official statistics. Whether these institutional changes will succeed in increasing public trust in official statistics remains to be seen. But that widespread public distrust of the numbers may not be accidental whenever high political stakes are invested in performance information and the institutional rules (even after the new Statistics Act) allow government ministers a comparatively long time interval to produce their positive 'spin' on performance numbers before they are published.

Where might we go from here?

In the 1980s heyday of the Thatcher government, much was made of the slogan 'there is no alternative' to sum up the view that free-market capitalism was the only viable economic theory for a modern democracy;[25] and some see the development of quantitative indicators linked to performance-based management as a similarly inexorable tide of history. Many have argued that rankings and ratings of public services are here to stay in an information age,[26] and any future Westminster government will certainly find itself pressed to extend and develop that approach by the performance management industry. So there is much that is likely to underpin the continued emphasis on measured performance indicators in public services, whoever is in government. And that means some of the fundamentals of the status quo are probably destined to remain, along with some of the underlying problems listed above. But the alternatives to PIs in the management of public services certainly aren't problem free either.

However, at least three policy options that go beyond incremental tinkering with the status quo merit some attention. One possibility is the option of re-engineering PIs for a colder bureaucratic climate, either of prolonged fiscal squeeze or of an active turn to 'smaller state' policies for public services. A second is the option of developing a 'data club' approach to public service performance information among the countries of the UK and perhaps beyond. And a third is the option of a general shift from targets and rankings to intelligence of various kinds in the use of PIs. Each of those options is briefly discussed below.

(a) PIs for a colder bureaucratic climate

If the 2010s turn out to be dominated by fiscal squeeze and/or an ideological mood stressing the need for lower taxes and a smaller state, we might expect a corresponding pressure for fewer performance indicators, and particular pressure on those PIs that are the most expensive to collect, such as the university RAE ratings mentioned earlier. After all, it is far from self-evident that it is central government that has to take on the role of ranking and rating hospitals, schools, universities or cities, when that task is performed by media or independent rating agencies in most other countries, even within the UK. Nor is it obvious that central government departments are always the best-placed actors in the public service delivery system to set and monitor detailed performance targets, as against local authorities or middle managers. And as mentioned above, various official statistical series came to be scrapped in earlier periods of cutbacks in the twentieth century. If that was the sort of climate facing PIs in the next decade, a major and testing challenge for the newly-created Statistics Board would be to resist the removal of key quantitative evidence (for instance about distributional outcomes) on which policies of state reduction or service cutbacks might be evaluated, and to maintain a balance between the cost and the validity of performance numbers against pressures for cheaper but possibly inferior data sources. That would need more research than has hitherto been conducted on the added value of more detailed PIs as against cheaper and less intrusive summary ones.[27]

But if that sort of climate was one in which we might expect a shift towards PIs with lower collection cost, rather fewer PIs overall, and a shift in the balance between official taxpayer-funded PIs and those produced by media or the private or independent sector, even a government that was committed (either ideologically or by force of circumstance) to shrinking the state and cutting public spending would still need such indicators. If cutbacks and a drive to shrink the state moved back into the centre of the policy agenda, the emphasis of PIs would need to move towards input-reduction targets, with increased weight on productivity indicators. After all, given that several research studies have suggested that increased resources do not necessarily improve public service outcomes, it would follow that input reductions need not necessarily be at the expense of service quality or quantity.[28]

The difficult challenge for those presiding over any such regime would then be to choose the right targets for input reduction, which would probably not be any easier than was the design of effective quality targets to accompany resource expansion in the 'spend, spend, spend' era of the 1990s and 2000s. Small-state ideologists will naturally be attracted to the sort of staff reduction targets applied to government departments under the Thatcher and Major governments up to 1994 (and reintroduced by the Labour government in 2004). But the experience of those targets showed that reducing the official civil service payroll did not necessarily reduce costs and in some cases increased them, as former 'civil servants' took exit packages designed to encourage them to leave, only to return as more highly paid 'consultants'. To prevent that sort of gaming, running-cost targets and staff-reduction targets would need to be closely integrated, and productivity indicators developed further and in a different direction.

(b) PIs for a four-country (or more) data club?

If the 2010s continue to be dominated by centrifugal political forces on the components of the United Kingdom, there might not still be a political unit called 'Britain' by the end of that decade. And even if Britain continues to exist as a political unit, it certainly cannot be assumed that all three countries of Great Britain will routinely be governed by the same political party or coalition, as they were at the outset of devolution a decade ago. So the difficulties mentioned earlier of using uniform performance information to enable the British countries to learn from one another's public service management policies are not likely to go away, and even if it wanted to, a Westminster government could not simply dictate the public service performance data policies of the other countries. How far the UK-wide remit of the Statistics Board could serve as a viable basis for developing more comparable performance numbers remains to be seen—and will obviously depend on political circumstances.

What might be developed, though, and perhaps encouraged by the Statistics Board, is a 'data club' approach, in which the British countries (however they turn out to be constitutionally related in the 2010s) agreed to develop more standardised and stable PIs for key public services, or at least work out ways of translating from one to another. Perhaps such a data club could even be extended beyond the British countries, for example to take in the ten Canadian provinces. By 'data club' is meant mutually-agreed arrangements for data-sharing across organisations or jurisdictions, for the development of common conventions or methods of translation and for the terms on which data shared with other members of the club is to be used.

A notable example of the data club approach is the COMET system for sharing of data about underground railway performance among the various metro operators around the world.[29] Of course the development of such a data club would require some process of intergovernmental agreement (or at least agreement among cities, associations of local authorities or healthcare providers), and is not the sort of quick-win 'eye-catching initiative' that has instant tabloid- and politician-appeal. But the long-term payoffs in creating a laboratory for learning about effective public service performance could be substantial, and an intergovernmental agreement on such matters might have the additional advantage of working as a counterweight to the already-noted political-bureaucratic impulse constantly to change performance measurement systems and thus undermine the ability to track changes over time against policy initiatives and thus allow evidence-based learning.

(c) PIs for 'intelligence'

Third, the apparent lack of payoffs to elected politicians from target and ranking systems (as opposed to payoffs to the performance indicator industry) might fuel a further rethink of the extent to which performance indicators should be used as high-stakes political targets as against rankings or intelligence data. The reaction that started to set in against targets in Labour's second term in the early 2000s has already meant that the number of top-level PSA targets has shrunk dramatically to about a tenth of the 336 or so that originally appeared in 1998, as greater awareness of the limits of target systems (well known to scholars, management theorists and Soviet historians) has developed in government and among the wider public—that is, ratchet effects, threshold effects and output distortions. Similarly, the draconian Michelin-star-type rating systems devised for English local authorities and health trusts in the early 2000s are currently morphing into fuzzier systems through a mixture of technocratic tinkering and political rethinking, and there is a rising tide of criticism of the effects of the testing regime that underpins school league tables in England.

Of course, there are good reasons for governments to want to use performance indicators as targets for high-stakes public management policies, and indeed both Conservative and Labour governments did exactly that over house-building numbers in the 1950s (and over arms manufacture in both world wars). Nor are targets likely to disappear in the management of caseload in public service organisations in areas like tax, welfare and job placement, for which they have been a common tool for at least sixty years. But at the top political level, it is possible to imagine an option in which the balance of use of public service performance indicators shifts from target and ranking systems towards relatively more emphasis on use as 'intelligence'— to inform user choices, provide a basis for learning about improvement, and serve as a way of evaluating policy but without mechanical consequences for managers' careers.

That would imply a world in which the use of performance indicators in England came to resemble that of Scotland and Wales rather than vice versa, for instance by the abandonment of official school league tables as all the other UK countries have done, and in which the league tables for healthcare and local government came to look less like the Michelin restaurant guide than the OECD's annual health statistics, which contain a dense mass of indicators (well over a thousand in that case), but any attempts at composite ranking are left to think-tanks, pressure groups or private enterprise of one kind or another. That does not imply a world in which high-level targets on things that really matter to elected governments would disappear altogether (indeed, such targets might be more effective if they were fewer and more selective), nor a world in which international rankings and ratings are likely to disappear. All it implies is a changed balance among the use of PIs for targets, rankings and intelligence, with relatively more emphasis on the latter and correspondingly less on the first two. But of course the lack of a firm corpus of evidence on the costs and benefits of the different uses of PIs, as noted earlier, means that any such shift runs the risk of swapping one *ad hoc* evidence-free use of performance information for another.

Conclusion

Although there is currently perhaps something of a backlash, at least among sections of the public-management professoriat in the United States, against the current state of performance management through quantitative perform-ance indicators,[30] there is no very clear idea among those critics as to what could replace it. The key challenge for Britain or its component countries in the 2010s would seem to be more one of how to use PIs more intelligently than of doing away with them altogether.

Acknowledgements

The author would like to thank Ruth Dixon, Tom Gash, David Halpern, Peter Smith, Varun Oberoi and Deborah Wilson for valuable comments on an earlier draft.

Notes

1 C. Hood, 'Public management by numbers: why does it vary? Where has it come from? What are the gaps and the puzzles?', *Public Money and Management*, vol. 27, no. 2, 2007, pp. 95–102.
2 In contrast to Rudolf Klein's well-known interpretation of the NHS as embodying an implicit bargain between the state and the medical profession, in which 'central government controlled the budget [and] doctors controlled what happened within that budget'. See R. Klein, *The New Politics of the NHS*, 4th edn, Harlow, Prentice-

Hall, 2001, p. 64. See also M. Moran, *The British Regulatory State: High Modernism and Hyper-Innovation*, Oxford, Oxford University Press, 2003, for the argument that there was a long-term shift from 'club government' across several sectors of British society towards more formal regulation.

3 An exception, though whether it could be called highly politically salient is debatable, is that of university research ratings, in which the four UK funding organisations have up to now cooperated to organise a common rating system. It remains to be seen whether that arrangement will survive into the 2010s.

4 See D. Wilson and A. Piebalga, 'Performance measures, ranking and parental choice: an analysis of the English school league tables', *International Public Management Journal*, vol. 11, no. 3, 2008, pp. 344–66.

5 C. Propper, M. Sutton, C. Whitnall and F. Windmeijer, 'Did "targets and terror" reduce waiting times in England for hospital care', *The B.E. Journal of Economic Analysis and Policy*, vol. 8, no. 2, 2008, Article 5; G. Bevan and C. Hood, 'What's measured is what matters: targets and gaming in the English healthcare system', *Public Administration*, vol. 84, no. 3, 2006, pp. 517–38.

6 C. Hood, 'Public management by numbers'.

7 See P. Smith, 'Performance budgeting in England: experience with public service agreements' in *Performance Budgeting and Funding*, IMF, 2006. As Smith explains, the PSAs were only the topmost level of a performance target system which comprised numerous lower level targets, some set by the Treasury and others by departments as targets 'cascaded' down the delivery chain.

8 A 'P45' is the official form employers in the UK have to give employees when they leave. 'P45 targets' thus meant targets that meant dismissal if they were missed.

9 A useful source for the New Labour years is M. Barber, *Instruction to Deliver: Tony Blair, Public Services and the Challenge of Achieving Targets*, London, Politico's, 2007.

10 Definitively analysed by A. Dunsire, *Control in a Bureaucracy*, Oxford, Martin Robertson, 1978. But measured performance regimes themselves can involve contradictory targets, as shown for English local authorities by I. McLean, D. Haubrich and R. Gutierrez-Romero, 'The perils and pitfalls of performance measurement: the CPA regime for local authorities in England', *Public Money and Management*, vol. 27, no. 2, 2007, pp. 111–17.

11 O. James and P. John, 'Public management performance information and electoral support for incumbent English local governments', *Journal of Public Administration Research and Theory*, vol. 17, no. 4, 2007, pp. 567–80; G. Boyne, O. James, P. John and N. Petrovsky, Does public service performance affect top management team turnover? ESRC Public Services Programme Discussion Paper no. 0802, 2008. http://www.publicservices.ac.uk/wp-content/uploads/dp0802-final.pdf

12 See Ipsos MORI, *Importance of Key Issues to Voting*, 2008. http://www.ipsos-mori.com/content/turnout/importance-of-key-issues-to-voting.ashx (accessed August 2008).

13 See P. Whiteley, M. C. Stewart, D. Sanders and H. C. Clarke, 'The issue agenda and voting in 2005', *Parliamentary Affairs*, vol. 58, no. 4, 2005, Table 2, p. 810.

14 See, for example, R. Lau, 'Two explanations for negativity effects in political behaviour', *American Journal of Political Science*, vol. 29, no. 1, 1985, pp. 119–38.

15 See http: http//www.channel4.com/fc/quote,jsp?id/=144 and http/news.bbc.co.uk/1/hi/programmes/newsnight/4497373.stm (both accessed August 2008).

16 C. Goodhart, *Monetary Theory and Practice: The UK experience*, London, Macmillan, 1984.

17 Of course, where the disaggregated components of the volatile composite indices remain constant, they can be, and have been, used for effective learning about determinants of performance by comparisons across local authority areas.

18 See Propper et al., 'Targets and Terror', pp. 8–9.

19 See Hood, 'Public management by numbers', pp. 99–102. At a seminar in Oxford in June 2007, Sir Michael Barber advanced the view that targets are better used to raise public service performance from the utterly unacceptable to the more-or-less satisfactory level than from satisfactory to excellent, but that proposition is only hinted at in his *Instruction to Deliver*.

20 See D. Dranove, D. Kessler, M. McClelland and M. Satterthwaite, 'Is more information better? The effect of report cards on health care providers', NBER Working Paper 8697, Cambridge, MA, NBER, 2002.

21 See, for example, R. F. Elmore, 'Forum: testing trap: the single largest and possibly most destructive federal intrusion into America's public schools', *Harvard Magazine*, vol. 105, no. 1, 2002. http://harvardmagazine.com/2002/09/testing-trap.html (accessed August 2008).

22 For documentation of validity and reliability problems in widely used composite indices of health and local authority performance in England in the 2000s, see R. Jacobs and M. Goddard, 'How do performance indicators add up? An examination of composite indicators in public services', *Public Money and Management*, vol. 27, no. 2, 2007, pp. 103–10, and McLean et al., 'Perils and Pitfalls'.

23 See European Commission, *Eurobarometer 67: Public Opinion in the European Union*, 2007. http://:ec.europa.eu/public_opinion/archives/eb/eb67/eb67_en.pdf, p. 505 (accessed August 2008). See also T. Holt, 'Official statistics, public policy and public trust' (2007 Presidential Address to the Royal Statistical Society), *Journal of the Royal Statistical Society A*, vol. 171, no. 2, 2008, pp. 5–6.

24 Office of National Statistics, 'No change in public confidence in official statistics, News Release, September 2005. http://www.statistics.gov.uk/ddfdir/pco0905.pdf (accessed April 2006).

25 I. McLean, 'There is no alternative: Margaret Thatcher and Tony Blair', in *Rational Choice and British Politics*, Oxford, Oxford University Press, 2001, pp. 204–31.

26 See, for instance, W. T. Gormley, Jr. and D. L. Weimer, *Organizational Report Cards*, Cambridge, MA, Harvard University Press, 1999, p. 233.

27 See Dranove et al., 'Is more information better?'.

28 For a discussion of how to measure public service productivity, see H. Simpson, 'Productivity and Public Services', CMPO Working Paper 07/164, Bristol, University of Bristol, 2007; for research on the link between input changes and outcomes in education, see E. A. Hanushek, 'The failure of input-based schooling policies', *Economic Journal*, vol. 113, 2003, pp. F64–98.

29 See R. Anderson, 'Transport performance and the data clubs approach', presentation to 'Where Does Britain Rank?', International Public Services Rankings Conference, 2005. http://www.publicservices.ac.uk/pastevents/wp-content/uploads/r_anderson_rankingsconf.pdf (accessed August 2008).

30 See, for instance, B. Radin, *Challenging the Performance Movement: Accountability, Complexity, and Democratic Values*, Washington, DC, Georgetown University Press, 2006.

The Future of the State

MATTHEW FLINDERS

Introduction

ALTHOUGH David Cameron's speech on the future of the state to the Google
Zeitgeist Conference in October 2007 represented a significant contribution to
contemporary thinking on this topic, his emphasis on the evolution of the
state in the 'post-bureaucratic era' arguably fails to pinpoint the most pressing
opportunities and challenges in relation to the delivery of public services. The
Leader of the Conservative party's speech did, however, reflect the fact that
the future of the state is currently a topic of deep and sustained thinking by
both the leading political parties. This is because the future of the state is
likely to be one of the biggest political themes of the twenty-first century. And
although discussions about the structure and role of the state are unlikely to
attract great media or public attention, it is possible to argue that debates
about the modern state's practical capacity and legitimate role underpin
discussions about nearly all contemporary political challenges (migration,
pensions, obesity, global warming, terrorism and security, illegal drug use,
globalisation, individual rights and responsibilities, AIDS-HIV, teenage
pregnancy, social exclusion, etc.). The future of the state is, therefore, one of
the biggest themes of our times because beliefs about its capacity and
legitimate role affect and shape the options that are viewed as realistic
across all policy areas. The central argument of this article is that, although
the structure of the state and its relationship with the public is likely to change
during the twenty-first century, its role in socio-economic terms is actually
likely to grow rather than diminish.

In order to set the scene in terms of the growth of the modern state and its
current complexity, a simple example is instructive. When Lord Shelburne
became the first Home Secretary in 1782, his department consisted of just one
chief clerk and ten civil servants but in 2008 the Home Secretary is responsible
for over 70,000 staff working across six directorates within the core of the
department, four executive agencies, twelve executive non-departmental
public bodies (NDPBs), ten advisory NDPBs, eight tribunal NDPBs, three
'other' NDPBs, and a significant number of 'third sector' organisations (TSOs)
and private sector organisations (PSOs) working under contract with the
department to deliver specific services. As such this article does not and
cannot claim to offer a definitive analysis of the future of the state but instead
has three quite simple aims:

1. to provide an objective sense of what has happened since the election of

Published by Blackwell Publishing Ltd, 9600 Garsington Road, Oxford OX4 2DQ, UK and 350 Main Street, Malden, MA 02148, USA

New Labour in May 1997 and the implications this may have for the future of the state;

2. to identify current and future major social trends and challenges as well as the public attitudes towards these challenges; and,

3. to set out a range of conventional (and slightly less conventional) policy options that could realistically be adopted by an incoming government over the next decade given the specified socio-economic conditions, and contextual opportunities and constraints.

The state, for the purposes of this article, refers to the bureaucratic structure through which civil public goods and services are delivered or socio-political interactions regulated. This would generally be taken to include those classes of public officials and civil servants who may work within central or local governance or within any number of quasi-autonomous public bodies—the public sector in the broadest sense. This article takes each of the three aims (noted above) in turn and therefore begins with a review of New Labour's approach to the modernisation of public services, but before embarking upon this, it might be helpful to set out the contours of the modern state in terms of resources and roles in order to provide some reference points for the subsequent analysis of recent developments and future options.

The British state is a large and complex bureaucratic entity. In March 2008, 5.76 million people were employed within the public sector (around 19.5 per cent of total employment). Having declined during 1991–8, the March 2008 figure for public sector employment is 556,000 higher than a decade earlier (public sector employment under New Labour peaked at 5.83 million in 2006).[1] The National Health Service is the third largest employer in the world with over 1.3 million staff (one in every 40 people or 2.5 per cent of the population). Total managed public expenditure in 2008–9 is expected to be £618 billion, around 41 per cent of GDP (see Figure 1).

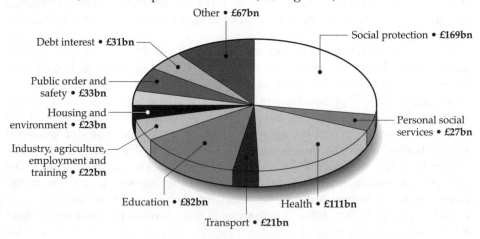

Figure 1: Government spending by function, 2008–9
Source: HC 388 *Budget 2008*, p. 11.

What is significant about these statistics is not just the sheer size of the British state but also its apparent capacity to withstand far-reaching attempts to reduce its responsibilities and size. In the early 1980s the British state employed over 5.5 million people and this figure has hardly fluctuated over the past thirty years. Public expenditure as a percentage of GDP exhibits a similar pattern of stability as it fluctuates within a relatively narrow band (48.9 per cent in 1975, 44.6 in 1980, 45.8 in 1985, 40.1 in 1990, 42.4 in 1995, 40.0 in 2000 and 42.0 in 2005).[2] Moving from the resources to the roles of the state, it is possible to identify five main functions and, from this, chart how the emphasis of each of these has changed over time (see Table 1).

In simple terms the central shift in terms of the role of the state in recent decades has been from a *provider* to a *commissioner* of public services. And yet it is important not to overstate the extent of this shift. Over 90 per cent of children are still educated in state schools; over 90 per cent of the public are still treated in state hospitals; and, over 90 per cent of prisoners are held in state prisons. This is a critical point. As the next section will illustrate, although attempts have been made to alter governance frameworks (as is the case with Trust Schools) while also drawing upon the resources of PSOs and TSOs (like City Academies and Specialist Schools), the extent of this shift is limited. Indeed, debates about the future of the state, and each of the sections in this article, tend to be united by a set of questions: How to re-draw the respective boundaries between the public, private and third sectors? What are the respective strengths and weaknesses of each sector? How should specific decisions about whether a specific service or policy is appropriate for contracting out be made?

New Labour and the state, 1997–2008

New Labour did not inherit a blank canvas when it assumed office on 1 May 1997, and in order to understand its subsequent reform agenda it is critical to appreciate both the dominant theory of the state and also its institutional legacy. The debate in the 1970s concerning state-overload, delegitimation and ungovernability in Britain created a sociopolitical context that was sympathetic to the assumptions and policy prescriptions of the New Right.[3] As a result new public management (NPM) became the dominant prescriptive paradigm from the 1980s onwards within which the state's role, structures and relationships with citizens came to be understood and, as a result, reformulated.[4] NPM embraced a preference for privatisation, contracting out, targets, contracts, market-like relationships, performance-related pay and a general preference for *output-orientated* legitimacy (prioritising efficiency and results in service delivery) over *input* or *process-orientated* legitimacy (emphasising the democratic process).[5] The institutional legacy of NPM was a highly fragmented organisational landscape including hundreds of generally single-purpose public bodies, each enjoying varying levels of day-to-day autonomy from their sponsoring department. The danger in terms of

Table 1: Role of the state

Role	Criteria
Provider	The state might choose to provide a service where: 1. direct lines of accountability need to be maintained, and the cost of any failure of accountability is too high for the state to take the risk, for example the armed forces; 2. there are strong strategic reasons for keeping a process in-house, for example ensuring that the state has sufficient information about the process so that it can act as an 'intelligent customer' for similar services.
Legislator	The state might choose to legislate where legal intervention is needed to provide an incontrovertible (statutory) basis for any aspect of policy.
Commissioner	The state might choose to commission a service where: 1. the service can be delivered through the market and any market failure can be addressed through taxes, subsidies, regulation or other means; 2. a market can be established: contracts can be written (outcomes and quality are quantifiable and measurable); there is an appropriate number of suppliers and commissioners; risks can be transferred; contract costs (bargaining and opportunism) are low; 3. commissioners have sufficient information about suppliers and the market; 4. service users are able to make informed choices and provide signals to commissioners. NB. Not all of these criteria necessarily need to be met.
Information provider	The state might choose to provide information where citizens are unlikely to be able to make effective choices without state oversight or regulation of information.
Regulator	The state might choose to regulate a service where the state is not providing a service but still has a duty, either to secure outcomes on efficiency grounds, to ensure that the service is being provided effectively or in line with certain standards (for example standards in private care homes; regulation of electricity markets).

Source: Cabinet Office, *Building on Progress: The Role of the State*, May 2007, p. 10.

public policy was that such a dense and fragmented institutional terrain, and particularly the existence of so many potential veto points, would undermine delivery capacity. Sir Richard Wilson admitted when Cabinet Secretary, 'I would not claim that the manner in which we implemented all these reforms over the years was a model to emulate. There was not enough overall vision or strategic planning'.[6]

This was critical for the Labour party because NPM had not only affected the state in structural terms, in a manner that had arguably left ministers less able to address society's 'wicked issues' (i.e. persistent and intractable, mainly social, problems which reach across departmental boundaries), but it also affected the reform agenda for any future government due to the fact that NPM was generally conflated with modern understandings of 'good governance'. To depart from the general ethos and trajectory of NPM would therefore have arguably been a risky strategy for a new government that was determined to appear financially competent and discerning in terms of public sector management. In this regard NPM formed a powerful type of path dependency, involving significant 'sunk costs', which affected New Labour's options for the state. However, before 1997 the Labour party was well-aware of the internal and external challenges to the state and how these might not only affect their capacity to govern in the future but would also force them to explore alternative models of state delivery.[7] But in this regard the values and prescriptions of NPM were not interpreted as anathema to the traditional commitment of the Labour party to the state and the provision of public services. Indeed the promise of an albeit softened form of NPM (i.e. 'best value' instead of compulsory competitive tendering) dovetailed with New Labour's search for a 'third way' between the simple public–private dichotomy. At the same time the promise of increased efficiency savings—'more bang for each buck'—that could then be reinvested into the public sector helped reassure the party's traditional supporters within the public sector and trade unions.

There is now an extensive literature on New Labour's public sector reforms and it is neither possible nor necessary to review this body of work in this chapter.[8] It is more profitable to simply sketch out the way in which New Labour has approached the 'modernisation' of the state and then draw out a number of underlying principles and tensions. The main argument of this section is therefore that New Labour has displayed a commitment to the state but that this commitment has been accompanied by very clear expectations in terms of reform and delivery. Table 2 provides a review of the core tenets or principles of New Labour's approach to reforming the state.

New Labour has arguably maintained the Labour party's traditional commitment to the state and public service provision but has attempted to locate this faithfulness within the paradigm of NPM (as reflected in the core tenets and principles contained in Table 2).[9] Although this commitment may have waned in recent years (as frustration within the government over the pace and extent of reform has grown), the basic commitment in terms of resources is clear: public sector spending has increased significantly and the number of people working within the public sector has increased by around 15 per cent. It is, however, important to acknowledge a change of emphasis between New Labour's first and second terms. In the first term the government committed itself to stay within the spending plans of the previous Conservative government for its first two years in office. As a result the main

Table 2: New Labour and the state: core tenets and principles

Rhetoric	Translation
'what matters is what works'	The belief that the public was no longer interested in who provided services, only in their quality.
'contestability'	A willingness to remove services from current providers and re-allocate responsibility.
'earned autonomy'	The opportunity to be granted increased operational freedoms by demonstrating excellence in service delivery within centrally prescribed policy frameworks.
'hub model of government'	A structural preference for a small strategic core commissioning specific services from a number of semi-autonomous service providers.
'shared responsibility'	An attempt (albeit embryonic) to redefine the relationship between the individual and the state vis-à-vis rights and responsibilities.
'depoliticisation'	A commitment to relocating responsibilities for decisions about public services to organisations operating beyond the direct control of elected politicians.

emphasis of the government was on achieving greater central steering capacity through a number of policies and measures designed to deliver 'joined-up' or 'holistic' government.[10] However having secured the confidence of the city, notably through granting operational independence to the Bank of England, and been returned for a second term with an increased legislative majority, New Labour's second term involved a distinct shift in policy. The 2002 budget included a five-year plan for the NHS based upon an annual increase in spending of 7.4 per cent; and the subsequent Comprehensive Spending Review included similar financial packages for education, transport, police and prisons. These spending plans represented a major shift from the financial prudence of the government's first term and reflected a degree of confidence in the capacity of the state to deliver public goods. But this strategy was also politically risky. Ministers understood that the increased resources had to deliver clear improvements in service standards and it was in this context that that the Institute for Public Policy Research (IPPR) emphasised,

If in five years time, after a sustained period of increased funding, citizens feel that those services are still failing to deliver there could be a major political backlash.[11]

Towards the end of New Labour's first term there had been clear indications that members of the government were becoming frustrated with a perceived lack of progress and concerned that their planned increases in real-term spending on public services would not lead to significantly improved levels of service provision. This was clear from the Prime Minister's (in)famous speech to the British Venture Capitalist Association in 1999—'you try getting change in the public sector and public services—I bear the scars on my back after two years in government'.[12] This speech was to prove significant because it marked a stark shift in the style, pace and rhetoric of reform away from a co-operative emphasis on 'joined-up' government to a more antagonistic drive towards improving public service delivery. As noted above, the 'third way' had always been more willing to advocate and embrace a more flexible approach to the delivery of public services and this theme would now enter the political discourse in the form of 'contestability'.

The principle of contestability is very simple—public services can be delivered by a host of providers including organisations from the public, private or 'third' sectors and, as a result, where services are deemed to have fallen below acceptable levels they will be transferred to an alternative provider. Contestability therefore represented a significant refinement from traditional social democratic values due to the way it maintained a commitment to public services but detached this commitment from public sector delivery organisations as the default tool of governance. It was therefore an important ideological departure: a fact confirmed in the Prime Minister's October 2001 speech on public service reform in which he emphasised that there should be no 'no barriers, no dogma, no vested interests that stand in the way of delivering the best services' and highlighted the 'promotion of alternative providers and greater choice' as forming a key element of his government's agenda.

In developing greater choice of provider, the private and voluntary sectors can play a role. Contrary to myth, no-one has ever suggested that they are *the* answer. Or that they should replace public services. But where use of them can improve public services, nothing should stand in the way of their use. In any event, round the world, the barriers between public, private and voluntary are coming down.[13]

Before we examine the degree to which the rhetorical emphasis on contestability has actually affected the contours of the state in terms of bringing PSOs and TSOs into the delivery of public services, it is important to understand that this approach to the state dovetails with a preference for what can be termed the 'hub' model of government. This involves a preference for a smaller policy-orientated central department that acts as a 'hub' and seeks to commission and co-ordinate the delivery of services from a host of arm's-length delivery mechanisms.[14] The role of the government is therefore to 'steer but not row', an aspiration captured in notions of the 'strategic' or 'enabling' state. And yet as the National Audit Office has found in relation to a range of policies, particularly those crossing departmental boundaries, operating the 'hub' model is problematic due to the existence of dense and complex chains of delegation through which services are delivered.[15] And yet the notion of contestability, with its implicit emphasis on diversity, risks augmenting the already convoluted delivery landscape. This point encourages us to examine the degree to which New Labour has implemented

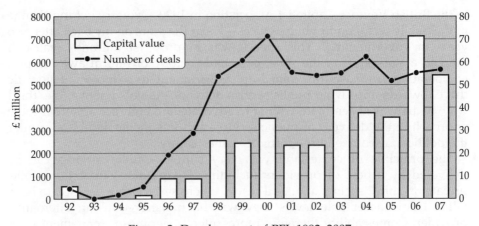

Figure 2: Development of PFI, 1992–2007
Source: HM Treasury, *Infrastructure Procurement: Delivering Long-Term Value*, 2008, p. 7.

partnerships with the private and third sectors for the delivery of public services.

Taking partnerships with the private sector first, it is clear that, despite their misgivings in opposition, the Labour governments have since 1997 developed and extended the schemes designed to draw upon the resources of the private sector, notably the private finance initiative (PFI), that were first introduced by the Conservative governments in the early 1990s.[16] New Labour's *Partnerships for Prosperity*, published just months after gaining office in 1997, represented an acknowledgement that the party had significantly diluted its traditional antagonism to private sector involvement in public projects. It also sought to demonstrate the new government's fiscal prudence and awareness of modern public management techniques. An associated benefit of these partnerships was also that they essentially offered a 'buy now, pay later' scheme for the government through which new public sector infrastructure and services could be delivered without increasing borrowing or taxation. In many cases PFI contracts are signed for terms in excess of thirty years in which a PSO will design and build and even manage a facility (hospital, prison, etc.) in return for a regular fixed annual payment from the government. In 2008 there were over 800 PFI partnerships in operation including 185 health facilities, 230 schools, 43 transport projects, nine waste management sites and 180 other projects including housing estates, prisons, museums and defence facilities.[17] As Figure 2 illustrates, the PFI scheme has been vigorously promoted since 1997.

And yet it is important to put in perspective the role of PSOs. The PFI programme plays a significant but relatively small and stable part of the British state, representing around 10 per cent (£50 billion) of annual public sector investment (Figure 3). It is also true to note that, in the context of New Labour's modernisation agenda, the use of public–private partnerships

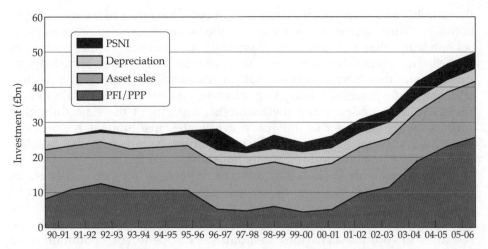

Figure 3: Total investment in public services, 1990–2006
Source: HM Treasury, *PFI—Strengthening Long-term Partnerships*, 2006, p. 15.

continues to represent a highly salient issue within and beyond the Labour party. Although it is increasingly clear that contracts with PSOs can deliver efficiency gains in some policy areas (like roads and prisons), it is also clear that they can be extremely inefficient in other areas (notably the provision of information technology infrastructure).[18] The vaunted risk transfer associated with these contracts has often proved elusive in reality, as PSOs are rarely penalised for poor performance. As the Public Accounts Committee noted,

Departments are too willing to bail out PFI contractors who get into trouble. Contractors should expect to lose out when things go wrong just as they expect to be rewarded when projects are successful. The taxpayer must not be expected to pick up the tab when things go wrong.[19]

Contracts with PSOs also have implications in terms of accountability and public scrutiny because the provision of information is often prevented through the application of 'commercial confidentiality' exemptions and, even where information is released, achieving clarity for where the responsibility lies for failings is often prevented due to the development of 'blame games' between those organisations involved.[20] Long-term partnerships with PSOs also bring with them a clear path dependency in terms of the way they may constrain the flexibility of future governments by obliging them to honour the contractual payments agreed by the previous government. Put in different terms, if the number of PFI contracts were significantly increased this would reduce the resource flexibility of commissioning agencies in the future while also inhibiting flexibility in policy terms. (The termination or re-negotiation of long-term contracts with PSOs under the PFI is possible but very expensive.) Moreover, due to the legal basis of contracts, should the government need to cut public spending it would be the non-PFI expenditure that would carry disproportionately deeper cuts.[21] In terms of the relationship between 'third sector' providers and the state, it is also important to acknowledge that the notion of 'contestability' encourages the pooling of expertise in competitive institutions that are reluctant to share knowledge or disseminate the 'best practice' that provides them with a competitive advantage. As a result delegating discrete responsibilities to alternative providers risks undermining the *intellectual* capacity of the state through a process of de-skilling that not only eviscerates institutional history and epistemic potential but also creates information asymmetries that weaken its bargaining position and reduce its holistic knowledge base.[22]

Partnerships with PSOs are clearly not a panacea for the challenges of modern governance but they do represent one option in the government's (and any future government's) growing portfolio of delivery mechanisms. Another form of partnership within this portfolio attempts to draw upon the resources of voluntary, charities, foundations, co-operatives, community and religious groups—the 'third sector'—as delivery mechanisms for public services. This represents a distinctive element of New Labour's adoption of NPM-inspired measures because it has gone to great lengths to demonstrate that, unlike the previous Conservative governments, public service provision is no longer viewed as a choice between the public or private sectors. The benefit of this position is that not only does it assuage those who are concerned with the growing role of the private sector but it also fits within a modernising agenda based around increased pluralism and competition to drive innovation and efficiency. TSOs are therefore critical in terms of the development of a mixed economy of service providers, coupled with the provision of greater choice for users, greater contestability for commissioners, and the personalisation of services for users. Moreover, for those committed to the 'third way' and a progressive governance agenda, TSOs provide a counterbalance to an emphasis on the private sector, represent a continuation of NPM goals like challenging organisational rigidities and self-seeking behaviour, while at the same time resonating with traditional social democratic values (e.g. active citizenship, civil renewal, voluntarism, devolution).

As a result, New Labour has sought to develop new opportunities for TSOs in mainstream policy areas for shaping, commissioning and delivering public services.[23] However, despite nearly a decade of measures designed to foster increased partnership working, the significance of this sector remains limited. The annual total funding for TSOs from the public purse between 1998 and 2008 has remained between £5 billion and £6 billion (generally no more than 1 per cent of public spending) and a large element of this figure is specific to the funding of Housing Associations.[24] The reasons for the limited role of TSOs are institutional and cultural. Institutional because much of the funding for TSOs is filtered through a complex delivery chain which makes the process very complex and the transactions costs very high for potential partners. Moreover, contracts are often short-term (annual) but involve burdensome monitoring requirements.[25] The cultural hurdles to greater third sector involvement are less tangible but no less significant. Although New Labour may be sure that TSOs can and should play a significant role in the future of the state, many of the organisations themselves are less sure. Many TSOs do not want to be 'mainstreamed' because they fear the distinctive qualities of their organisation—independence from government, unique resources, capacity for innovation, bottom-up organisational structures, core values—may be lost through their *de facto* incorporation as a delivery arm of the state and the associated processes of standardisation and professionalisation.[26] In short, the relationship between the government and the third sector remains embryonic and tentative.

Having reviewed New Labour's strategy in respect to the reform of the public sector, it seems appropriate to review the evidence in terms of whether this strategy has been 'successful' in terms of, for example, improving the efficiency of the state or increasing service provision levels. And yet assessing 'what has worked' is highly dependent upon timescales and emphasis. In many areas the results of specific policies that have drawn heavily on PSOs and TSOs, like the targets for reducing heart disease or the introduction of Sure Start, will not be clear for decades (if not generations). There is also a strong constituency that seeks to argue that any marginal productivity gains in service levels need to be offset against the high costs of those achievements in terms of their impact on the specific qualities and values (equality, collective provision, public service ethos, etc.) that, although hard to quantify in economic terms, contributed to the distinctive qualities of the public sector.[27] Setting those momentarily aside and reviewing the work of the National Audit Office, Audit Commission and Healthcare Commission, the general conclusion on the impact of New Labour's reforms is that that public services (measured on a range of indicators like waiting times, class sizes, crime levels, etc.) have improved since the significant public spending increases from 2001 onwards.[28] The improvements may not have been as dramatic as ministers would have liked for their increased investment (and much of it has been absorbed in increased wage costs), but improvements have occurred.

However, the paradox of New Labour's modernisation strategy (and a key challenge for any future government) is that the public does not perceive or believe that public services have improved even when their own individual experience of services has been better than expected. This is illustrated in a series of Populus surveys that have focused on the public services, specifically health, education and transport, and have revealed a significant disparity or 'perception gap' between how the public perceives services (generally negatively) as opposed to their actual experience (generally positive).[29] It is often said that, when a boxer fights in their opponent's country, dominating every round of the contest is not enough to secure a win—only a knockout will do. The paradox of the 'perception gap' can be viewed as the same dilemma in a different context—not only must the government ensure the state *delivers* improved public services, but it must also *convince the public* that this is the case. (Convincing the public, however, is made more difficult by the public's lack of faith in official data and statistics.) This is a point that leads us to consider public attitudes and social trends as challenges for the state.

Social trends, challenges and public attitudes

The central argument of this chapter is that, although the structure of the state and its relationship with the public is likely to change during the twenty-first century, its role in socio-economic terms is actually likely to grow rather than diminish. Arguments concerning the 'end of the state', the 'crisis of the state', the 'disappearing state', or the 'retreat of the state' are therefore, from this perspective, likely to prove ill founded. Indeed, even the most cursory glance at the main challenges for the state in the next decade (see Table 3) suggests a leading role in relation to socio-economic governance. To the ten broad challenges set out in Table 3 could be added any number of major policy areas that demand urgent attention—childhood obesity, mental health, illegal drug use, pension provision, AIDS-HIV, teenage pregnancy, social exclusion—not to mention the raft of new policy challenges or opportunities for which the state is expected to take responsibility arising from ongoing innovations in science and technology (human embryology, nanotechnology, genome research, reproductive technology, etc.).

While many of these challenges are well-documented and recognised in the government's 2006–7 policy review on the role and future of the state (and may also be examined by other parts of the Future Options II project), this section seeks to sharpen our understanding and push forward debates about the role of the state by emphasising a contextual dimension (a social trend or public attitude) that has generally been overlooked in official reports and academic analyses but helps explain the existence of the 'perceptions gap' (discussed above)—public attitudes to the state.

Public attitudes towards the state have shifted markedly in recent decades as the relatively positive and optimistic public attitudes about the role and capacity of the state that had characterised much of the twentieth century gave way from the 1970s onwards to a more sceptical public. In Britain concern about the reach and efficacy of the state first surfaced in the 1970s in debates about state-overload, delegitimation and ungovernability and it was in this context that neoliberal ideas about the role and limits of state intervention flourished and were implemented in the guise of NPM.[30] What is critical in terms of outlining the relative strengths and weaknesses of any future reform option is that public attitudes towards the state remain overwhelmingly negative. As numerous public opinion surveys and studies illustrate, the public appears to have lost faith in the capacity of the state to solve social problems and no longer sees the state as an effective means of delivering public goods.[31] YouGov surveys in 2008, for example, not only suggest increased scepticism amongst the public about whether the expansion

Table 3: The state: ten challenges

Challenge	Meaning
1. Fiscal sanity	Controlling public spending in relation to current and future commitments.
2. Crisis of competence	Ensuring the state has staff with the correct blend of education, training, experience and values to ensure the delivery (directly or indirectly) of high quality public services.
3. Information overload	Developing data capture, analysis and storage systems that facilitate predictive forecasts and modelling through which the state can improve its responsiveness and capacity.
4. Governing without boundaries	How to govern effectively in a network-based environment in which traditional boundaries (social, geographic, etc.) are less significant.
5. E-government	Recognising the second-wave potential of information technology by integrating operations between agencies and embracing a customer-centric view.
6. Identifying core functions	Adopting a strategic view to contestability that recognises there are legitimate issues around which services should be delivered directly as opposed to through TSOs or PSOs.
7. Results-orientated management	Achieving a results-based culture that focuses on demonstrable results and innovation while preserving a public service ethos.
8. 'Green' leadership	Establish a framework of incentives and sanctions that promote environmentally responsible behaviour.
9. Security and privacy	Capturing the societal benefits of IT (data storage, wireless connections, internet and email, etc.) while managing the risks (inappropriate usage, illegal access, etc.).
10. Surprises	A number of recent events (bird flu, SARS, floods, etc.) have underlined the need for the state to be prepared for catastrophic and non-routine management challenges.

Source: Adapted from IBM Center for the Business of Government, *Ten Challenges Facing Public Managers*, 2008.

in public spending is being efficiently spent but also growing resistance to paying higher taxes.[32]

More specifically, it appears that public faith in the capacity of the state to respond to public demands fell in the 1990s, recovered slightly in the wake of New Labour's election in 1997, but has now fallen back to more or less what it was in the mid-1990s. Public attitudes and social trends matter because they make some possible future options more acceptable than others. They therefore create an environment in which some options are simply removed from the public agenda by virtue of the perception that they offend against certain dominant public values or beliefs. The next section emphasises the narrowness and insularity of the current debate on the future of the state by both the Conservative and Labour parties and seeks to place a wider range of options within the sphere of public debate and contestation.

Future options

Political arguments about the state are changing. Traditional arguments used to be focused around over-simplistic dualisms: whether the state should be large or small; whether the state was part of the problem or part of the cure; 'public' good—'private' bad (or vice versa). These false dualities have given way to a more sophisticated and nuanced debate that recognises the benefits of a broader range of service providers and the need to taper delivery mechanisms to specific services. It has been recognised that the state can play a positive role in both developed and developing countries, but that it can also play a negative role when utilised without careful planning. In this regard it is the scope and effectiveness of the state's activities, rather than the size of its budget or personnel, that are the key issues. This strand of thinking has been particularly evident within the Conservative party's recent discussions about the 'post-bureaucratic state', because the party has not only demonstrated a capacity for deeper thinking about the future options for the state but it has also realised that promising the public unrealistic efficiency savings is an ultimately self-defeating strategy.[33] And yet it is also possible that these more open and sophisticated debates about the role and future of the state are taking place within a very narrow ideological tunnel. It is a tunnel, as was illustrated in relation to New Labour in the second section (above), which remains conditioned and bounded by the almost uncontested assumptions of NPM with its implicit (neoliberal) beliefs about the superiority of markets and market-derived management methods.

This tunnel vision was evident in the final recommendations of the 2007 official policy review on the future of the state that embraced an unashamedly NPM-inspired set of ideas and inspirations based around eight core principles: increased choice; 'personalisation'; 'empowerment'; 'active citizens'; 'ends not the means'; 'payment by results'; 'joint responsibility'; and the notion of a 'strategic' or 'enabling' state [hub model].[34] Although this set of principles contains a certain internal coherence or shared logic, they do also deny the existence of a much broader range of options that are simply not discussed. The report is therefore more of a blinkered final decision than a broad *review* of all the options followed by the rationale on which a specific course of action has been selected. The report is also heavy on aspirations (bordering on clichés) but light on practical recommendations that would achieve these objectives. The same can be said of the Conservative party's emphasis on the 'post-bureaucratic' state which is hard to distinguish from the Labour party's 'strategic' or 'enabling' state apart from its greater emphasis on the 'tremendous possibilities' of information technology.[35]

Let us be honest about the future of the state. The challenges outlined briefly in the second section (above), and in great detail within the government's various policy reviews, indicate that the pressures on the state are likely to grow significantly over the next decade. The state is a large and complex bureaucracy and to suggest that it is about to become 'post-bureaucratic' is nonsensical especially in light of the fact that the history of information technology within British government is disastrous. What evidence does the Conservative party really have that the 'information revolution' is going to deliver benefits on the scale it is claiming? Once again the key factor limiting a full debate on the future of the state is contextual—it is the political environment. This makes it very difficult for politicians to openly discuss practical options that might be unpopular with the public and therefore politically risky. In order to cultivate a more open and honest debate about the future of the state, thereby locating a broader range of options within the sphere of public contestation, it is necessary to be honest about (1) its merits, (2) its limits and (3) the depoliticisation of the state.

Option 1—Trumpet the public

Towards the end of the twentieth century the increasing role of the private and third sectors sparked concern about the future of the state. This was a particular theme of Gordon Brown's platform to become Leader of the Labour party:

[W]e must have the strength to face up to fundamental questions that cannot be side-stepped about the role and limits of government and markets—questions in fact about the respective responsibilities of individuals, for markets and communities including the role of the state . . . As long as it can be alleged that there is no clarity as to where the market requires an enhanced role, where we should enable markets to work better by tackling market failure, and where markets have no role at all, an uncertain trumpet sounds and we risk giving the impression that the only kind of reform that is valuable is a form of privatisation and we fail to advance—as we should—the case for renewal and a reformed public realm for the coming decades.[36]

The government's subsequent policy review in 2007 stated, '[A] new set of issues is emerging, in which the distinction between public and private must be discussed openly'. And yet a debate has not occurred, and certainly very little discussion of 'the case for renewal and a reformed public realm for the coming decades'. To reiterate a point made above, recent statements on the future of the state remain blinkered by a very narrow and neoliberally inspired agenda in which assumptions are made about the innate superiority of the market or market mechanisms. The evidence, however, for these assumptions is equivocal. The comparative research of Pollitt and Talbot finds that there is no research that suggests that the implementation of NPM 'consistently produces enhancements in efficiency or effectiveness'.[37] Stiglitz similarly emphasises that 'there does not seem to be any basis for the *presumption* that markets yield efficient outcomes' (emphasis added) which is obviously not the same as assuming that state intervention is necessarily a superior alternative, but it does at least encourage a more impartial and refined debate on how the selection of delivery mechanisms should be carefully targeted.[38]

One option for a future government would therefore be to 'face up' to exactly those issues highlighted by Gordon Brown (above) and set out their views on the limits of the market alongside an acceptance that the public sector does offer a range of resources (democratic legitimacy, public sector ethos, institutional memory, etc.) that simply cannot be replicated by alternative providers. This point is related to the role of NPM as a dominant paradigm or narrative which tends to emphasise the value of market-like relationships and yet it precludes a discussion of what the state *can* and *does* deliver in areas where the market does not (or cannot) play a role. Acknowledging the *merits* of public sector provision alongside its *disadvantages* would not only facilitate a more balanced debate and a broader range of subsequent options but it would also open political space in which politicians could adopt a more radical option—tackling the 'expectations gap'.

Option 2—Manage public expectations (as well as the state)

Contemporary debates about the future of the state or the public sector veil a much deeper dilemma regarding public expectations vis-à-vis the state and the capacity of political actors to control or suppress public expectations within a political marketplace. In this context options for the future of the state are inevitably tied up with the maximisation of economic efficiency to release resources to either improve or increase service levels. The truth is that there is very little fat left on the bone. Although not publicly acknowledged in these terms, this was the core finding of both the Gershon Review (2004) and James Review (2005) into public sector efficiency and reform. Their conclusion, that efficiency gains in the region of £20 and £35 billion, respectively, were possible, represents only 3.5–6.0 per cent of total annual spending. Every large organisation, be it public, private or voluntary, needs a certain amount of surplus capacity in order to cope with unforeseen crises or surges in demand. Just as a human body with no fat is as unhealthy as a body with too much fat, a bureaucracy running with no spare capacity is similarly susceptible to administrative fatigue, failure and breakdown. Therefore one potentially far-reaching although politically difficult option for a future government would be to focus on the *demand side* of the argument rather than the *supply side*.

Current Labour and Conservative thinking on the future of the state is based on the premise that public expectations about the state are rising.[39] Higher public expectations are fuelled by a number of societal factors—rising living standards, better education, rising incomes in real terms, less deference—but they are also driven by the implicit logic of NPM, and therefore the tendency of politicians to compare public services with those provided by the private sector. As a result the public are encouraged to expect the same standards of personalisation, choice and control in their interactions with the public sector that they enjoy with organisations within the private sector where the mode of exchange is purely financial. The simple fact is that by indulging in this behaviour without massive increases in resources, politicians are deluding the public and simply fuelling frustration with the public sector. As Peter Riddell has argued in this context 'Something has to give. We cannot have it all, but don't bet on any party saying so'.[40]

As Director of the Prime Minister's Policy Unit during 1997–2001, David Miliband developed the notion of an 'expectations gap'.[41] This gap consisted of the difference between the public's expectations of what the state *should* deliver and what the state *could* realistically deliver given the resources it was provided with. The important aspect of Miliband's understanding of this dilemma stemmed from the fact that he was well aware that, although New Labour's modernisation agenda for the public services could marginally increase performance, it was never going to close the gap. The most important role for ministers, Miliband argued, was not necessarily driving forward reform but suppressing (or at least not inflating) public expectations about what the state could deliver. And yet introducing and maintaining a mature debate such as this would be difficult in the highly charged and adversarial context of Westminster. In reality the innate irrationalities of the political business cycle—incentives to promise too much, opportunities to make irrational decisions that offer short-term political benefits but carry long-term public costs, technical decisions being taken by individuals with no specialist knowledge, the manner in which the efficiency of the state is undermined by its inability to make credible commitments, etc.—are well known and have in recent years stimulated a shift towards the depoliticisation of the state that could be extended by a future government.

Option 3—Depoliticise

Given the almost uncontested nature of NPM as the paradigm of 'good governance', attempting to publicly acknowledge the merits of the public sector (Option 1 above) would actually be quite a radical step for any future government. At the same time emphasising the limits of the state and seeking to cultivate an environment in which public expectations about the capacity of the state were more realistic (Option 2 above) would also be a brave option for any future government. However, a third and final option for a future government committed to radically advancing the reform agenda would be to institute a sharper separation between the state and politics. This separation would take the logic of NPM with its technocratic beliefs and assumptions to its logical conclusion by transferring responsibility to unelected specialists who were insulated from political pressures. As noted above, depoliticisation of this nature has formed a central plank of New Labour's modernisation agenda as ministers have sought to distance themselves from the temptations of the political business cycle, most clearly (but not exclusively) in relation to economic policy.[42]

Depoliticisation is therefore associated with the range of tools, mechanisms and institutions through which politicians can attempt to move to an indirect governing relationship with parts of the state, while at the same time seeking to persuade the public that they can no longer be reasonably held responsible for a certain decision, issue or policy.[43] This strategy is founded on rational and technocratic arguments regarding the complexity of modern politics in which decision-making in many areas now demands specialist economic, technical or scientific knowledge. Another politically attractive element of this strategy is that it also creates a 'buffer zone' between politicians and elements of the state that are viewed as either 'failing' or inherently problematic because of the moral questions they pose. These issues are demonstrated by the creation and role of the National Institute for Clinical Excellence (NICE). This independent body was created in 1999 on the basis that decisions about the availability of drugs and medicines on the NHS demanded scientific skills that most health ministers lack. However, the existence of spending restraints on NHS Trusts combined with NICE's role of assessing clinical performance relative to the cost of the medication means that, in effect, the organisation is imposing a government-set form of economic rationality, or what the think-tank Civitas claims is 'a covertly politicised system of rationing'.[44] The benefit of this option for any future government is, as NICE has proved, that depoliticisation provides a useful blame-shifting capacity to shield them from the public backlash against unpopular decisions.[45] And yet the option of depoliticisation is also highly problematic because it brings with it no guarantee that the public will accept that politicians are no longer responsible for certain services, and in this context Christopher Hood has suggested that 'blame boomerangs' are likely to occur in circumstances where a minister attempts to shift responsibility for problems onto officials.[46] Moreover, as events with Network Rail and Northern Rock have demonstrated, although public faith in the capacity of the state might be declining, the public will still expect politicians to intervene and the state to act as guarantor of last resort.

Nevertheless, in terms of the options for rolling out and extending this strategy, debate has recently focused on the depoliticisation of the NHS. Although not a new idea (having been examined in 1944, 1956, 1979, 1983 and 1994), this idea has recently gained prominence via the King's Fund and the British Medical Association.[47] In 2006 the idea received support from a number of New Labour ministers, notably Andy Burnham and James Purnell, and in 2007 depoliticisation for the NHS was recommended by the Conservative party's Public Service Improvement Policy Group and was subsequently adopted as party policy.[48] A 'once in a generation review' of the NHS is currently being undertaken under the leadership of Professor Lord Darzi and the Prime Minister's May 2008 mini-Queen's Speech included an NHS Reform Bill which is expected to deliver a new NHS constitution to enshrine certain principles and a new governance framework.[49] Whether this might at some point in the future embrace the proposals for depoliticisation is yet to be seen.

The three options briefly considered in this section are clearly neither comprehensive nor mutually exclusive. An additional option might have focused on the widespread devolution of tasks to the local level and in this vein could have built upon recent political statements concerning 'double' and 'treble' devolution.[50] In terms of combining the options outlined above, it would be rational to combine a strategy of depoliticisation alongside an explicit attempt to cultivate a more measured public view on the capacity of the state. However, the intention of this section was to demonstrate the existence of choice as part of a wider project to cultivate a more sophisticated and applied debate about the future of the state. It is to re-stating this project within the context of the central argument of this chapter that we now turn.

Conclusion

The central argument of this chapter is that, although the structure of the British state and its relationship with the public is likely to change during the twenty-first century, its role in socio-economic terms is actually likely to grow rather than diminish. In this context the notion of a 'post-bureaucratic state' might have some value as a provocative, rhetorical tool through which to stimulate discussion about the state, but it has very little analytical or empirical leverage in terms of responding to pressing social challenges. Like NPM before it, the concept of a 'post-bureaucratic state' was originally developed in the United States. This fact reminds us that, although this chapter has been concerned with the British state, the vast majority of the issues, challenges and options discussed are relevant in a wide range of both developed and developing countries. There are, however, facets of this debate that remain distinctively British. Central amongst these is the notion that 'there is no alternative'.

The 'logic of no alternative' and particularly that associated with the discourse of globalisation has formed a central element of British statecraft for some period.[51] In this context, this chapter has attempted to articulate a political discourse—an ideational counter-offensive—that re-emphasises the existence of choice and the nature of contingency. Events and crises, as is so often the case, have also created an environment in which politicians and policy-makers are reconsidering the basic ideas that have shaped the nature of the state for so long. In the face of global financial crises during September 2008, the British and American governments (and others) quickly freed themselves from the shackles of free market theory, and embarked upon extensive state intervention into the economy. Options did exist, and the role or capacity of the state to mitigate the consequences of market failure to some degree was obvious. The implications of this crisis for the future of the state should not be over-stated—the political responses were most specifically concerned with reorientating the structures of economic management rather than reviewing the core functions or framework of the state—but it is at least likely that the event will broaden the horizons of contemporary debates regarding the future state and in so doing form the latest stage in a 'restating the state' project that was first formally initiated in the pages of this journal some years ago.[52]

Notes

1 Office for National Statistics, *Public Sector Employment*, London, ONS, June 2008.
2 HM Treasury, *Public Finances Databank*, London, HM Treasury.
3 A. King, 'Overload: problems of governing in the 1970s', *Political Studies*, vol. 23, no. 2/3, 1975, pp. 284–96; A. Birch, 'Overload, ungovernability and delegitimation', *British Journal of Political Science*, vol. 14, 1984, pp. 135–60.
4 T. Christensen and P. Laegried, *Transcending New Public Management*, London, Ashgate, 2007.
5 This distinction is taken from F. Scharpf, *Governing in Europe*, Oxford, Oxford University Press, 1999.
6 R. Wilson, 'The civil service in the new millennium', speech given at City University, London, 5 May 1999.
7 See P. Mandelson and R. Liddle, *The Blair Revolution*, London, Faber and Faber, 1996.
8 J. Newman, *Modernizing Governance*, London, Sage, 2001.
9 See E. Shaw, *Losing Labour's Soul?* London, Routledge, 2007.
10 For a review of this agenda, see M. Flinders, 'Governance in Whitehall', *Public Administration*, vol. 80, no. 1, 2002, pp. 51–75; G. Kavanagh and D. Richards, 'Departmentalism and joined-up government: back to the future?', *Parliamentary Affairs*, vol. 64, no. 1, 2001, pp. 1–18.
11 IPPR, *Building Better Partnerships*, London, Institute for Public Policy Research, 2002.
12 See Cabinet Office, *Building on Progress: The Role of the State. Policy Review*, London, Cabinet Office, 2007.
13 A. Blair, 'Prime Minister's speech on public service reform', speech to the Office for Public Service Reform, London, October 2001.
14 See Cabinet Office, *Better Government Services*, known as the Alexander Report, London, Cabinet Office, 2002.
15 See, for example, HC 801 *Tackling Childhood Obesity*, February 2006.
16 For a review and discussion concerning the different forms of public–private partnerships, see M. Flinders, 'The politics of public–private partnerships', *British Journal of Politics and International Relations*, vol. 7, no. 2, 2005, pp. 543–67.
17 HM Treasury, *PFI—Strengthening Long-term Partnerships*, London, HM Treasury, 2006, p. 16.
18 IPPR, *Building Better Partnerships*.
19 HC 764 *Delivering Better Value for Money from the Private Finance Initiative*, 28, report from the Public Accounts Committee, Session 2002–2003, para. 5.
20 See IPPR, *Opening It Up: Accountability and Partnerships*, London, Institute for Public Policy Research, 2004.

21 E. Shaw, 'What matters is what works: the Third Way and the Private Finance Initiative', in S. Hale, W. Leggett and L. Martell, eds, *The Third Way and Beyond*, Manchester, Manchester University Press, 2004.

22 L. Budd, 'Post-bureaucracy and reanimating public governance', *International Journal of Public Sector Management*, vol. 20, no. 6, 2007, pp. 531–47.

23 For a review, see J. Kelly, 'Reforming public services: bringing in the third sector', *Public Administration*, vol. 85, 2007, pp. 1003–22.

24 Home Office estimate at current prices.

25 See HC 75 *Working with the Third Sector*. Report by the Comptroller and Auditor General, Session 2005–2006.

26 For a discussion, see M. Taylor and D. Warburton, 'Legitimacy and the role of the UK third sector organizations in the policy process', *Voluntas: International Journal of Voluntary and Non-Profit Organisations*, vol. 14, no. 3, 2003, pp. 321–37.

27 See N. Lawson, *Machines, Markets and Morals*, London, Compass, 2008.

28 See, for example, Audit Commission, *Is the Treatment Working?* London, Audit Commission, 2008.

29 See www.populus.co.uk notably 'Public Services: Experience v. Perception', March 2006.

30 King, 'Overload'; W. Parsons, 'Politics without promise: the crisis of "Overload" and "Ungovernability"', *Parliamentary Affairs*, vol. 35, 1982, pp. 421–35; Birch, 'Overload'.

31 For a full review of the available data, see C. Hay, *We Hate Politics*, Cambridge, Polity, 2007.

32 See www.yougov.co.uk

33 See, for example, D. Cameron, 'Fairness and equality in the post-bureaucratic age', speech to the Centre for Policy Studies, London, March 1998. http://www.cps.org.uk/latestlectures/

34 Cabinet Office, *Building on Progress*.

35 Centre for Policy Studies, *The Role of the State in the Post-Bureaucratic Age*, London, CPS, 2008.

36 G. Brown, 'A modern agenda for prosperity and social reform', speech to the Social Market Foundation at the Cass Business School, London, 3 February 2003.

37 C. Pollitt and C. Talbot, *Unbundled Government: A Critical Analysis of the Global Trend to Agencies, Quangos and Contractualisation*, London, Routledge, 2004, p. 331.

38 J. Stiglitz, 'Redefining the role of the state', paper to the MITI Research Institute, Japan, 1998.

39 Cabinet Office, *Building on Progress*.

40 P. Riddell, 'Parties let us believe we can have it all', *The Times*, 8 May 2008.

41 See A. Rawnsley, *Servants of the People*, London, Penguin, 2001, p. 330.

42 P. Burnham, 'New Labour and the politics of depoliticisation', *British Journal of Politics and International Relations*, vol. 3, no. 2, 2001, pp. 127–49; J. Buller and M. Flinders, 'The domestic origins of depoliticisation in the area of British economic policy', *British Journal of Politics and International Relations*, vol. 7, no. 4, 2005, pp. 526–44.

43 M. Flinders and J. Buller, 'Depoliticisation: principles, tactics and tools', *British Politics*, vol. 1, no. 3, 2006, pp. 1–26.

44 Civitas, *England Versus Scotland: Does more money equal better health?* London, Civitas, p. 24.

45 For detailed analysis, see M. Flinders, *Delegated Government and the British State*, Oxford, Oxford University Press, 2008.
46 C. Hood, 'The risk game and the blame game', *Government and Opposition*, vol. 37, no. 1, 2002, pp. 15–37.
47 King's Fund, *A New Relationship between Government and the NHS*, London, King's Fund, 2003; British Medical Association, *A Rational Way Forward*, London, BMA. See also B. Edwards, *An Independent NHS: A Review of the Options*, London, Nuffield Trust, 2007.
48 J. Purnell, *The Guardian*, 23 September 2006; A. Burnham, *A Health Constitutional*, London, Progress, 2006; D. Cameron, Speech to the King's Fund, 9 October 2006; Public Services Improvement Policy Group, *The National Health Service: Delivering Our Commitment*, London, Conservative Party, 2007.
49 NHS, *Constitution: A Draft for Consultation*, July 2008.
50 D. Miliband, Speech to the National Council for Voluntary Organisation, London, 21 February 2006; J. Purnell, Speech to the Centre for Economic and Social Inclusion, Birmingham, 25 June 2008.
51 C. Hay and M. Watson, 'The discourse of globalisation and the logic of no alternative', *Policy & Politics*, vol. 31, no. 3, 2003, pp. 289–305.
52 See A. Gamble and A. Wright, eds, 'Restating the state?', special issue of *Political Quarterly*, vol. 75, no. S1, 2004.

Social Justice and Inequality in the UK: Eradicating Child Poverty?

PETER KENWAY

Why child poverty?

THIS CHAPTER is concerned primarily with the subject of child poverty, something which New Labour has pledged to abolish by 2020. Its premise is that whoever is elected at the next General Election—and in elections for the devolved administrations since they all, too, support this goal—will strive to honour that pledge. Yet notwithstanding the importance which the political class attaches to this commitment, to focus a discussion of the options for 'social justice and inequality' on 'child poverty' is certainly a brutal reduction in scope. How can it be justified? There are two reasons.

First, even though child poverty remains widespread, the government's strategy for dealing with it shows no sign of being able to deliver further progress; in short, the social justice 'flagship' is becalmed. On top of this is the fact that while the Labour government's goal of ending child poverty marked a sharp break with its Conservative predecessors, most of the Labour government's policies for dealing with poverty are an extension of what has gone before rather than a rupture with it. In that sense, the challenge is no less serious for the Conservatives than it is for New Labour.

Second, 'child poverty' is not an isolated problem. Being as much to do with work as with worklessness, it is linked directly to a host of issues to do with low quality employment. As we shall see, it cannot be separated from poverty among working-age adults. As a result, the problems besetting the child poverty flagship are symptomatic of wider social justice difficulties, and the policy options considered towards the end of the chapter have ramifications that go well beyond child poverty.

The chapter is divided into two main parts. The first part is devoted to an overview of the New Labour strategy in this area, including a description of that strategy, its roots and the support for it, and its record according to the latest official statistics. The second part begins by developing criteria to use to identify possible options, going on to sketch out and justify four such options. This is followed by a short conclusion which argues that what is now needed is a paradigm shift, prompted by the anomaly of in-work poverty.

Published by Blackwell Publishing Ltd, 9600 Garsington Road, Oxford OX4 2DQ, UK and 350 Main Street, Malden, MA 02148, USA

New Labour's programme to reduce child poverty[1]

The roots of New Labour's approach

New Labour's strategy for reducing child poverty directly, by raising household incomes, can be characterised as comprising four main elements:

- There is stress on shifting parents, especially lone parents, from worklessness to work, backed by the view that work is the best route out of poverty.
- This shift is encouraged—and the claim that work is, indeed, an escape from poverty is validated—by the tax credit system, and underpinned by the National Minimum Wage (NMW). The value of social security benefits for working-age adults has been allowed to fall steadily relative to average earnings, rising only in line with prices.
- The childcare strategy further supports a shift into work, through both the supply of childcare and the provision of money to pay for it (again via tax credits).
- (Near) universal Child Benefit raises the income of all families with children irrespective of their means.

The only genuinely new element introduced since 1997 is the NMW. On its own, the NMW contributes little to the avoidance of child poverty: two adults (with two children) have to work at least 80 hours a week between them at the NMW in order to avoid poverty without the help of tax credits. What the NMW does, however, is to limit the government's financial exposure by preventing unscrupulous employers cutting wages to a point where the employee is entitled to the maximum amount of tax credits.

The heavy lifting, therefore, is performed by a hybrid of two different approaches, both of which go back long before 1997. The first—the belief that income from work would enable people to avoid poverty, as long as it was boosted by extra money for families with two or more children—was a cornerstone of the analysis beneath the Beveridge Report. The Family Allowance, introduced in 1946, provided that extra. Child Benefit (1977) is its direct successor, albeit in much mutated form.[2]

The second approach—the use of means-tested benefits to boost the money of low-income working families—goes back nearly 40 years to the introduction of the Family Income Supplement in 1971. The current arrangements for Child and Working Tax Credit can be seen as its great grandchild, via Family Credit (1988) and Working Families Tax Credit (1999). The linking of the value of working-age social security benefits to prices rather than earnings also dates from the late 1980s, another legacy of the 1986 Social Security Act alongside the introduction of both Family Credit and Income Support.[3]

Although New Labour has certainly pushed this hybrid much further than its predecessors, it has done nothing to disturb the priority of the principles enshrined in the 1986 Act. In particular, both the pre-eminence of means-testing and the up-rating principle for benefits (in line with prices) remain intact. In short, New Labour has sought to reach its social democratic goal using a Conservative route map.

New Labour's record on child poverty

So how has this strategy fared? New Labour's first anti-poverty measures were introduced in 1999. Official statistics are now available up to 2007/08: in effect, nine years of data since the official 1998/99 baseline. Starting with lone parent employment, the proportion employed has risen by a fifth over the period, from 47 per cent in 1998 to 57 per cent in 2008. Though New Labour would wish to go further, this could fairly be deemed a success.[4]

As far as poverty itself is concerned, the 4.0 million children in 'relative' poverty ('after housing costs') in the UK in 2007/08 was 400,000 lower than in the baseline (see footnote 1 for a discussion of how poverty is measured). This fall is less than half what is required to reach the government's first milestone—a reduction in child poverty of a quarter, or about 1.1 million—which was supposed to have been reached by 2004/05. However, this net fall of 400,000 reflects a larger fall, of some 800,000, up to 2004/05, followed by a rise in the latest three years, of some 400,000.[5]

What lies behind this reversal in fortunes? More detailed data show that the problem lies with 'in-work' poverty, that is, children in families where one or more of the adults are doing paid work.[6] Table 1, for Great Britain, shows the number of children in poverty by their family's work status, in 1998/99, 2003/04 and 2007/08. As can be seen, while poverty among children in workless families has continued to fall, 'in-work' child poverty fell from 2.1 million to 1.7 million in 2003/04 (the low point), since when it has risen all the way back to 2.1 million again. Although it is tempting to look for an explanation of 'what went wrong' in 2004, other statistics suggest that the problem is longer standing. The number of working adults in poverty, but *without* dependent children, rose steadily under New Labour, from 1.2 million in 1998/99 to 1.8 million in the three years to 2007/08.[7] Similarly, estimates of the number of children in working families who 'need' tax credits have risen from 2.4 million in 1998/99

Table 1: The number of children in poverty, by the work status of the family, selected years, Great Britain (millions)

	Children in poverty in working families	Children in poverty in workless families	'In work' as a proportion
1998/99	2.1	2.2	48%
2003/04	1.7	1.9	47%
2007/08	2.1	1.7	55%

Source: Institute for Fiscal Studies. Limited data for Northern Ireland before 2002–3 means that these more detailed statistics are for Great Britain only.

to 3.1 million in 2007/08.[8] The net effect of all this is that the proportion of all children in poverty whose parents are in in-work poverty now stands at 55 per cent, the highest it has been since at least as long ago as 1979.

Rising above the detail, four things of political significance stand out:

- While the anti-poverty strategy was working fairly well up until about 2005, it has, at best, ceased to do so since then. At worst, things are now going backwards.
- The main problem lies with in-work child poverty, where the net improvement under New Labour is now zero.
- Although progress only ceased in the middle of this decade, the forces driving in-work poverty upwards have been evident since at least the late 1990s.
- The adverse trends in in-work poverty impact working-age adults too, especially those without dependent children.

Breadth of support for the current strategy

One of the more curious features of New Labour's anti-poverty strategy is the way that its dependence on means-testing has come to enjoy the overwhelming support of anti-poverty campaigners, for whom more money devoted to tax credits is seen as the best—frankly the only—way of reaching the government's next (still distant) milestone of halving child poverty by 2010. The most influential report to this effect estimated the cost at between £4 billion and £5 billion, an estimate which has been regularly updated since.[9] On the latest evidence, support for tax credits among campaigners seems unabated.[10]

So long as this strategy continued to deliver steady progress, the consensus that it represented was a source of strength. Now that progress has ended, however, it is a source of weakness, since its very pre-eminence has ensured that other ideas about how to abolish child poverty remain sparse in number and under-developed. This is what makes the current situation so difficult. On the one hand, there is a need for a big shift in strategy—not from left to right, but away from a consensus view with bipartisan roots; and on the other, there is little to go on to suggest what this shift might actually be.

Before leaving tax credits, however, there are two more points to note about them and the strategy of which they are part. The first is that they are on a scale that is broadly commensurate with the scale of the problem, that is, they affect millions of people. If child poverty is to be further reduced, never mind abolished, measures that operate at this scale will be needed, even if they are not enough on their own.

Second, both tax credits and the rules on benefit uprating are designed to work by altering the incentives and disincentives that individuals face when making decisions such as whether to take a new job or not. This 'incentive building' approach seeks to make work more attractive, assuming that individuals are capable and rational agents. By contrast, a 'capability-building' approach tries to leave people better equipped to flourish in the environment in which they find themselves. A substantial example of this 'capability-building' or 'personal improvement' approach in New Labour's anti-poverty programme is 'Sure Start'.

The focus on 'early years'

The main exception to the focus on direct measures to address child poverty is the programme of actions aimed at overcoming the disadvantages that young children in low income households tend, on average, to face. By far the most important of these is Sure Start, which began in 1999, and whose most visible manifestation is a developing network of children's centres to meet the health, education, childcare and wider support needs of under-fives and their families.[11] The number of such centres is rising rapidly, from around 1,000 in late 2006 to some 2,900 by March 2008.[12] The target for 2010 is 3,500 corresponding to a centre in every area. Allied to this, though separate, is the policy of providing a free, part-time place for every three and four year old in a nursery, playgroup or pre-school setting.

With academic evaluations of Sure Start beginning to show positive outcomes,[13] it is possible that those looking back several decades hence may conclude that it was the legacy of Sure Start, rather than the direct interventions to alter household incomes, that was actually New Labour's lasting contribution to reducing child poverty.

Except for childcare, which by allowing parents to take paid work may raise income now, the full impact of these centres on child poverty may not be visible until the children benefiting from them today have themselves become parents; in other words, some time in the 2020s. The fact that the ultimate effects of such a programme are long in the future cannot be held against it. But if the current policy mix contains direct measures with a short-term effect and indirect ones that take a generation, what is supposed to happen in the meantime?

This tension highlights an area where New Labour's strategy has been striking for what it has *not* done, namely, to improve the prospects of young adults with the fewest qualifications. By 'young adults', we mean those aged 16 and over (or 18 and over if still in full-time education) and under 25—that is, a mixture of late teenagers and those in their early 20s. All of these people, it should be noted, were still children in 1999 when Blair made his pledge to abolish child poverty.

The bald poverty numbers for this group are striking enough: almost 1½ million (of whom just 200,000 are lone parents) living in poverty.[14] Even more striking are the statistics on qualifications and employment, and the connections between them for those at the bottom:

- Among 16 year olds, 10 per cent got fewer than five GCSEs at *any* level in 2006/07, a proportion only slightly down on 1999/00.[15] Among 19 year olds, a quarter were not qualified to NVQ2 or equivalent in 2006 while one in twelve had no qualifications at all. These proportions, too, are unchanged since the late 1990s.[16]
- Among those in their late 20s, the risks of adverse labour market outcomes in the future associated with poor qualifications are quite stark. For example, among 25 to 29 year olds with no qualifications, 20 per cent lack but want work while 70 per cent of those in work are low paid. For those with only low GCSEs, these risks are 20 per cent and 40 per cent, respectively.[17]

Like tax credits, New Labour's focus on early years enjoys widespread support. Yet the neglect up until recently of those leaving childhood with the fewest qualifications—or indeed those 16 and 17 year olds who are not in employment, education or training (NEETs)—means that even if Sure Start turns out to be a wonderful success, a whole generation will have gone by before its beneficial impact on the deeper causes of child poverty—that is, in the capacities and capabilities of parents—starts to be felt.[18]

Options for 2010

Criteria for possible options

A cursory reading of what can be seen as the main policy documents of both government (*Ending child poverty: everybody's business*) and opposition (the report of Duncan Smith's Social Justice Policy Group, *Breakthrough Britain*, to the Conservative party) confirms that there is already a plethora of policies, actual and proposed, which to a greater or lesser extent are relevant to child poverty.[19] There is not space here to subject these policies to detailed scrutiny. Nevertheless, if we are to proceed in any kind of manageable way, reaching conclusions that do not appear wholly arbitrary, we need some criteria to help identify the kinds of policy that are likely to be needed in order to approach the goal of ending child poverty.

On the basis of the analysis of the record to date, we suggest that there are two criteria which any strategy, or overall approach, must meet. They are:

- first, that the approach addresses in-work poverty; and
- second, that that the approach addresses the overall 'environment' of incentives, disincentives and opportunities within which individuals make their decisions.

The argument for the first criterion rests directly on the analysis of the New Labour record. In summary, it is the failure to reduce in-work poverty that has brought the previously successful approach to a halt. While the reversal in fortunes is quite recent, the underlying adverse trend is long standing. Finding a way to reduce in-work poverty is the priority.

The argument for the second criterion proceeds from the observation that if even a very general policy like tax credits, operating directly on incomes, can only dent child poverty, how plausible is it that an alternative strategy, which depends on 'improving' or capability-enhancing literally millions of people, can do better? For a start, can it be pursued on a large enough scale? Even if it can, doesn't it overlook the point that since part of the value of personal improvement (e.g. an extra qualification) lies in the advantage that it confers over someone else, such an advantage may disappear if everyone 'improves'? Similarly, while personal strengths and weaknesses may very well explain why one person is poor and another is not, it does not follow that such characteristics can explain why some people, as opposed to nobody, are poor. Ultimately, something in the wider social and economic environment has to change if something like poverty is to be abolished. Improved incentives and opportunities are almost certainly necessary, but not *sufficient*.

Against these criteria, the two documents referred to above fare rather differently. As far as the first criterion is concerned, the government document does clearly acknowledge the problem of in-work poverty and suggests that it may now enjoy the same status as the problem of poverty arising from worklessness. By contrast, the Social Justice Policy Group report commits itself firmly to the view that 'work is the key route out of poverty for virtually all working households'.[20] To this author at least, such a confident assertion is reminiscent of the early days of New Labour—see, for example, *Opportunity for all*[21]—before the difficulty of the task had sunk in, and certainly before the evidence of both the extent and persistence of in-work poverty had been appreciated. Its failure even to acknowledge the problem, never mind admit its centrality, must be judged a serious shortcoming.

By contrast, the Conservative document does set greater store by the idea of altering the wider incentives and disincentives facing individuals, not only in relation to employment but to important family and personal choices too. This may be not only to do with the report's broad scope, but also that this type of idea has typically tended to find more favour among Conservatives.

The absence of any comparable idea in the government document is striking. If there is a dominant motif in emergent government thinking in this area it is the idea of 'progression', which includes working more hours, or staying in a job longer, or getting a better job on the back of improved skills. As we will explain below, all these ideas make sense. Yet there is no sense either of the barriers that might confront people who want to 'progress', nor of whether 'progression' on its own can be remotely sufficient. It is as if, having placed so much faith in tax credits, New Labour has now given up entirely on the idea that further measures of that type have any part to play.

Four options

Against that background, we now suggest four options which, we believe, are in accord with the criteria set out above. These should be understood, at least in the first instance, as being complementary to the other policies of the kind just discussed. They are also complementary to one another. The four are:

- to cut 'taxes' for low income working families;
- to restore out-of-work adult benefits to levels that allow a minimum standard of living, for example through a revival of the 'entitlement-based' approach to social security;
- to replace the current arrangements for childcare funded by means-tested benefits, with a system of free, universal childcare; and
- to alter the poverty goal and/or change the way that poverty is measured.

Cutting taxes at the bottom

One of the more striking aspects of New Labour's anti-poverty strategy is that while it has relied so heavily on tax credits, it has neglected the wider tax and social security systems of which they are part. The most egregious example of this was the abolition in 2008 of the 10 pence starting rate of income tax, something which the government itself had introduced in 1999 in order, in the Treasury's words, to improve 'work incentives by allowing individuals to keep more of what they earn'.[22] At least one result of this episode is that it has raised the question of whether the tax system could be used as part of an anti-poverty strategy, with two related but distinct objectives in mind.

The first objective is to reduce the amount of tax that low income, working households pay. More than half of both children and working-age adults in poverty belong to working families.[23] Almost all of them will be paying tax and it is certain that some of them (without dependent children) will have an income below the poverty line by an amount that is less than the combined national insurance, income tax and council tax that they are paying.[24] Of these people it can actually be said that they are being 'taxed into poverty'. Of the rest, it can certainly be said that tax is making their situation worse.

The second objective is to reduce the very high 'marginal effective tax rates' that many of these households face. Anyone earning more than about £100 a week loses 31 pence of every *extra* pound of gross earnings to national insurance and income tax. But anyone in a household receiving tax credits (above the near-universal family element) also stands to lose a further 39 pence as a result of the 'taper' which reduces the amount of tax credit as income goes up. Taken together, this means an effective marginal rate above 70 per cent. For those receiving Housing Benefit or Council Tax Benefit, this rate can be as high as 95 per cent.

In one sense, higher marginal rates are an inevitable consequence of means-tested in-work support. If the 'poverty line' really marked a threshold where life on one side of it was dramatically different from life on the other, such rates could still be justified as the price that had to be paid for taking people over the threshold. But in modern Britain, that is not the case: all sorts of factors—including credit, debt, savings, support from friends and family, the durability of many household goods, etc.—mean that *no* threshold can be that important. In these circumstances, the capacity to improve one's income *further*, via overtime, a pay increase or a small second job (in effect, the government's idea of progression) ought to be an important part of the story. The trouble is the high marginal effective tax rates stand in the way.

A substantial reduction in these marginal tax rates (by say 20 per cent) could only come about as the result of a comprehensive review of how the tax, tax credit and social security systems impact on low income working households. A paper for Sir James Mirrlees' review of a twenty-first-century taxation system, which included an option along these lines, focused on tax credits and benefits and confirms the potential here.[25] Estimated to cost £9 billion per year, this option would take several years to implement. A substantial reduction, on the scale suggested above, would cost more, take longer and require changes to the income tax system too. While there must always be doubt about how far it is possible to go, there is little doubt about the direction that needs to be followed.

A return to the contributory principle

Relative to earnings, out-of-work social security benefits for working-age adults have fallen by a fifth since 1997; anyone dependent on them alone is in 'deep poverty'.[26] Looking further back, the real value of these benefits (after allowing for inflation) is no higher than it was 25 years ago.

The basic argument for tolerating this situation is that it increases the financial incentive to enter employment. In response to this, two points can be made. First, factors influencing *individual* motivation are necessary but not sufficient to reach any particular *aggregate* level of employment. Since 1999, the overall employment rate in the UK has been stuck between 74 and 75 per cent.[27] As a result, there remain some 3.6 million people of working-age, or 10 per cent, in 2007 lacking but wanting paid work.[28] Second, many at the bottom of the labour market actually shuttle back and forth between work and unemployment—or 'labour market churning'. Hence the problem is not just entering work, but of staying there.[29]

The question that arises, then, is the value at which benefits might be set and the eligibility conditions that might be attached. While the former will preoccupy the Treasury, it is the latter that is the political concern. Since 'something for something' is the phrase currently in vogue, it must be time to look again at Beveridge's proposals: 'benefit in return for contributions, rather than free allowances from the State, is what the people of Britain desire'.[30]

An immediate application of this principle would be an increase in the value of *entitlement-based* Job Seeker's Allowance (a Beveridgian relic in the current system), that increase being justified on the grounds that those benefiting from it have already contributed towards it. A more general application of the principle would look at what other criteria might meet such an eligibility condition, for example, remaining at home to care for others or taking part in training, apprenticeships or education.

Expanding free childcare to encourage 'all working'

Unlike the first two options which were both about money, the third option counts as 'indirect' in the terms employed in this chapter. In short, it is the suggestion that the UK, or its constituent parts, should move towards the provision of free, universal childcare. It should be said straightaway that such an idea would be controversial. Besides concerns about behaviour and education, which would lead some to argue that society actually does not want parents to spend less time with their children than they do now, there would also be the objection that what was once a liberation—the 'right' to work—is on the point of turning into its opposite, namely a duty to do so. Why, therefore, should this option even be contemplated? The answer is because both equity and effectiveness demand it.

More than four-fifths of children in in-work poverty belong to families who are only 'part working'. Alongside those who are self-employed, this includes both those families where the working adults had part-time jobs only or, in couple families, where one was working full-time and the other not at all. An obvious implication—and another instance of the New Labour idea of 'progression'—is that to escape poverty the adults in these families should work 'more'. But this raises two questions.

First, what is preventing them? The availability of affordable, quality childcare is part of the answer. A recent government report suggests that New Labour's childcare strategy, which uses tax credits to help parents meet the cost, is not succeeding in providing support for those who need it most. It also finds that earlier progress in extending the use of formal childcare has come to a halt, and that both cost and affordability remain barriers to its use.[31]

Second, why should they work more? At first glance, getting working families to work 'more' may look like a natural progression from the long standing aim of getting workless families to work. When judged by the statistics, however, there is a big difference, for whereas four-fifths of children belong to working families, only half of them belong to 'all-working' ones.[32] While it can therefore be said that it is the norm for a child to belong to a working family, it is not necessarily the norm for them to belong to an all-working one. Any suggestion that poor working families should be 'all-working' is to set a different, harder standard for them than for the rest.

The answers to both of these questions point in the same direction. If we want low income, working families to work more, equity requires that we seek to make 'all-working' the norm across society, not just among those on low incomes. That necessitates universal provision. And if that provision is to be both affordable, high quality, and fully utilised, it needs to be free.

There is one more consideration. Although the government has set a target of 80 per cent for the employment rate, that rate has remained stuck between 74 and 75 per cent throughout this decade. To reach 80 per cent, a large number of new jobs are needed: why not in childcare? The childcare workers will need to be highly trained—a profession, rather than a workforce—not only to achieve a high quality of provision but also to ensure that the jobs can be well paid, thereby avoiding the ultimate irony of one person's route out of in-work poverty being another person's route into it.

This option has to be set against the counter-arguments of dead-weight costs at the high income end, and the need for childcare to be of especially high quality at the low income end if it is to lead to gains for the children concerned. Additionally, some have argued that it would be better to focus efforts among the more disadvantaged on supporting parents to do a good job at home, rather than pushing their children into childcare and their parents into low quality work.[33] With strong arguments on both sides, this will be an area of sharp political argument in the decade to come.

Altering the goal or changing the measure

The last option is different again. Both the goal of ending child poverty, and the way this is measured, have barely changed since they were first announced. This stability has served public understanding and has helped establish the importance of the subject, even when the headline results have been disappointing. But in the end, these choices are value-laden, so the start of a new administration would be the time to consider them anew.

In broad terms, there are two types of changes which could be made. The first concerns the subject. New Labour has explicitly identified children, thereby implicitly identifying their parents who live with them too. Through its actions, it has also clearly identified pensioners. By contrast, it has paid little attention to the remainder—working-age adults without dependent children.

The basic argument for reconsidering the goal is that it is no longer sustainable. As it is, the focus on children to the exclusion of working-age adults has led to a situation in which the maximum value of state child support exceeds the maximum amount payable for adults. That gap will continue to widen. This pattern is far removed from what the official poverty statistics imply about the relative incomes that adults and children need in order for different sized families to have the same standard of living.[34]

More importantly, once we recognise the centrality of 'in-work' poverty, the roots of this large and growing aspect of *child* poverty are largely the same as the roots of (the rising level of) in-work poverty among *adults* without dependent children. A switch to a more general poverty target (even if it did not go so far as to pledge anything so bold as an end to adult poverty) would arguably offer a more balanced approach.

The other possible change is to adopt a different measure of poverty. There is, of course, a substantial literature on this subject, including a growing debate about the need to consider 'well-being' in a broader sense than just income.[35] For politicians and policy-makers, however, one question matters far more than any others, namely, whether to persist with a 'relative' measure or switch to an 'absolute' one.[36] Anecdotally, the 'absolute' standard would seem to enjoy more popular support and would be easier to deliver, so it would not be surprising if politicians were attracted to it.

In response, two things can be said. First, it should not be thought that an 'absolute' standard is easier to defend. It is actually *more* arbitrary than the 'relative' standard, being in effect a 'relative' standard at a fixed point in time, and also produces nonsense over a long period of time (e.g. 'most people in poverty in the 1960s by modern standards'). Second, as a recent report from the Rowntree Foundation shows, a well-founded absolute standard would not necessarily lead to a lower poverty line than the current 'relative' measure.[37]

Concluding remarks

If the exclusive focus on 'child poverty' was a brutal reduction in the subject matter of this chapter, the identification of just four options for child poverty is a further brutal reduction of the view of what needs to be done. Ultimately, the justification for this is the belief that New Labour's strategy is exhausted and that what is now needed is something akin to a paradigm shift. The large ideas sketched out here are an attempt to prompt people towards thinking about what that shift might be.

It is important to be clear, however, that it is not mere exhaustion that demands such a shift, but rather the extent and trajectory of in-work poverty. In Kuhnian terms, this is an 'anomaly' which simply cannot be accommodated within a strategy that is predicated on the idea that work is the route out of poverty. New Labour may finally have adopted various circumlocutions in order to allow it to acknowledge the inevitable; but there is no sign that it has grasped the extent of the challenge it poses.

At the risk of pushing the metaphor too far, talk of paradigm shifts should not obscure the fact that matters of 'normal' administration remain vital too. Sure Start is a good example. On the one hand, it is still a young programme, the basic requirement being to nurture it for several years before its full impact is seen. On the other hand, big issues of implementation and principle remain,[38] such as who should run children's centres (voluntary sector or local government?) or what their ethos should be (top down, government-led, or bottom up, shaped by those who are using them?). Similarly, keeping the tax credit system in good order represents a substantial challenge in its own right.

Putting this more prosaically, whatever options are chosen, a 2010 government will be building on the legacy of New Labour efforts to reduce child poverty. In so far as it has fallen short, Labour has done so because it has overestimated what it was able to do, rather than what it needed to.

Acknowledgements

The views expressed in this paper are those of the author alone. The author is grateful to Adam Coutts, David Halpern, Samantha Callan and Asheem Sigh for helpful comments and suggestions.

Notes

1 All measures of poverty reported here use official statistics and official definitions. In keeping with this, 'poverty' is a *household-level* concept. While most households consist of one or two adults, with or without dependent children, some one in eight also include other adults, usually other family members, mainly grown-up children. 'Child poverty' therefore arises when a household containing (dependent) children is 'in poverty'. Poverty is measured relative to median income, a household being counted as 'in poverty' if its net income (after council tax and income taxes) is less than 60 per cent of *median* household income in the current year. Incomes are 'equivalised' for household size (to allow for the fact that while a family of four clearly needs more money than a single person in order to achieve the same standard of living, they do not need four times as much). For more on these definitions, see appendix 1 of Department for Work and Pensions, *Households Below Average Income 1994/95 to 2006/07*, 2008, at http://www.dwp.gov.uk/asd/hbai/hbai2007/appendicies.asp. This measure of poverty using relative income (that is, relative to the median in the current year) does *not* mean that what is being looked at here is something called 'relative' poverty. Although it is very commonly described as such, it is wrong in principle and betrays a misunderstanding of what poverty is: in short, poverty is measured relative to average income because poverty itself is *inherently* relative, that is, to quote the pioneering work of Peter Townsend in the 1960s and 1970s, when 'resources are so seriously below those commanded by the average individual or family that they are, in effect, excluded from ordinary living patterns, customs and activities'. As a result, what is being measured is not some lesser thing call 'relative poverty' but poverty itself.

2 The mutation is that whereas Family Allowance (set at five shillings per child per week) was available for second and subsequent children only, Child Benefit is not only available for all children but is also worth more for the first child than for others. This latter feature dates from 1991. Prior to that, that is, from 1978, one year after its introduction as a replacement for Family Allowance, Child Benefit was set at a uniform rate for all children in the family. But until 1999 Child Benefit for children in lone parent families was always about 60 per cent higher than that for children in two parent families. After that, this differential declined rapidly, and was abolished altogether in 2007.

3 See, for example, Joseph Rowntree Foundation, 'The effects of the 1986 Social Security Act on family incomes', *Social Policy Research* 54, 1994, at http://www.jrf.org.uk/knowledge/findings/socialpolicy/SP54.asp

4 *Labour Force Survey* at http://www.poverty.org.uk/28a/index.shtml?2

5 The latest government figures for 2007/08 show that child poverty increased by 100,000 between 2006/07 and 2007/08, after increases in the previous two years of 100,000 and 200,000. Source: DWP, *Households Below Average Income 1994/95 to 2007/08*, 2008, table 4.3tr, at http://research.dwp.gov.uk/asd/hbai/hbai2008/excel_files/chapters/chapter_4tr_hbai09.xls

6 For a strategy based on work as the route out of poverty, in-work poverty on the scale observed is extremely damaging. Yet one of the curious features of the discussion of something so conceptually straightforward is the extent to which the idea itself remains contested. It is, for example, quite clear that in-work poverty and low pay (understood as a low rate of pay) are not one and the same thing. Low pay is, after all, a characteristic of an individual worker. Whether that translates into a low household income depends also on the hours that person works, how many people (adults and children) belong to their family, whether anyone else in it works (and if so for how much and for how long), whether the family is taking up the tax credits and any other benefits it is entitled to; what taxes they are paying; and so on. As a result, it is not surprising that the proportion of low paid workers living in poverty has been estimated at just 14 per cent (J. Millar and K. Gardiner, *Low Pay, Household Resources and Poverty*, Joseph Rowntree Foundation, 2004). Consistent with this, more recent analysis, which took as its focus the average hourly pay of all working adults in the household, found that 23 per cent of 'low paid households' were in poverty. However, it also found that 65 per cent of those in in-work poverty belonged to low paid households. When considering how far policies to increase low pay might affect in-work poverty, it is essential to take *both* of these percentages into account (V. Winckler and P. Kenway, *Dreaming of £250 a week: a scoping study on in-work poverty in Wales*, New Policy Institute and Bevan Foundation, 2006 at http://www.npi.org.uk/reports/in-work%20poverty%20in%20wales.pdf). So while it is perfectly true that the first shows that measures to address in-work poverty through raising low pay will be fairly *inefficient* (since most beneficiaries are not in work poverty), the second shows that such measures will nevertheless be fairly *effective* (since most of those in in-work poverty are low paid). It will be noted, however, that recommendations on low pay do not figure among the options considered in the third section of this chapter.

7 *Households Below Average Income*, via http://www.poverty.org.uk/23/index.shtml. The coverage is for Great Britain.

8 *Households Below Average Income*, via http://www.poverty.org.uk/09/index.shtml. The coverage is for Great Britain. This measure of need is made up of those children in working families who are either in poverty (whether or not they receive tax credits) or who escape it by an amount less than the tax credits they receive.

9 D. Hirsch, *What Will it Take to End Child Poverty? Firing on All Cylinders*, York, Joseph Rowntree Foundation, 2006, p. 13, at http://www.jrf.org.uk/bookshop/eBooks/9781859355008.pdf

10 See, for example, a 2008 call for 'next generation of tax credits to "build on progress"', at http://www.cpag.org.uk/press/200508.htm

11 Separate Sure Start programmes are run in Scotland and Wales (as part of

Cymorth, the unified children and youth support fund). There are also Sure Start centres in Northern Ireland.

12 Hansard, 6 June 2008, co. 1175W (Parliamentary answer by Beverley Hughes, MP), source: http://www.publications.parliament.uk/pa/cm200708/cmhansrd/cm080606/text/80606w0002.htm#080606139002305

13 See, for example, National Evaluation of Sure Start Research Team, 2008, *The Impact of Sure Start Local Programmes on Three Year Olds and Their Families*. Accessible at: http://www.ness.bbk.ac.uk/impact.asp. It should be noted, however, that this assessment followed an earlier, first evaluation which was not able to be positive: National Evaluation of Sure Start Research Team, 2005, *Early Impacts of Sure Start Local Programmes on Children and their Families* (report 13), at www.surestart.gov.uk/_doc/P0001867.pdf .

14 Original source: *Households Below Average Income, 2003/04 to 2005/06*, at http://www.poverty.org.uk/24a/index.shtml?2

15 Original source: statistical releases from the DCSF (for England) and the National Assembly for Wales (for Wales), at http://www.poverty.org.uk/15/index.shtml?2. It should be noted that the lack of progress compares unfavourably with the trend for the 'headline' statistic of five GCSEs at grade C or above.

16 Original source: Labour Force Survey (LFS), at http://www.poverty.org.uk/17/index.shtml?2. It should be noted that the DCSF dispute the capacity of the LFS to measure these things properly. But while they believe that the LFS understates the (positive) trend in these numbers over time, they also believe that it overstates academic achievement. These matters are discussed more fully on the poverty website (reference as above).

17 Original source: Labour Force Survey, at http://www.poverty.org.uk/17a/index.shtml?2. 'Low pay' is defined here as an hourly rate of pay of £7 or less in 2007.

18 It is true that the Education and Skills Bill going through Parliament in the 2007–8 session (http://services.parliament.uk/bills/2007-08/educationandskills.html) can be seen as partly answering some of these needs, for example in the duty it imposes on 16 and 17 year olds to continue taking part in education or training, or the duty placed on the Learning and Skills Council to pay the tuition fees for 19–25 year olds seeking their first level three qualification. But some of this is still a long way off: for example, the participation duty only comes into effect in 2015, meaning that it does not apply to any child that was alive back in 1999.

19 HM Treasury, DWP and DCSF, 2008, *Ending child poverty: everybody's business*. http://www.hm-treasury.gov.uk/media/3/F/bud08_childpoverty_1310.pdf; and Social Justice Policy Group, 2007, *Breakthough Britain: ending the cost of social breakdown*, http://www.centreforsocialjustice.org.uk/default.asp?pageRef=226. It should of course be acknowledged that the proposals in the latter report only have the status of recommendations to the Conservative party.

20 Social Justice Policy Group, 2007, *Breakthough Britain: ending the cost of social breakdown*, vol. 2, p. 6, at http://www.centreforsocialjustice.org.uk/client/downloads/economic.pdf

21 Department for Work and Pensions, *Opportunity for all*, 1999, at http://www.dwp.gov.uk/publications/policy-publications/opportunity-for-all/

22 http://www.hm-treasury.gov.uk/pre_budget_report/pre_budget_report_1999/pbr_1999_press_notices/pbr_pn_ir3.cfm

23 Sources: http://www.poverty. org.uk/23/index.shtml?2 and http://www.poverty.

org.uk/08/index.shtml for adults (between 25 and retirement) and children, respectively.

24 See, for example, table 1 in *Memorandum to the Treasury Select Committee by the New Policy Institute: Budget Measures and Low Income Households*, at http://www.publications.parliament.uk/pa/cm200708/cmselect/cmtreasy/326/326.pdf

25 M. Brewer, E. Saez and A. Shephard, *Means-testing and tax rates on earnings*, paper prepared for the Report of a Commission on Reforming the Tax System for the 21st Century, chaired by Sir James Mirrlees, Institute for Fiscal Studies, 2008, at http://www.ifs.org.uk/mirrleesreview/press_docs/rates.pdf

26 Source: benefit levels from DWP at http://www.poverty.org.uk/06/index.shtml?2. 'Deep poverty' is where household income is below 40% of median income.

27 Source: ONS Labour Market Statistics (series MGSU).

28 Source: Labour Force Survey, at http://www.poverty.org.uk/27/index.shtml?2

29 Source: Juvos cohort, ONS, at http://www.poverty.org.uk/33/index.shtml?2

30 W. Beveridge, *Social Insurance and Allied Services*, 1942, para. 21.

31 A. Kazimirski, R. Smith, S. Butt, E. Ireland and E. Lloyd, *Childcare and Early Years Survey 2007: Parents' Use, Views and Experiences*, Department for Children, Schools and Families, 2008, http://www.dfes.gov.uk/research/data/uploadfiles/DCSF-RR025A.pdf. The paraphrased views attributed here to that report are based on the first, second, sixth and eighth paragraphs of the 'conclusions' on pp. 18 and 19.

32 Source: analysis of *Households Below Average Income, 2005/06*.

33 See, for example, *Breakdown Britain*.

34 A ratio of about three to one for a single adult relative to a child, and a ratio of about two to one for any second and subsequent adult relative to a child.

35 UNICEF, Child Poverty in Perspective: An Overview of Child Well-being in Rich Countries, *Innocenti Report Card 7*, Florence, UNICER Innocenti Research Centre, 2007.

36 It should be noted that these popular labels are thoroughly misleading since both measures are, inevitably and invariably, relative to the modern mode and standard of living. A better pair of terms is 'contemporary' and 'fixed', to distinguish the fact that the former moves year by year in line with average income, whereas the latter does not, being uprated only in line with prices.

37 J. Bradshaw, S. Middleton, A. Davis, N. Oldfield, N. Smith, L. Cusworth and J. Williams, *A minimum income standard for Britain: what people think*, York, Joseph Rowntree Foundation, 2008, at http://www.jrf.org.uk/bookshop/eBooks/2226-income-poverty-standards.pdf. For working-age adults, and families with children, this report's standard was around 70 per cent of median income, rather than the normal 60 per cent.

38 For some implementation issues, see, for example, the conclusions in House of Commons Committee of Public Accounts, *Sure Start Children's Centres*, 38th Report of Session 2006–07, 2007: http://www.publications.parliament.uk/pa/cm200607/cmselect/cmpubacc/261/261.pdf

Social Mobility: Concepts, Measures and Policies

JO BLANDEN

Introduction

ON 23 JUNE 2008 the Prime Minister stated that 'Raising social mobility in our country is a national crusade in which everyone can join and play their part'[1] and announced that a Social Mobility White Paper would follow, which it did in January 2009. The Conservatives and Liberal Democrats also share in the desire for more mobility with David Cameron pledging to take 'the banner of sensible, centre-right reform' to social mobility in December 2006[2] and the Liberal Democrats supporting its own independent Social Mobility Commission. Indeed, we might see the social mobility agenda as dating back to 1990 when the then Prime Minister John Major stated his desire for a 'genuinely classless society'.

But what does social mobility mean, and what policies would promote it? Leading sociologist John Goldthorpe has been rather sceptical of the government agenda on this topic, saying that 'like motherhood and apple pie, it [social mobility] is hard to be against'.[3] Is this true; is the concept of social mobility, as politicians see it, too vague to be operationalised?

In this chapter I aim to uncover what politicians mean when they talk about social mobility and compare this to academics' understanding of the term. I then provide some discussion of the types of policies that might be pursued if politicians are serious in their desire to improve it.

What does social mobility mean?

The Prime Minister's June speech on mobility provides a good basis for us to assess what social mobility means to him:

It is a mission of social mobility that the next generation, whatever their background, should have the opportunity to do better than the last.

This is a measure of absolute mobility; we are comparing the outcomes of children with reference to their own parents' outcomes. If we think of 'doing better' as having greater income, then economic growth will do the job, provided it is not shared too unequally across the population. Indeed, we can imagine a case where the children of poorer families are just £1 richer than their parents; were and the children of the rich have twice the income of their parents, this would be social mobility. We can also imagine a case where those from poorer families have twice the living standards of their parents but the

Published by Blackwell Publishing Ltd, 9600 Garsington Road, Oxford OX4 2DQ, UK and 350 Main Street, Malden, MA 02148, USA

richest in society are a little poorer than during their upbringing. This would not count as mobility for everyone. This 'economic growth plus' definition of social mobility therefore does not seem to be quite strong enough.

An alternative conception of doing better is captured by sociologists in the idea of social class. Social class is determined by occupation, but sociologists believe it captures much more than this: it is related to permanent income levels, job security and job autonomy (Goldthorpe and McKnight, 2004) and tends to be strongly related to health outcomes, civic engagement and the outcomes of children. The social class approach to mobility (also known as social fluidity) has been explored by British sociologist John Goldthorpe and his colleagues for the last thirty years. The first challenge is to find a way of grouping occupations. An example is provided in Table 1.

There are a number of criticisms of measuring outcomes by social class.

1. The meaning of social class changes as the nature of work changes; the huge shift from manual to non-manual employment in the last several decades is a testament to this.
2. The broad social class categories conceal a large amount of variation in outcomes within them.

Social fluidity can be examined using a cross-tabulation; comparing father's social class ('the origin') with son's social class ('the destination'). An example of a social class contingency table is given in Table 2, drawing on data on those born in 1970 and included in the British Cohort Study. Absolute upward mobility considers how many people move up the social hierarchy compared to their origin destination. In this case, 42 per cent of the sample is moving up, the most common trajectory in this data.

Table 1: Goldthorpe–Erikson social class schema

I + II Service class	Professionals, administrators and managers; higher-grade technicians; supervisors of non-manual workers
III Routine non-manual workers	Routine non-manual employees in administration and commerce; sales personnel; other rank-and-file service workers
IVa + b Petty bourgeoisie	Small proprietors and artisans, etc., with and without employees
IVc Farmers	Farmers, smallholders and other self-employed workers in primary production
V + VI Skilled workers	Lower-grade technicians; supervisors of manual workers; skilled manual workers
VIIa Non-skilled workers	Semi- and unskilled manual workers (not in agriculture, etc.)
VIIb Agricultural labourers	Agricultural and other workers in primary production

Table 2: Social class contingency table, British Cohort Study

Origin	Destination							
	Non-skilled manual	Skilled manual	Lower grade technical*	Self-employed	Routine non-manual	Prof & manager, lower**	Prof & manager, higher	Σ
Non-skilled manual	3.6	1.5	2.0	1.1	0.8	2.5	1.2	12.7
Skilled manual	5.6	3.8	4.3	1.6	1.6	5.0	3.6	25.5
Lower grad technical*	1.9	1.4	1.7	0.9	0.7	2.3	1.6	10.5
Self-employed	1.9	1.3	1.2	1.6	0.5	2.7	1.8	11.0
Routine non-manual	0.7	0.6	0.7	0.2	0.7	1.8	1.5	6.2
Prof & manager, lower**	1.6	1.5	1.8	1.1	1.3	5.9	5.5	18.7
Prof & manager, higher	0.9	0.7	1.1	0.6	1.3	4.4	6.6	15.6
Σ	16.2	10.8	12.8	7.1	6.9	24.6	21.8	100

Figures given are generally proportions of the population. Σ gives row and column totals as proportions of father or son populations.
* Includes supervisors of manual workers
** Includes small employers
Source: Blanden et al. (2008).

Some of this upward mobility is due to a general movement towards higher status occupations; measures of relative mobility net this out. Relative mobility assesses the outcomes of children relative to others with different family backgrounds. One simple demonstration of this would be to say that just over 30 per cent of children born into the two lowest social classes migrate to the top two as adults, and 65 per cent of those born with fathers in the top two social classes remain in these classes as adults. The chances of getting into the top two social classes are twice as high for those born there than for those trying to get up from the bottom. This paints a rather different picture of mobility. In other words, given that everyone has a better chance of being in the top groups in the second generation, the chances of being in the higher social classes are much greater for those whose parents were there already.

Sociologists have statistical models for drawing out the key features of social class contingency tables. These are powerful tools which enable researchers to make detailed comparisons of both relative and absolute mobility patterns across countries and time. Unfortunately for sociologists they are also quite difficult for the layperson to understand, meaning that the details of sociological research into mobility have not been taken on that widely in policy circles.

Economists also have a tradition of measuring observed mobility, using income and earnings as measures of family background and outcomes (reviewed in Solon, 1999). The measures used in this approach are relative, not absolute. One of the ways that economists measure mobility is through 'transition matrices'. This involves breaking the income distribution of the parents' generation into equal sized groups (usually fifths or quarters) and showing what proportion of the next generation move into a higher income group in their own generation, how many go down, and how many stay the same. Movement away from the starting point is seen as mobility. Notice, though, that using this approach, upward mobility equals downward mobility. If some sons move up, others must go down. An example transition matrix for sons from the British Cohort Study is given in Table 3. A third of

Table 3: Income mobility transition matrix for British Cohort Study

Parental income quartile when son aged 16	Sons' earnings quartile when aged 30 in 2000			
	Bottom	2nd	3rd	Top
Bottom	0.38	0.25	0.21	0.16
2nd	0.29	0.28	0.26	0.17
3rd	0.22	0.26	0.28	0.25
Top	0.11	0.22	0.24	0.42

Source: Blanden et al. (2005).

the sons in this sample are in the same income groups as their parents, with immobility particularly concentrated among the richest and poorest.

One of the problems with the transition matrix approach is that it is unable to take account of how large movements within groups are. If those moving from the first to the second quartile are just tipping over the boundary between the two groups, this is less mobility than if they were moving into the middle or top of their new group. The transition matrix approach cannot account for this. To overcome this limitation, economists commonly adopt a regression approach which takes accounts of all the mobility between generations. This produces the intergenerational elasticity—a result of 0.3 would say that on average 30 per cent of any income difference between two sets of parents would be passed on as the percentage income difference between their children. The extent to which this matters depends on how wide the income distribution is. If inequality is increasing between generations, then we may prefer a measure that takes this into account, and this is given by the intergenerational correlation. The statistical approach is also based on an entirely relative conception of mobility; the amount of upward and downward mobility balance.

The intergenerational elasticity and correlation have their own limitations. In their commonly used forms, they assume that the average association between parent and children's incomes is constant; they cannot show if income differences among particularly rich or poor parents have a stronger effect on their children. Because of this, they may abstract from many of the interesting details of mobility.

Economic progress from one generation to the next (absolute income mobility) is the combination of relative social mobility plus economic growth. There is no reason in principle why absolute economic mobility cannot be measured directly. But in order to do this we would need to have comparable measures of income across generations, adjusted for purchasing power; a tall order. This has been attempted recently for the US Pew Foundation. Isaacs et al. (2008) find that two-thirds of Americans are doing better than their parents while one-third are falling behind. For America, at least, the assumption that economic growth will ensure absolute mobility appears unfounded. It is a notable gap in our knowledge about social mobility in the UK that we do not have this information.

In his June 2008 speech the Prime Minister states that 'there will be potentially unlimited opportunities for the forward march of social mobility, opened up by the changes in the wider global economy'. This assertion rests on the acceptance of the principles of the Leitch Review, that if the UK gains comparative advantage in skills compared to the rest of the world then this will attract many new high skilled jobs. By making skills forecasts that put the UK among the most high-skilled economies, Leitch predicts that we will have 5 million new skilled jobs by 2020. This conception of social mobility seems to be clearly linked with the sociologists' notion of absolute social class mobility.[4]

The evidence that globalisation leads to a shift towards high-skilled employment and a shift away from low-skilled employment seems to be disputed by recent research from both sides of the Atlantic. Autor et al. (2003) and Goos and Manning (2007) both find increases in employment at both the top and bottom of the occupational ladder; while a paper by Autor and Dorn (2008) asserts that the growth in low-skilled service jobs is particularly pronounced precisely because of the growth at the top; more high-paid workers demand more low-skilled workers to cook, clean and look after their children.

Given these observations, it cannot be accepted without question that globalisation combined with improved skills will lead to substantial occupational upgrading and economic growth. And, *even if this were the case*, economic growth and upgrading would not necessarily lead to absolute social mobility for all, and great care would need to be paid to how the fruits of growth were distributed. This point is pursued in the policy section.

In summary, it seems that politicians are more closely wedded to an absolute measure of mobility, possibly linked to occupational improvements across generations. Politically this is no surprise; absolute mobility is couched as everyone doing better, while improving relative mobility means that some people's children will do worse relative to others.

The evidence on mobility in the UK

There are profound difficulties with assessing whether social mobility is at its optimal level (Roemer, 2004). Measuring social mobility in one country or at a point in time is actually not very informative about whether mobility is high or low as we would expect some link between economic/social status across generations for a variety of reasons. This may not mean that the opportunities for mobility are restricted. It is only by making comparisons of mobility across countries and over time that we can see mobility in the UK today as 'relatively strong' or 'relatively weak'. Comparisons can also take us further in terms of policy recommendations as we seek explanations for the differences we find.

The examination of the 1958 and 1970 British birth cohorts has shown a fall in relative income mobility of those growing up in the 1980s compared with those growing up in the 1970s. This finding is based on transition matrices and regression approaches that relate sons' earnings in his early 30s to parental income when he was 16. Research on more up-to-date data has shown that little has changed for cohorts born since 1970 (Blanden and Machin, 2008). These findings have been influential in contributing to the sense that the UK has a mobility problem, and these results have been extensively quoted by politicians of all stripes (albeit sometimes inaccurately).

Studies of the UK's comparative position on economic mobility tend to draw unfavourable comparisons with the Scandinavian countries where the economic structure appears to be more fluid across generations. Some commentators ask whether this is a fair comparison as the Nordic nations are so much smaller and have considerably less diverse populations. However, there are other nations which appear to have more income mobility than the UK: Germany and Canada, for example. Information on other European countries such as Italy, France and Spain is somewhat difficult to come by. The estimation of economic mobility relies on good information on incomes for parents and children which must be obtained over several decades. When this is not available, compromises must be made, which means that, while Italy and France look as immobile as the UK, their position as poor mobility performers is somewhat in dispute.

The messages from research based on social class are rather different and tend to point towards similarity and stability; as indicated in the title of Erikson and Goldthorpe's (1993) book *The Constant Flux*. Results from the 1958 and 1970 cohorts show both absolute and relative mobility to be unchanged. How can this be reconciled with the sharp fall observed for income mobility? One possible explanation is that there are problems with the measures or samples used; investigation indicates that this is not the case (Erikson and Goldthorpe, 2009; Blanden et al., 2009). In fact, it is possible for both of these findings to coexist. Father's social class and parental income are quite distinct, with differences in father's social class able to predict only 20 per cent of income differences. Changes in income mobility within fathers' social class groups appear to be driving changes in mobility across the cohorts.

An additional piece of evidence which points towards suboptimal mobility in the UK comes from Feinstein (2003) who considers the evolution of children's cognitive performance by their socio-economic group. He finds that for a group born in 1970 even those from the lower socio-economic status (SES) group who do well (top quartile) in test scores at 22 months have their relative performance bypassed between the ages of 5 and 10 by those who are in the bottom quartile of test score achievement at 22 months but in the highest SES group. This result has been taken to imply that the interaction of schooling with SES has more influence on outcomes than early ability; those from poorer families are not getting the chance to make the most of their talents. Such explicitly unequal opportunities would clearly work against relative improvements and, to the extent that children's talents may be wasted, might also limit prospects for absolute mobility.

Links with policy

As has been made clear already, the meaning of social mobility is not entirely straightforward, and therefore when discussing policy agendas for mobility we must be careful to ensure we keep in mind impacts on both relative and absolute mobility.

Education and early intervention

Absolute mobility requires the current generation to do better economically or occupationally than the last. High productivity and occupational success are strongly predicted by educational achievements and skills. Therefore to equip the next generation to be mobile we must ensure that they obtain a good education. More than this, we might need to place particular attention on improving the outcomes of the poorest children to ensure this group is not left behind, and counter the forces identified by Feinstein.

Relative mobility requires a rather stronger intervention: the gap between the outcomes of those from richer and poorer backgrounds needs to narrow. It is not enough that those from poorer backgrounds keep up; they must progress faster than their better-off peers. The history of UK education indicates that this is a difficult goal. As shown by Blanden et al. (2005), as university participation rates expanded over the 1980s and 1990s, the lion's share of additional opportunities went to those from richer backgrounds. There was absolute mobility as all groups did better, but the gaps in improvement were so pronounced that relative mobility fell.

When Tony Blair came to power in 1997 he famously said that his three policy priorities were 'Education, education and education'. Since 1997 there has been a raft of policy initiatives aimed at improving educational outcomes, particularly those of the disadvantaged.[5] The Excellence in Cities Programme provided additional funding for poorer schools while the Education Maintenance Allowance gave financial incentives for those with lower family incomes to stay on in education beyond age 16. Both policies have been shown to be moderately successful (Emmerson et al., 2005) but are unlikely to have substantial impacts on future rates of intergenerational mobility, either measured absolutely or relatively.

Another key dimension of government policy on schools has been the competition and choice agenda. There is an argument that by allowing schools to compete for pupils, schools will be incentivised to improve their performance, which should benefit all. Diversification of schools has been encouraged by allowing schools to specialise by subject area and through the private sector sponsorship of academies. So far, evidence on the success of competition and choice in driving up outcomes across the board has been limited (Gibbons et al., 2008). School choice reveals particular tensions between the politics of absolute and relative mobility. Quite understandably all parents want access to the best schools for their children. The difficulty is that places at the best schools are naturally rationed and it tends to be better-off parents who are able to secure places in these schools for their children. Improving relative mobility would require access to the top schools to be given preferentially to poorer children; a policy likely to be highly unpopular with the middle classes.

All three major parties have policies which explicitly aim to narrow educational gaps. In the 2009 Social Mobility White Paper, the Government announced £10,000 'golden handcuffs' to encourage the best teachers to commit to the most disadvantaged schools. An objection to Labour's school-based approach is that many of the most disadvantaged pupils do not go to the most disadvantaged schools. Instead, the Conservatives and Liberal Democrats propose a Pupil Premium which will give schools additional funding for each disadvantaged student on their rolls, increasing the incentives to take these pupils. These types of policies, if well-targeted and backed up by real money, could make a real difference in terms of helping poorer children catch up and improving relative mobility.

The research evidence seems to point to early interventions as crucial, with evidence to suggest they give the most 'bang for your buck' in terms of improving outcomes and narrowing inequalities.[6] Once again the type of mobility we are pursuing will influence the way that early childcare and education is provided. The stronger the commitment to relative mobility is, the more highly targeted interventions will need to be. Sure Start is an example of an intervention that could pay dividends in the long term, but there have been tensions here too, as noted by Polly Toynbee in the *Guardian* in June 2006:[7]

Another No 10 adviser has been telling the prime minister that Sure Start has been 'captured' by the middle class. Good grief, securing some middle-class enthusiasm for Sure Start is vital for its political survival. Most policy-makers are desperate to entice the middle classes into housing estates and struggling schools: services only for the poor rapidly become poor services.

The balance between universalism and targeting is a difficult one, and it is without doubt that the focus on absolute mobility is in part due to the tricky politics of 'getting everyone on board'.

Inequality and child poverty

There is clearly a very strong link between the child poverty and social mobility agendas, although the links are rather complex and require some examination. Take this statement from *Ending Child Poverty: Everybody's Business*:

Childhood experience lays the foundations for later life. Growing up in poverty can damage cognitive, social and emotional development, which are all determinants of future outcomes. While some children who grow up in low-income households will go on to achieve their full potential, many others will not. Experiencing poverty in childhood affects children's outcomes as adults, and these, in turn, affect their children, thus creating cycles of deprivation. (HM Treasury, 2008, p. 25)

In summary: low levels of social mobility combined with high levels of child poverty are going to lead to poor future outcomes for today's children.

However, ending child poverty will not necessarily lead to improved outcomes for children if it is not money in itself that matters for children's development. If poor parents are poor because they lack skills and motivation, then tipping their incomes over the poverty line through redistribution will not necessarily lead to much improvement in their children's life chances. For this reason, government policy on ending child poverty through work and redistribution tends to be discussed hand-in-hand with the type of targeted interventions mentioned in the previous section.

On the reverse side, child poverty can be thought of as a driver of low social mobility. In a society where there is substantial inequality, those at the bottom are likely to be substantially disadvantaged compared to those at the top. The reduction of child poverty is not only more important in the light of sub-optimal social mobility but may also be a cause of it.

I have already mentioned that the UK is often compared unfavourably with the high mobility Nordic countries; these nations are also striking for their low inequality and consequent low rates of child poverty. A summary of the relationship between child poverty and social mobility for those born around 1960 is given in Figure 1.

Further investigation of the relationship between inequality and mobility in Blanden (2009) shows strong relationships between both inequality and poverty and mobility. Indeed, results show that the relationship between inequality in childhood and social mobility is stronger than the relationship between child poverty and mobility. A real desire to promote relative economic mobility would require a narrowing of income gaps at both the top and the bottom. Given the government's relaxed attitude to top-end inequality, this may be another reason why increasing absolute mobility is a more palatable option.

John Goldthorpe puts it more strongly than this. He asserts that the focus on social mobility or equality of opportunity has been in large part a substitute for a New Labour policy on 'equality of condition' through redistribution. Indeed, he goes further and states that those economies that have succeed in achieving high levels of relative mobility have done so only as a by-product of policies that focus on narrowing the income distribution.

Conclusion

One conclusion that has emerged very strongly from this article is that, despite how ubiquitous the term 'social mobility' is in policy circles, there is some confusion over what is meant. Academics tend to distinguish between absolute and relative mobility and also to differ in the measure of outcomes used, focusing either on income or social class. Recent statements, particularly from the government, tend to indicate that absolute mobility is the primary concern.

Politicians' fondness for absolute measures of mobility is understandable. Absolute mobility is essentially a win-win story while relative mobility is conceptually a zero-sum game (although not if we think of economic growth operating at the same time). Increased relative mobility is also a more demanding target as it requires a continual narrowing of the gap between

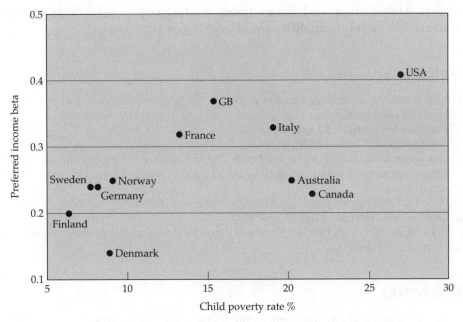

Figure 1: Child poverty and relative economic mobility

Notes: Intergenerational persistence is the preferred intergenerational elasticity taken from Blanden (2009). Child poverty rates are based on 60 per cent of median income and are from the Luxembourg Income Study. The poverty figures are for 1982 or as close as possible to that date; it should be noted that child poverty in the UK rose substantially after 1982.

the outcomes of children from richer and poorer (or higher and lower class) backgrounds.

Policies to increase relative mobility need to be strongly targeted. As well as far-reaching policies to address gaps by family background in education and beyond, it also seems probable that a radical re-examination of attitudes to inequality would be required. Both of these policies would require real political commitment and difficult choices. The achievement of absolute mobility should in theory be easier; it requires that there is economic progress and that the gains from this progress *are not too unevenly distributed*. Even then, policies that lead to substantial economic progress for the majority of the population are not easy to come by.

Another difficulty with policies that attempt to influence mobility is that they take a long time to bear fruit. It was not until the early 2000s that we were able to investigate the mobility of those born in 1970 and even then this was only possible because of very detailed longitudinal data. This difficulty in evaluation only helps to strengthen the impression of a rather vague policy agenda. A future government of whatever colour will need to be much clearer and franker about what improving social mobility means to them and have concrete intermediate targets that relate clearly to their objectives; for example narrowing the socio-economic gradient at different points in the education system. However, a real commitment to targeted policies that address (particularly early) inequalities could bear real fruit.

Notes

1 Speech by Prime Minister Gordon Brown to the Specialist Schools and Academies Trust, 23 June 2008.
2 *The Observer*, Sunday 3 December 2006.
3 Goldthorpe and Mills (2008), p. 96.
4 This impression seems to be confirmed by the discussion in the Cabinet Office discussion paper, 'Getting on, getting ahead', which was published after this article was drafted.
5 McNally (2005) provides a helpful review of recent reforms.
6 Carneiro and Heckman (2003) *inter alia*.
7 P. Toynbee, 'Labour's best achievement hangs in the balance, but they do nothing', *Guardian*, 30 June 2006.

References

Autor, D. and D. Dorn, 'Inequality and specialization: the growth of low-skilled service jobs in the United States', Cambridge, MA, MIT, mimeo, 2008.

Autor, D., F. Levy and R. Murnane, 'The skill content of recent technological change: an empirical exploration', *Quarterly Journal of Economics*, vol. 118, 2003, pp. 1279–333.

Blanden, J., 'How much can we learn from international comparisons of intergenerational mobility?', Centre for Economics of Education Discussion Paper, forthcoming (2009).

Blanden, J. and S. Machin, 'Up and down the intergenerational ladder in Britain: past changes and future prospects', *National Institute Economic Review*, No. 205, 2008, pp. 101–16.

Blanden, J., P. Gregg and S. Machin, 'Educational inequality and intergenerational mobility', in S. Machin and A. Vignoles, eds., *What's the Good of Education?* Princeton, NJ, Princeton University Press, 2005, pp. 99–114.

Blanden, J., P. Gregg and L. Macmillan, 'Intergenerational persistence in income and social class: the impact of within-class inequality', mimeo, 2009.

Cabinet Office, 'Getting on, getting ahead: a discussion paper: analysing the trends and drivers of social mobility', 2008. http://www.cabinetoffice.gov.uk/media/cabinetoffice/strategy/assets/socialmobility/gettingon.pdf

Carneiro, P. and J. J. Heckman, 'Human capital policy', in J. J. Heckman, A. B. Krueger and B. M. Friedman, eds., *Inequality in America: What Role for Human Capital Policies?* Cambridge, MA, MIT Press, 2003, pp. 77–240.

Emmerson, C., S. McNally and C. Meghir, 'Economic evaluation of education initiatives', in S. Machin and A. Vignoles, eds., *What's the Good of Education?* Princeton, NJ, Princeton University Press, 2005, pp. 191–216.

Erikson, R. and J. H. Goldthorpe, *The Constant Flux*, New York, Oxford University Press, 1993.

Erikson, R. and J. H. Goldthorpe, 'Income and class mobility between generations in

Great Britain: the problem of divergent findings from the datasets of birth cohort studies', *British Journal of Sociology*, forthcoming (2009).

Feinstein, L., 'Inequality in the early cognitive development of British children in the 1970 cohort', *Economica*, vol. 70, 2003, pp. 73–98.

Gibbons, S., S. Machin and O. Silva, 'Choice, competition and pupil achievement', *Journal of the European Economic Association*, vol. 6, 2008, pp. 912–47.

Goldthorpe, J. H. and A. McKnight, 'The economic basis of social class', CASEpaper 80, London, LSE, 2004.

Goldthorpe, J. H. and C. Mills, 'Trends in intergenerational class mobility in modern Britain: evidence from national surveys 1972–2005', *National Institute Economic Review*, No. 205, 2008, pp. 83–100.

Goos, M. and A. Manning, 'Lovely jobs and lousy jobs: the rising polarisation of work in Britain', *Review of Economic Studies*, vol. 89, 2007, pp. 118–33.

HM Treasury, *Ending Child Poverty: Everybody's Business*, London, HM Treasury, 2008.

Isaacs, J., I. Sawhill and R. Haskins, 'Getting ahead or losing ground: economic mobility in America', report for the Pew Foundation, The Brookings Institution, Washington, DC, 2008, available at http://www.economicmobility.org/assets/pdfs/Economic_Mobility_in_America_Full.pdf

McNally, S., 'Reforms to schooling in the UK: a review of some major reforms and their evaluation', *German Economic Review*, vol. 6, 2005, 287–96.

Roemer, J., 'Equal opportunity and intergenerational mobility: going beyond inter-generational income transition matrices', in M. Corak, ed., *Generational Income Mobility in North America and Europe*, Cambridge, Cambridge University Press, 2004, pp. 48–57.

Solon, G., 'Intergenerational mobility in the labor market', in O. Ashenfelter and D. Card, eds., *Handbook of Labor Economics*, Volume 3A, Amsterdam, North Holland, 1999, pp. 1761–800.

The Tax System under Labour

PAUL JOHNSON

WRITING a review of tax policy during the last period of Conservative government was a relatively straightforward exercise. The big ideas were pretty clear and pretty consistently acted upon. There was a major move from direct taxes, particularly income tax, to indirect taxes, particularly VAT. There were dramatic cuts in higher and basic rates of income tax, following directly from a stated belief in the importance of incentives. The overall effect of these changes was clearly regressive. In addition there were real moves towards simplification of the system, a widening of the tax base through, for example, gradual phasing out of mortgage tax relief and the married couples allowance, and some important reforms of the taxation of savings. There were individually significant reforms of corporation tax and Capital Gains Tax, and the replacement of capital transfer tax by inheritance tax. The income tax system moved from a joint to an individual basis. And then, of course, there was the poll tax debacle.

It is much harder to put together anything like such a coherent narrative of tax reform since 1997. If there has been a 'big idea', it has been the introduction of tax credits as a means of increasing both redistribution and work incentives. This has been a massive reform. About £20 billion are currently spent annually on the various elements of working tax credit and child tax credit. Arguably though, and certainly in the opinion of this author, this was more about reforming the welfare benefit system than about the tax system as such.

This paper gives a broad overview of tax policy change from 1997 and then focuses on just two issues which define much of the Labour approach to tax policy. The first is the direct tax system and how it has, or has not, been used as an instrument of redistribution. The second is the use of the tax system as a tool of economic policy aimed at changing behaviour.

Overview

At the macro level the tax take rose by about 2.1 per cent of national income between 1996/97 and 2007/08, equivalent to £29.5 billion in today's terms. Announced tax increases—like increases in NI contributions and removal of dividend tax credits—and fiscal drag have played equally important roles.[1] Fiscal drag, resulting from increases of tax allowances in line with inflation when earnings are rising faster, has in fact been crucial to Labour policy and helps explain why the number of people paying income tax rose from 25.7 million in 1996–7 to 31.6 million in 2007–8 and why the number paying it at

 Published by Blackwell Publishing Ltd, 9600 Garsington Road, Oxford OX4 2DQ, UK and 350 Main Street, Malden, MA 02148, USA

the higher rate rose from 2.1 million to 3.7 million over the same period. Whilst the overall increase in tax take is not massive in historical terms, it does represent the fourth highest increase among OECD countries over that period. Of course, taxes are raised for a reason and spending has also risen since 1997.

As we have already observed, putting a narrative around this overall change is challenging. A number of early tax changes were largely opportunistic. The imposition of a windfall tax on the privatised utilities is now largely forgotten. Its stated aim was to tax those who had made excessive gains from the rise in share values associated with privatisations where share values had risen very fast, in part reflecting under-valuation of the original shares. Its effect, of course, was to tax those who happened to be holding shares at the time the policy was announced—not, on the whole, the same people who benefited from any original under-valuation. The removal of dividend tax credits, which raised £5 billion annually largely as a result of an increased tax take from pension funds, was another early cash raiser, the controversy surrounding which was considerable. The reduction of the VAT rate on domestic energy from 8 per cent to 5 per cent was another populist measure introduced in the wake of the 1997 election victory—one which presumably some of those within government who take environmental issues seriously now regret.

Beyond that, some continuation of Conservative policies is evident. Mortgage interest relief was finally put out of its misery by the Labour government in 1999 with the Married Couple's Allowance disappearing a year later. There have been further cuts in the basic rate of income tax and, as under the Conservatives, a significant rise in the numbers paying higher rates. Like the Conservative government, when an increase in direct taxation was deemed necessary, Labour chose to increase the rate of that much less satisfactory—but apparently less visible—tax, National Insurance contributions. And for his first two years in office Chancellor Brown also continued with, and indeed made more punitive, the fuel duty escalator which saw tax on petrol rise much faster than inflation.

Of course the fuel duty escalator ended in 2000 with an abrupt policy *volte face*. Since then fuel duties were raised even in line with inflation only once between April 2000 and November 2006 with the result that real levels of fuel duty had fallen back to roughly their initial 1997 level by 2007.

Indeed the problems with following a consistent policy on fuel duty exemplify well two other rather interesting aspects of Labour tax policy. One has been the difficulty faced in making a reality of another apparent 'big idea', i.e. giving a much more salient role to environmental taxes. The other has been the astonishing number of policy turnarounds. Perhaps the two most damaging tax events of the entire Labour period in government occurred in the chaos (and chaos is not too strong a word) surrounding the reform to Capital Gains Tax and the abolition of the 10p starting rate of tax, both originally announced in 2007. What is less remarked upon than the chaotic nature of these reforms is that both were essentially about undoing major, and largely economically illiterate, reforms introduced by the Labour government in its first term. Other less celebrated policy climb-downs include the introduction and subsequent abolition just four years later of a zero per cent starting rate of corporation tax.

The starting rate of corporation tax was intended as an incentive for 'investment and enterprise'. It represents another strand in Labour tax policy—the desire to use changes to particular elements of the system to incentivise behaviour deemed to be desirable. The zero per cent starting rate was abolished because its major effect was not to stimulate a boom in enterprise. Rather it was, entirely predictably (and predicted at the time), to alter the legal form in which individuals decided to operate. Other efforts to use the tax system to change behaviour included the original changes to Capital Gains Tax (undone in 2007/08), which offered incentives for holding on to assets, in particular 'business' assets, for longer periods and the introduction and considerable extension of tax credits for research and development. There has been a host of smaller initiatives.

Finally in this brief overview one should mention the one big change that has not happened—the reform, or even revaluation, of Council Tax. No doubt well aware of the problems caused to the last Conservative government by local taxes, Labour has reviewed them to death through the interminable process of the Lyons Review (2007) and then simply sat on its hands. That's not to say that nothing has happened—average council tax bills have risen by about two-thirds in real terms since 1997 (whilst payments remain based on the relative value of properties in the early 1990s).

Chancellor Brown never really set out to be a tax reforming Chancellor, and lasting and substantial tax reforms are certainly not going to be among his political legacies. But, as we shall see, this does not mean that he was inactive in this field.

Redistribution and direct taxes

Table 1 shows how changes to the personal tax and benefit system from May 1997 to 2008 have impacted on the incomes of the different income groups. Using household level data from the Family Resources Survey, it divides the population into deciles (tenths), from the poorest to the richest, and, using the IFS tax and benefit model, shows how the incomes of each decile have been affected by direct tax and benefit changes since 1997 (after adjusting only for price inflation). The first column of figures shows by what percentage the incomes of that decile have, on average, been raised or reduced by the tax and benefit changes. We include all changes to the direct tax system, including changes to employee and employer NI contributions, and increases in Council Tax, as well as all changes to the benefit system including tax credits. The systems being compared are those of May 1997 when the current government came to office and that of 2008, including the impact of the abolition of the 10p tax rate and associated compensation packages.

Table 1: Percentage changes in incomes resulting from tax and benefit policies between 1997 and 2008

Decile	Percentage change in income from tax and benefit changes	Percentage change in income from benefit changes only
1 (poorest)	16	18
2	14	15
3	10	12
4	7	8
5	4	5
6	3	4
7	2	3
8	0	1
9	−1	0
10 (richest)	−2	0

Note: Calculations from IFS Tax benefit model (TAXBEN) based on 2005–06 Family Resources Survey. Includes direct tax changes and benefit changes. Tax credit changes counted as benefit changes. All percentage changes rounded to nearest full number. 2008 system compared to May 1997 system uprated with price inflation.
Deciles are deciles of income under the 2008 system. So the first figure, for instance, shows that the poorest tenth of the population under the current tax and benefit system are 16 per cent better off than they would have been under the 1997 system.

Immediately obvious from the table is that the combination of these changes has been substantially redistributive. The bottom three deciles—the poorest 30 per cent of the population—have seen their incomes rise by 16 per cent, 14 per cent and 10 per cent, respectively, purely as a result of tax and benefit changes. These are substantial increases. By contrast the top three deciles have seen very little impact, on average, on their incomes. The top decile has been made worse off by 2 per cent, the 9th decile is worse off by 1 per cent and the 8th decile is essentially unaffected on average by tax and benefit changes. (Although we don't show it here, it is interesting to note that about a third of the losses by the top decile are in fact accounted for by rises in levels of Council Tax, the one tax not in the direct control of central government and not, one assumes, a deliberate element of government tax strategy.)

The tax and benefit changes included in this table have involved a significant net giveaway to households. This is more than explained by increases in benefits and tax credits. Direct taxes by themselves have risen by just over 1 per cent of household income on average—or just over £8 per household per week, and that doesn't include effects of changes to Inheritance Tax, Capital Gains Tax or stamp duties, indirect taxes, like VAT and excise duties—which have in fact changed little on average over the period—or taxes like Corporation Tax which don't fall directly on households (though which are, of course, eventually paid by them).

Given the pattern of changes observed in the first column of the table, it is not surprising to learn that the vast majority of the redistributive changes have arisen as a result of changes to the benefit (including tax credit) system. Other than at the very top, where tax changes have been enough to more than claw back any increases to benefits to which richer households may have had access, the effects of the benefit system dominate. This is demonstrated in the second column of the table which shows the effect of the benefit system (including tax credits) only. The residual tax effect is small at every point. Whilst the benefit system has been used as a major tool of redistributive and social policy, the tax system quite clearly has not. Even some of the most significant changes, a 3p cut in the basic rate of tax alongside increases in employer and employee NI contributions (NICs), are to a large extent offsetting. And the majority of the tax effect on the top decile is accounted for by the combination of Council Tax and *employer* NI increases.

Other important changes—including following through from the previous government the business of abolishing the Married Couple's Allowance and Mortgage Interest Relief, as well as rationalising to some extent the relationship between NI and Income Tax—have had limited distributional effects though they have been welcome reforms to the system. Also following the pattern of the 1979–97 Conservatives, this Labour government has reduced the basic rate of tax whilst increasing the apparently less visible NI rates. Perhaps more importantly for the future has been the decision to remove the cap on employee NICs for the first time. Following a welcome alignment between the income tax and NI system, NICs are now levied on employees at 11 per cent of earnings between the 'primary threshold', now set equal to the income tax allowance (£105 in 2008), and the Upper Earnings Limit (UEL) of £770 per week, and 1 per cent on all earnings above the UEL.

This additional 1 per cent charge above the UEL, introduced in 2002 as part of the package claimed to be to help fund big increases in NHS spending,[2] effectively means that the marginal tax rate on higher earners is now 41 per cent rather than the 40 per cent it had been since 1988. There is, of course, in reality no link whatever between the NI system and spending on the NHS. And having taken the plunge and started to charge NI above the UEL for the first time, the government has surely made it easier to increase the rate from 1 per cent at some point in the future. There is also scope for a much more radical bringing together of income tax and NICs—something which governments of all stripes have shied away from until now.

One element of the direct tax system that was in place for nearly all of this period, but which does not appear directly in these calculations, is the 10p starting rate of tax. It was introduced in 1997 explicitly to help poorer taxpayers and improve work incentives. Its demise was announced in 2007 alongside a cut in the basic rate of tax. A set of compensatory policies centred on raising the personal allowance were announced in 2008 following the furore over its abolition which would have left many low earners worse off. Of course, if the money from abolishing the 10p rate had been used to increase allowances in the first place, rather than to cut the basic rate of tax, then all these problems could have been avoided.

To give a sense of scale, the Treasury's 2007 tax 'ready reckoner' suggests that changing the basic rate by 3p costs about £12 billion annually. Changing the personal allowance by £100 costs about £700 million. So if the government had not cut the basic rate from 23p to 20p in the pound, it could instead have raised personal allowances by more than £1,500 thereby removing around 1.5 million people from the income tax system altogether.[3]

The question obviously arises as to why Chancellor Brown in 1997 thought the 10p rate to be a good idea and yet by 2007 had changed his mind. It is in fact the first part of that question which is the real puzzle. There never was a coherent case for a 10p tax rate on grounds either of redistribution or work incentives. It is *always* a more effective route to helping the lowest earning taxpayers to spend a certain amount of money raising the personal allowance rather than to introduce a new lower rate of income tax. Raising allowances takes those with the lowest incomes out of tax altogether. And the impact of the 10p tax rate on work incentives was miniscule because it is overwhelmingly the benefit system which matters for them. As Andrew Dilnot and Chris Giles put it back in 1997:

Given the objectives of the Labour manifesto (fair taxation and increasing work incentives), increasing allowances or reforming means-tested benefits will always be more effective for the same cost than introducing a 10% starting rate of tax. They will also avoid unnecessary complication of the tax system.

There must be a strong suspicion that adjustments to rates of income tax make better slogans than more sensible reforms to the direct tax system.

As was demonstrated rather clearly in 2008, undoing such complications can be messy, expensive and politically challenging—points that future Chancellors would do well to bear in mind.

None of this should be taken to understate the remarkable quantities of money that have gone into the *benefit* system in general and the tax credit system in particular. This has been crucial in arresting the growth of inequality and in helping millions of poor families—with a particular focus on families with children and pensioners. The tax credits which have seen hugely increased rewards for those in work have also transformed work incentives for many low earners with children, even if their implementation has been very badly flawed. Their impact on incentives and incomes could have been replicated through reform to the previous Family Credit system but, as William Davies (2007) concludes in his survey of the experience of tax credits, much of the problem arose from the extent to which 'perhaps more than any other big New Labour initiative, the policy was built around presentation—in this case the need to call a benefit a tax and to pay it through the pay packet'.

Changing behaviour

If it is hard to find a narrative for personal tax changes since 1997, there clearly has been a theme running through another set of tax reforms—the desire to use taxes to alter behaviour, and in particular to overcome perceived market failures of one sort or another and thus to improve productivity. To some degree the use of tax credits to increase work incentives falls within this set of policies. Other significant changes in this area include two—the initial Capital Gains Tax (CGT) reforms offering lower rates for assets held longer, and the introduction of a zero per cent starting rate of corporation tax—which have since been abolished. Of those that remain, the biggest is the R&D tax credit which was estimated to reduce tax revenues by £490 million in 2007/08 as well as incurring public expenditure costs of an additional £170 million.

Because the range of changes has been so considerable, it is hard to make judgements about the effectiveness of all these efforts to improve productivity. Some, like the R&D tax credit, have at least been focused on areas where there is a clear economic case for believing that there might be a market failure. Others, such as the original CGT changes, were based on much shakier foundations. All have complicated the system. And it is not only the proliferation of, and later changes to, particular schemes which have added uncertainty and complexity. As far as companies are concerned, even ignoring any of the many other changes that have been implemented, corporation tax rates were changed in seven of the eleven years from 1997–2008 with further changes planned for 2008–09 and 2009–10.

Here we will look at the three major examples already mentioned—CGT changes, the R&D tax credit and the starting rate of corporation tax. There are many more—tax reliefs, tax rules for pensions, etc.—that we don't have space enough to go into here, though some were very substantial.[4]

Let us turn first to Capital Gains Tax. This is a tax on the increase in value of assets held by individuals. It is not a huge tax but it is important, raising £4.8 billion in 2007–8 or just under 1 per cent of total revenue. And it is important not least because of the role it plays in preventing tax avoidance—if income can be taken as a capital gain and there is no tax on capital gains, then a way of avoiding income tax is created. In a complex way this is what allowed private equity fund managers to pay very low rates of tax on their gains. This in turn played a part in prompting the reforms of 2007–8.

The Chancellor, Mr Darling, in his 2007 Pre-Budget report, announced a major simplification of CGT, abolishing taper reliefs and indexation allowances and announcing a single rate of tax of 18 per cent. He said that his goal was 'to make the system more straightforward and sustainable; to ensure it sets consistent incentives for investment and enterprise; and to ensure it remains internationally competitive'. All laudable aims, and something he would largely have achieved with this reform. Unfortunately the subsequent furore over the changes, which would have led to owners of existing business assets paying more tax than expected, led to a partial climb-down and re-complication of the tax regime with the introduction of a £200 million 'entrepreneurs' relief' available effectively to owner managers and owners of unincorporated business. This is not the place to go over the details of the changes, though the process of change was a problem in itself. As Stuart Adam (2008) put it in an excellent review of what happened, the main lesson of the reform is that problems can be avoided by:

[p]roviding certainty, stability and predictability, and to introduce carefully thought out policies that will not need to be reformed or reversed in future. Yet the process of this reform has run exactly contrary to this lesson: an announcement was made without advance consultation; adverse reaction has prompted the announcement of a partial rethink, leading to instability and uncertainty; and the rethink is now being conducted under intense time pressure and lobbying, not the best environment for producing sensible policy proposals.

Rather like the problems involved in unwinding the 10p tax rate, the latest CGT reforms were actually about unwinding what nearly all commentators would view as a policy mistake at the start of the government's first term. This reform introduced a system of 'taper relief' which had the effect of reducing the amount of taxable gain for assets held for longer periods. Further generous reforms in 2000 and 2002 ensured that capital gains on any 'business assets' held for two years or more would be subject to a tax rate of just 10 per cent, as opposed to 40 per cent (for higher rate tax payers) on gains on assets sold less than a year after purchase. Capital gains on 'non-business' assets were subject to a tax rate declining from 40 per cent if held for less than three years to 24 per cent if held for ten years or more. There were two stated justifications for the introduction of this (rather extraordinary) reform. First, there was supposed to be a culture of excessive short-termist speculation damaging the economy. Second, taper relief was supposed to encourage long-term investment. There is little evidence either theoretical or empirical to support these rationales or to suggest that taper relief for CGT would be a good way of improving matters even if there were a problem. In any case, the CGT system has an inbuilt bias towards supporting long-term holding of assets, first because it is forgiven entirely at death and second because it only becomes payable on the realisation of the gain, not at the point at which it accrues.

The point is that the original reforms were badly thought out. They created complexity, benefited the well advised (and well off) and offered increased scope for tax avoidance. The original 1998 reforms also became significantly more generous as they were extended in both 2000 and 2002. Having created these problems, as with the 10p band, the government found it staggeringly hard to unwind them. The net effect has been a big tax bonus for those selling second homes and other assets on which they have enjoyed significant returns.

The next change, which illustrates quite nicely the desire to use the tax system to alter behaviour, is the introduction of a zero per cent starting rate of corporation tax. The intention was to increase incentives for entrepreneur-ship. For example, the Paymaster General stated in 2002 that the government:

recognises that businesses growing beyond a certain size will often be companies. We believe that cutting corporation tax is an effective way of targeting support at small and growing businesses . . . Surely small businesses will not look a gift horse in the mouth. We want to create growth and economic activity, and to sustain entrepreneur-ial activity.[5]

In 2003–4 an incorporated owner-manager whose business made £25,000 gross profit would have paid only 9 per cent of this in tax. The effect was predictable (and predicted). The numbers of self-employed businesses decid-ing to incorporate rose dramatically with incorporations rising from about 5,000 a week in April 2002 to 8,000 a week in April 2003. There is no evidence that this was anything other than a change in legal form. Tax revenues were hit. To understand what happened next we can do no better than to quote Crawford and Freedman (2008):

Government complained that the increase in incorporations was due to 'self-employed individuals adopting the corporate legal form where the change is made for tax reasons rather than as a step to growth' (HMRC, 2004). This was the inevitable result of the policy pursued: small businesses did not 'look a gift horse in the mouth'. Whilst businesses that intend to grow are likely to incorporate in order to raise external finance and to obtain limited liability, it does not follow that encouraging incorporation through the tax system will necessarily encourage growth. Rather, non-entrepreneurial and life-style businesses will quite reasonably utilise the advantages of incorporation so created. Finally the encouragement of incorporation in this way was accepted by Government to be misconceived. Following some complex and unpopular changes in 2004 designed to reduce the advantage of the 0% rate, both this legislation and the corporation tax starting rate were removed in 2006.

This is not to say that all attempts to affect behaviour through the tax system have left quite so much to be desired. In the corporate field, the introduction of R&D tax credits (which cost £660 million in 2007–8) was based on both reasonable a priori economic reasoning—that firms left to themselves will under-invest in R&D because of spillover effects which they cannot internalise—and on the basis of quantitative economic research suggesting that such credits could be effective. What has been perhaps most interesting about the experiment with R&D tax credits has been the way in which policy drifted over time. Originally aimed specifically at small companies, their existence appears to have created a process of lobbying which resulted in significant and expensive expansions to large firms. As with much else in the tax system, there has been a degree of instability associated with the R&D credit. As James Alt and colleagues (2008) put it, in a fascinating analysis of the political processes at play 'almost before the credit got out the door, the Government was thinking about altering it'. Its long-term impact remains uncertain.

Finally, of course, there are 'environmental taxes'. The economic rationale for using taxes to alter behaviour where there are environmental externalities is impeccable. The government has been, arguably unfairly, criticised over the fact that receipts from 'environmental taxes' have fallen as a share of overall tax receipts. Duty on petrol is so overwhelmingly the largest part of the total—£25 billion in 2007/08—that any conceivable change in receipts from the other so-called green taxes—climate change levy, landfill tax, aggregates levy and Air Passenger Duty, which between them raised less than £4 billion—cannot possibly make up for the falling share of fuel duty in taxes. The problem is that policy on petrol taxes seems to have been driven for eight years by memories of the lorry drivers' protests of 2000, with the result that real duty levels on petrol have fallen by more than 15 per cent since then. In the end, it is hard to see how this tax base will be maintained without a widespread move to some form of congestion charging. There is little sign of this happening.

As for other elements of the green tax agenda, the most important point to note is actually that instruments other than taxes have been more important than taxes themselves in attempting to reduce emissions. Indeed, where greenhouse gases are concerned, taxes have played only a very limited role. Much the most important mechanism here is the EU Emissions Trading Scheme—the priority now surely being to extend dramatically the auctioning of allowances such that, as with taxes, revenues are generated. Significant support for renewable energy and energy saving measures in homes has also been important. By comparison the Climate Change Levy, a limited tax on business energy consumption, has had some important effects, but is quantitatively small. And, of course, the reduction in VAT on domestic energy consumption was effectively an increase in the effective subsidy to energy consumption relative to a uniform VAT system.

For a comprehensive analysis of environmental taxation over the past ten years, the reader is referred to Andrew Leicester's review of 2006. He concludes with the following:

Whilst many recent developments in environmental taxation have focused on the business and industrial sectors, it seems that further reductions in emissions will depend on changing household behaviour, in terms of both domestic energy consumption and transport use. Policies designed to change behaviour through information and education alone may not be sufficient. Using the tax system to force consumers to face the environmental cost of their actions in the price they pay for particular goods and services may well be the best option from an economic efficiency point of view. However, any such measures will probably have to take into account concerns about equity, as they would undoubtedly have a proportionately greater impact on the poor than the rich. In addition, the political will required to introduce policies that directly impact on consumers is almost certainly much higher than the will needed for policies that largely affect business.

Evidence of the required 'will' is in scant supply.

Conclusions

There have been areas of the tax system where real progress and improvement have been made. They might not really be part of the tax system, but tax credits, for all their problems, have had very big impacts indeed on the incomes and work incentives of low earners. Bringing NI and income tax systems closer together has been a welcome move as has the final abolition of MIRAS. There has been some limited but important use of tax to address environmental externalities.

But the reality is that this has not been a government with a long-term and coherent strategy for tax reform. The debacles surrounding the undoing of two early reforms—to CGT and the 10p tax rate—are merely particularly salient and damaging symptoms of this lack of direction. The lack of political will even to revalue properties for Council Tax purposes, let alone reform the tax, has been unimpressive. Progress on 'green taxes' has also been held back by a degree of timidity particularly over taxes on petrol. It is genuinely curious that a government so set on reducing poverty and improving work incentives should have spent so much on cutting the basic rate of income tax and made so little progress on raising allowances. Equally incomprehensible has been the persistent belief that people won't take advantage of tax reliefs intended to promote supposedly desirable behaviour. It is to be hoped—though perhaps not expected—that all future Chancellors will have learned from the repeated experience of this government, that fiddling with the system to create reliefs and allowances is often more effective in ensuring that tax is avoided than in changing real economic behaviour.

Acknowledgements

I am particularly grateful to David Phillips for assistance and comments and to Robert Chote for helpful comments. All views expressed are my own and not those of the IFS.

Notes

1 In fact, between them they significantly more than account for the overall increase as they have had to offset other economic factors, such as weak earnings growth given the state of the economy.
2 Of course, this was no more than what one might generously call 'rhetorical hypothecation'—there is no link whatever between NI receipts and NHS spending.
3 Based on 2008–9 HMRC statistics, at http://www.hmrc.gov.uk/stats/income_tax/table2-5.pdf
4 Film tax relief, for example, which was introduced in 1997, was costing the exchequer a faintly astonishing £0.5 billion a year by 2006–07, despite 13 separate pieces of anti-avoidance legislation by 2005.
5 House of Commons Standing Committee F16 May 2002, cols. 114–115, quoted by Crawford and Freedman (2008).

References

Adam, S., 'Capital gains tax', in R. Chote, C. Emmerson, D. Miles and J. Shaw, eds., *The IFS Green Budget 2008*, London, Institute for Fiscal Studies, 2008.

Alt, J., I. Preston and L. Sibieta, *The Political Economy of Tax Policy*, 2008, available at http://www.ifs.org.uk/mirrleesreview/publications.php

Crawford, C. and J. Freedman, *Small Business Taxation*, 2008, available at http://www.ifs.org.uk/mirrleesreview/publications.php

Davies, W., 'Tax credits: the success and failre', *Prospect*, no. 135, 30 June 2007.

Dilnot, A. and C. Giles, *The IFS Green Budget Summer 1997*, London, Institute for Fiscal Studies, 1997.

HM Treasury, *Reform of Film Tax Incentives: Promoting the Sustainable Production of Culturally British Films*, London, HM Treasury, 2005.

Leicester, A., *The UK Tax System and the Environment*, London, Institute for Fiscal Studies, 2006.

Lyons, M., *Lyons Inquiry into Local Government*, London: The Stationery Office, 2007.

Regulation, Equality and the Public Interest

SHAMIT SAGGAR

Introduction[1]

THIS CHAPTER is designed to stimulate a wider debate about the role of
regulation and regulators in serving social objectives, and especially those
that relate to greater equality. Some of these wider social purposes are
familiar, such as the need for minimum standards in basic utilities, and
have been broadly accepted in the interests of society. Others have more to do
with uncovering hidden social and consumer detriment, often linked to
unrelated, yet important, changes in the economy.

The development of a basic public interest narrative, around which
regulators can shape and articulate their role, is a natural starting point.
This concept is positive-sum, i.e. it centres on the up- and downsides for all.
This is not a literal gain or loss. Rather it is a public interest discipline to work
out why, and to what degree, policy measures will deliver benefits for
particular social groups whilst also avoiding detriment to others.

This is a trade-off that was, historically speaking, implicit in relation to the
legacy bodies that preceded the new Equality and Human Rights Commission (EHRC). A public interest test, for instance, might be used to set the
boundaries of public space where individual identities can be projected. It
might also serve to specify the basis for benefits and burdens that accrue to
society at large rather than a particular sectional group. It may be used to
pinpoint the case for why one group's particular claims for recognition and
resources have also to meet the needs for solidarity and cohesion for all
groups. And it may be helpful in providing for some vulnerable groups the
support to help them make choices that better meet their needs as consumers
and as citizens. For example, being sufficiently empowered to seek out the
cheapest and most appropriate insurance product can be critical for some
players who are daunted by information overload in this complex market.

The article also touches on other sectors, industries and professions to draw
out comparisons relevant to the EHRC and also to identify what has delivered
lasting change. Some big corporate firms, for instance, have turned around
whole workplace cultures and become equal opportunities leaders where
previously they had been laggards. Additionally, some modern regulators
have been effective in protecting the public from consumer detriment in areas
ranging from food safety to digital switchover to long-term asset-backed
investment. This suggests that it is worth capturing how and why—in order
to borrow and learn about whether, and to what extent, this can happen more

Published by Blackwell Publishing Ltd, 9600 Garsington Road, Oxford OX4 2DQ, UK and 350 Main Street, Malden, MA 02148, USA

generally. Such evidence can also be used to inform policy interventions by the EHRC.

The chapter starts by scoping out the basic proposition that equality objectives and the social aims of regulation are interlinked. Secondly, it tests the applicability of this claim in relation to practice among a selection of regulators. Finally, it points to proposals to advance the use of public interest arguments in strategic approaches to equality, including some suggestions about the future role of the EHRC itself. It also presents a discussion of the leverage of selected public interest regulators in pursuing social inclusion objectives. This discussion aims to draw some simple judgements about social objectives and modern regulation, taking into account the degree to which risk-based regulatory frameworks and interventions do or do not support EHRC-centric objectives. Inevitably, therefore, this final section is interpretive in nature and is designed to add directly to debates and choices about the evolving role of the EHRC.

The issue: why it matters and to whom

Regulation and regulatory policy is a mainstay of modern effective and responsible government. Positive outcomes accrue from, *inter alia*, public health, clean food, reliable and safe medicines, clean and orderly financial markets, school attainment standards, trusted election results, and fairness for consumers at and beyond the point of sale. Modern regulators are involved in all of these areas and many more. Their presence and effectiveness is often unnoticed although, inevitably, major regulatory failures are often the subject of intense controversy and scrutiny.

Many modern regulators are constituted either to balance competing interests and/or to promote the public interest in their duties. The latter is not uniformly defined but usually includes standing apart from sectional concerns and biases. Such a public interest can also be thought of in terms of promoting and pursuing better and fairer outcomes for all.

Crucially, the improvement in outcomes may be disproportionately greater for some rather than others. It is one of the social roles of modern regulation, therefore, to ensure that (at its simplest) disproportional benefits are linked to disproportional barriers. In addition, it is important that regulators operating in the realm of social objectives are able to satisfy themselves that their interventions are designed to influence such disproportionate barriers.

In this context, equalities thinking and practice needs to be careful to ensure whether, or to what degree, groups actually experience poorer outcomes— penalties—after sensible factors are accounted for. The alternative is unattractive—to assume that a 'gap' always constitutes a case for correction. The implications of this discipline are significant. For one thing, it can affect greatly shared definitions of vulnerable and disadvantaged groups, not least in a political environment where entrenched identity groups and interests remain attached to pursuing their perceived needs for redress.

SHAMIT SAGGAR

More specifically this might also entail special regard being given to those in society who are least able to secure such outcomes for themselves. For instance, an energy or water regulator may compel utility firms to deliver a basic level of service to low income households. This action may be through explicit directives and requirements and/or via more subtle actions designed to deliver particular outcomes. In any case, the regulator thus serves the pursuit of a social objective that goes beyond creating efficient markets alone.

This means that regulation and regulators have, at least in part, locus over social issues and objectives. The link is sometimes embedded in their statutory purpose or equivalent, but it is more usually the result of a particular interpretation of roles and responsibilities, as well as through cumulative regulatory and quasi-regulatory practices.

The new EHRC should prioritise a better understanding of the role and work of public interest regulators in pursuing social inclusion objectives. This involves probing the question of how far the public interest is conceptually geared towards social objectives. It also involves examining the approach and track record of various regulators in practice. There is an obvious need to assess such work, however broadly or narrowly defined, so as to frame the issue of regulatory effectiveness. The role and impact of existing and future regulators in delivering EHRC-specific goals is important. This might be a long-term strategic priority for the EHRC in terms of successfully discharging its own statutory objectives and doing so in a way that aligns with its own resources, reach and influence. It is also significant in allowing the EHRC to build a more credible platform for its own long-term equalities agenda and reputation.

The public interest and regulatory social objectives

There are three main ways in which the issue of the public interest and modern regulation touches the EHRC. These can be summarised as follows:

- *Influencing existing regulators.* The natural starting point should be the degree to which the EHRC is successful in encouraging regulators to make greater and more innovative use of their powers, particularly in relation to social objectives. The existing remit (and interpretation) of key regulators such as the Office of Communications, the Food Standards Agency and the Financial Services Authority varies. Examining this experience is useful in terms of establishing a baseline review and better understanding of levers that have been utilised.
- *Public interest arguments.* The logical backdrop to a new equalities agenda is the style and grounds upon which the EHRC is able successfully to formulate public interest arguments for equality. This is, of course, implicitly connected to the track record of mainstream regulators in pursuing socially defined goals. The public interest case also chimes increasingly with (a) the changing climate of public understanding of

fairness and equity; (b) changing consumer expectations and demands that can affect which claims regulators act upon; and (c) the changing nature of future equality challenges.

- *The role of the EHRC.* Finally, building on the above platform, there is the question of the extent to which the EHRC should act as a regulator and/or in a quasi-regulatory oversight role. This is arguably the hardest question to set and judge at present, in part because it requires a detailed gap analysis of roles and capacity. It also hangs significantly on the statutory role assigned to the EHRC and the nature of monitoring and oversight that the EHRC is required to observe.

The challenge facing a given public interest regulator may not necessarily involve any explicit consideration of social inclusion oriented objectives. In many cases, the link is indirect and implicit, to the extent that one is recognised at all. However, there are a number of ways in which important socially defined goals are absorbed into the general task facing the regulator and can be used to inform judgements of effectiveness.

Some general examples make the case. Several arise from the policing by 'watchdogs' of consumer markets and the problems that can stem from the imbalance of knowledge and resources between providers and certain consumers. Others relate to delivering outcomes in a way that best promotes social cohesion. And others are essentially about using intelligent regulatory interventions to incentivise and accelerate changes that are already present but are neither widespread nor embedded. These 'nudges' can prove pivotal if they are well timed and focused on removing particularly disproportionate obstacles.

Example 1: Helping disadvantaged consumers

Helping consumers in a world of intense information access and potential overload may seem daunting. In part, it is because of scarcity of time and unfamiliarity with tools, that not all consumers are either able to protect their own interests and/or able to secure positive outcomes for themselves. For example, levels of basic numeracy and literacy have a bearing on access to complex financial services products. But there should be scope to encourage and promote positive, substantial change, whilst also discouraging other negative trends that are already apparent.

Supporting disadvantaged groups can go beyond assistance in navigating consumer choice. It can also extend to judgements about how to deliver backing for those seeking redress where market providers are responsible for inadequate goods and services. A regulator can step in to support individuals. But, significantly, it can intervene with various existing bodies that have to judge which complaints to follow up and which categories of consumers to prioritise. The former might entail special attention being given to complaints that arise from systemic weaknesses and flaws among providers (e.g. lack of supervision, conflicts of interest). The latter may involve outreach and access-centric changes to make it possible to complain for those that evidence shows find it hardest to register and pursue redress (e.g. using telephone-based, rather than paper-based, processes to create informality as a means of building trust).

Tackling the problems faced by disadvantaged citizens (public interest objective one) and consumer detriment (public interest objective two) are not necessarily separate matters. These may be closely interwoven, perhaps even different sides of the same proverbial coin. For instance:

- *The professions.* The traditional professions have not typically been associated with transparency of information. Publishing data about high performers (i.e. those individuals or practices that pursue standards of consumer or client care greatly in excess of the norm) and low performers (i.e. those who systematically fall below basic agreed minimum standards) has the potential to challenge rigorously such low performers, perhaps by threatening to 'shake things up' favourably. In these circumstances, consumers might be warned off bad performers, for instance. They might be attracted to top performers. And the members of professions themselves can quickly see who is leading the way (so they can further encourage them) and who is letting the side down (who might need to be censured and/or left to wither on the vine, so to speak). Crucially, transparent information will also identify the large group of professionals in between who have high aspirations but little practical knowledge as to what to do in practice (typically, these 'fence-sitters' will need advice, support and backing, ideally from their own professional ranks, if they are to deliver positive change).
- *New redress and advocacy mechanisms.* A possible future trend will involve new mechanisms and players who seek to support consumers and do so through advocacy and simplification of complex information. So, for example, there has already been an expansion of the claims handling industry, both in terms of the significant growth of professional groups claims handlers and also by virtue of important reforms in 'no win–no fee' contractual arrangements between clients and their legal representatives. But new websites to show consumers, especially vulnerable groups of consumers, and consumer lobbies and activists, how to complain and obtain redress, are further examples. These players will have a vested interest in encouraging a more complaining-oriented and litigious public, and will also want to project certain firms and industries in increasingly negative and confrontational terms (e.g. food producers, supermarkets, restaurant chains, mobile telephone firms, etc.). This can be a negative development if those with a vested interested simply want to 'right' each and every 'wrong', regardless of real merit or context. Therefore, regulators need to be wary of the danger of supply creating its own demand.
- *Understanding vulnerability.* On vulnerable or disadvantaged consumer

groups, economic regulators and competition authorities may hold somewhat outdated perspectives. They may need to raise their game in order to grasp new, hidden forms of disadvantage and the circumstances that contribute to some groups of consumers being poorly equipped to protect their own interests. This is mainly because there is a risk that particular groups or sections of society will be left behind in making efficient and informed use of modern markets. Similar concerns already exist in relation to parent or patient choice in state-funded schooling and healthcare.

That said, there is another (roughly opposite) risk. This stems from any (and potentially all) social, demographic or identity groups over-asserting the case for regulators (typically they refer to 'the government') to defend them, and/or promote their interests, and/or provide special support to allow them to obtain redress. This can be a negative development, chiefly because it often only takes a group to brand itself as necessarily 'vulnerable' or 'disadvantaged' on the basis of its raw statistical profile (e.g. group X has few among its ranks who have median earnings or above, or who have attended university—ergo its members automatically cannot navigate markets and public services well, or perhaps at all). This reasoning can be evidentially flawed, politically misleading and designed to get regulatory authorities to step in without first asking sensible questions. Some such questions might include, for example, checking to see whether sensible background causal factors were controlled for, just in case these were driving the patterns of disproportionate outcomes under scrutiny. Another example might be to assess whether, or how far, the starting point of different groups was comparable in terms of drawing large conclusions about outcomes. Finally, it might be helpful to inspect more closely whether widely differing outcome patterns were reduced or widened as a result of the effects of a particular institution, industry or sector. This may help to interpret unusual patterns, some of which might be endemic to performance and achievements that ran across a whole sector and were not limited to a single institution. It is also a trend that may intensify as a result of, *inter alia*, misguided government rhetoric, symbolic pilot efforts by a few regulators and others creating fresh, unmerited demand, and public authorities simply not having the confidence to develop properly thought out understandings of vulnerability themselves. Therefore, responsibility rests on the EHRC and others to balance these two risks more astutely in the future.

Example 2: Addressing market failures

The spectacle of vulnerable consumers who are less able than others to secure their interests may in fact be the result of other, underlying causes. The most important of these is likely to be the result of a market that gravitates to certain kinds of consumers whilst withdrawing from other kinds. This market failure is seen most clearly when there is a lack of universal provision or access, as might happen, for example, in postal services in rural areas or energy and telephony services for low volume users.

The main job of the regulator in this scenario is to find ways to ensure that market imperfections and failures are kept to a minimum. Regulators may also exist to act as an influence and control over government itself, in order to help set service standards for disadvantaged or vulnerable groups.[2] Failing that, the regulator may choose to be guided by the prospect of ensuring that firms and others adhere to some basic minimum standards that are available to all consumers or users. Finally, this is not incompatible with placing pressure on suppliers to offer services through hidden (and occasionally not so hidden) cross-subsidies. While this may be hard to defend at face value, it may be justified in terms of the general social benefits that accrue from all consumers having access to, for example, clean water and sanitation. In fact, the public health costs of allowing markets to reign with specific, known gaps in provision may be highly unpalatable.

There are a number of examples that illustrate the kinds of interventions or concerns of regulators. For instance:

- *Utility retail competition.* The Office of Gas and Electricity Markets (Ofgem) has recently begun investigating allegations that energy providers misled customers who already used prepaid meters into using more expensive services.[3] There are two pieces of evidence that alerted the regulator to the potential for mis-selling. First, in 2007, Ofgem found that two-thirds of electricity prepayment customers actually switched to more expensive providers for similar services. Secondly, just over a half of transferring prepayment gas customers also moved to more expensive providers. In a normal market, the regulator believed that switching customers of all kinds would results in lower tariffs (78 per cent of such customers reported that their primary motive was to save costs). Moreover, the regulator stated its concerns were based on: (a) the fact that low income households were disproportionately more likely to use prepayment for utilities; and (b) evidence that vulnerable consumers often lacked the capacity to research better deals and were thus heavily exposed to aggressive and potentially exploitative telephone and doorstep selling campaigns.[4]
- *Internet safeguards.* The Office of Communications (Ofcom) has been active in helping to ensure that regulation of access to the internet (rather than internet content) offers greater protection of young and vulnerable people online. One way has been to emphasise the 'user-friendly' orientation of filtering devices and applications. The Home Office has worked with Ofcom, industry and other stakeholders to create a British Standard for internet access control software. The standard aims to encourage the industry to make their products more effective and easier to use. The kite marks awarded to products which pass the standard are designed to help give confidence to the user and increase take-up, and also help parents to choose effective systems that can protect their children from unsuitable material on the internet.

Example 3: Promoting social and community cohesion

In addition to economic markets delivering for consumers, there can be public interest benefits in relation to communities. These can be centred around the links between individuals and also the responsibility that specific identity groups have to others in society. A key aim is to create communities in which there are high and resilient levels of trust between individuals and groups both within and across identity boundaries. Trust is reflected in many things and ways, but includes an open acceptance of certain differences between groups in society. In other words, trust is more likely to be found and to be sustaining when ethnic or religious difference is not only tolerated but actively supported.

There is a need to create communities with high trust between individuals and groups within them, and between different identity communities. This approach can certainly influence the 'good relations' mandate of the EHRC. For instance, it has direct implications in terms of what types of institutional arrangements, information transmission and use of media are most likely to generate such high levels of trust.

Support for particular policy interventions might involve examining whether—or how far—they make any one or a combination of the following three contributions. First, the value of such difference requires some overt recognition, however nominal, as being integral to the nature and character of a society.[5] The role of policy-makers and others in this context is to deliver interventions that are in the mainstream of building a cohesive and integrated society.[6] Take the example of shaping education policy to meet the needs of a plural society. This comprises three separate though related challenges, each of which amounts to a public interest justification for action:

- *Educational participation (Test #1).* This is centred on the 'who' aspects of education—the argument that public detriment may result from the long-term consequences of poor access, opportunity and attainment among particular social, economic, geographic or identity groups.
- *Educational content (Test #2).* This is about the 'what' aspects of education—thus public detriment may result if the educational curriculum is poorly geared to social cohesion and diversity goals.
- *Educational contributions (Test #3).* Finally, the 'how' aspects of education—whereby public detriment may result if younger people are inadequately prepared to live successful lives in plural societies where numerous predictable—and not-so-predictable—differences of background and outlook are commonplace.

Secondly, barriers to cohesion can be identified in a way that balances a range of causal factors, ranging from asymmetric economic relations through to simmering grievance and the effects of social isolation. This is important since it is challenging to identify and tackle such barriers in a way that is not crudely identified as promoting one sectional interest or another. Barriers, in other words, are defined not simply as those facing one group or another from enjoying greater benefits, but rather those preventing social cohesion across the board and affecting all in some manner.[7]

Thirdly, active support is also required to build narratives that accept complexity in the relationship between causes and effects. One of the biggest dangers for any intervention is that these narratives can be projected in misleading and unhelpful simplistic terms, for example in the link between poverty and extremism. The evidence base far from supports this picture, and therefore needs to be layered and nuanced. Ultimately it needs to build a counter-narrative that sees various interconnected reasons for the breakdown of normal trusting and respectful relationships.

Risk, regulation and strategic priorities

This chapter has described the role and importance of social objectives in the work of regulation and regulators. This has shown that various regulators carry out their duties with some regard to social inclusion, although the meaning and interpretation given to this term varies unevenly from case to case. Certainly, whilst social inclusion is *implicit* in the work of many regulators, it is seemingly *explicit* in the case of Ofcom. In this particular case, the strength of the argument is to place citizens' interests alongside an economic rationale to regulate for consumer interests. It is an argument that is not especially common among public interest regulators and is closely linked to the pre-legislative work of the Puttnam committee.[8]

We now turn to look at the question of risk-based regulation and the extent to which regulators might enjoy discretion so as to give greater priority to social inclusion-oriented objectives. The concept of risk, of course, depends heavily on context and the definition and nature of detriment and burdens to be averted. Nevertheless, it is significant because it acts as one way to draw together the work of a wide span of social, cultural, economic, health, social care, professional services and constitutional regulators. The concept of equality is poorly embedded in the remit or culture of most such regulators. But that is not to say that equality-related principles are not linked to the delivery of otherwise generally agreed goals and objectives.

The discussion below looks at three aspects of how regulation and regulators might give greater priority to equality issues and outcomes in the future:

- consumer empowerment and vulnerability
- redress and transparency
- risk disclosure.

Consumer empowerment and vulnerability

A common approach taken by regulators to consumer interests and policy has been to look for ways to support consumers to allow them to make better, more informed decisions. Empowering consumers may take the form of additional information being collected and disseminated by regulators. Additionally, it might involve formal consumer education campaigns, including some that go beyond trying to achieve a better deal for individuals and instead focus on whole groups of consumers, thus creating new demands on providers. And empowerment might include efforts to allow consumers to check and drive the behaviour of providers particularly in relation to obtaining redress and/or raising service standards.

For regulators, there is a challenge to understand better the most significant drivers of empowerment or vulnerability among consumers. These drivers can change over the next five to seven years, with important implications for government, consumers and businesses. The key issues for regulators at large will be:

- *Navigating an abundance of information.* Given that the information available to consumers is increasingly abundant, are there actions that regulators can take to ensure that consumers will be able to trust or make sense of such information? In particular, large amounts of complex information may find its way to vulnerable groups of consumers who are known to be poorly equipped to digest it, let alone be able to make informed decisions. In the case of broadband services or mobile telephony, there is existing evidence that excessive, untailored information is commonly misinterpreted and/or misused by very young or elderly consumers and those with low educational attainment. Similarly, the green or ethical claims made by providers can be poorly correlated either to underlying factual evidence and/or to particular consumer groups' ability to understand the nature or basis of such claims.
- *Product/service complexity.* A related concern is that products and services are becoming more complex and are increasingly sold in complex ways, such as bundles or via rental or lease arrangements. This practice raises the question of how far consumers have the capacity—or can be expected to have the time and skills—to comprehend reasonably the benefits and trade-offs involved. Bundled energy services are a good illustration of this problem whereby it can no longer be taken for granted that consumers with poor educational backgrounds are capable of drawing out relevant information and making informed judgements.
- *Demographic and technological trends and vulnerable consumers.* There are existing trends towards an older and more diverse society, although not enough is known about the micro-composition of such social categories in the future. Notwithstanding such distinctions, these underlying demographic trends themselves may point to more vulnerable consumers. A

further possibility might be that other dimensions of vulnerability might emerge in the future, partly based around geographical locations as well as the influence of support and advice networks, technological awareness, and proximity to positive and supportive peer influences.[9] These factors may also be magnified in the case of particular urban populations undergoing significant transitional change and adjustment.[10]

Redress and transparency

The expectations of consumers in many fields are increasing and, as part of this, there is a related assumption that they will become more inclined to complain, and even litigate, to get the product or service they want. This can be thought of as empowering if it allows them to use purchasing power or its equivalent to incentivise providers to raise standards of delivery. This is, after all, a basic element of a competitive marketplace and it may be possible to replicate such results in non-market settings.

That said, there are some points of caution before it can be assumed that such outcomes will always prevail. First, regulators (including self-regulatory bodies) need to ensure that the opportunity to complain and seek redress is itself as open and accessible as possible. In the past, particular organisations and industries have been notorious for presiding over exceptionally inaccessible redress schemes. Opening up greater accessibility might include:

- information and awareness campaigns, particularly among disadvantaged groups and communities, to publicise the existence of a redress option to begin with;
- targeted campaigns to encourage particular groups or communities to come forward and make formal complaints, especially where evidence exists to suggest that tacit discouragement has previously taken place;
- pro-active initiatives to assist particular groups and communities to submit, track and pursue fully complaints and claims for compensation. These can take the form of verbal-based processes in place of paper-based ones, less reliance on formal adjudication and more on informal conciliation, and direct efforts to reduce complexity and minimise jargon that might be off-putting to vulnerable groups;
- pilots of the above interventions in particular locations to (a) test the underlying level of demand for redress and (b) judge the wider extent of hidden demand at aggregate level;
- joint projects with community advocacy organisations dealing with vulnerable groups to obtain best practice guidance and support; and
- periodic opening up of the processes and procedures of independent redress to test against the expectations and norms of consumers who are known to be least likely to submit or pursue a complaint.

Related to this, it might be possible to develop kite marks and equivalents for making information about redress as accessible as possible to vulnerable groups. Such kite marks themselves might also be linked to new ways of accrediting reliable information that can be shown to aid the navigation of markets by consumers. In resourcing terms, it is likely that these schemes will be most cost effective if they are produced by trade associations or providers—and then tested for efficacy by external regulatory bodies.

A further step beyond the above would be for consumer redress organisations to see themselves, and act, as advocates for vulnerable and disadvantaged client groups. This would be seen as a novel and perhaps controversial development in many cases, not least because such a role might be interpreted (by some) as an implicit abandonment of the independence of such redress bodies. That said, a compromise position might be greater collaboration with advocacy and campaigning organisations so as to understand better the situation faced by vulnerable groups.

Finally, it is arguable that the principle of transparency can be used to make greatest use of the results of consumer or citizen redress. Thus, many regulators now accept that they are under a reasonable expectation to publish aggregate-level data about the overall volume and categories of complaints they receive and/or are able to resolve, and with enough detail to isolate the broad patterns of outcomes. This is widely seen in advertising standards regulation and the regulation of misconduct among medical professionals, for instance. It is a proposal that is being currently examined in relation to major financial services providers.[11] A further extension of this tool might be to publish in addition the findings in particular cases and on a non-anonymised basis where firms or providers have lost final adjudications. In such cases, the arguments are that: (a) consumers will be able to use such information about poor standards to make more informed decisions, and (b) providers will have an additional incentive to improve performance.

Risk disclosure

The issue of individual risk tends to preoccupy common understandings of the role of regulators. This, of course, does not always match with the approach taken to risk-based regulation whereby regulators are required to take into account many other dimensions including the potential impacts across more than single individuals. And risk-based regulation centres on the question of whether, or how far, particular interventions are required to address systemic weaknesses either in markets and/or in delivering basic outcomes.

However, the success of risk-based regulation hangs on a public interest rationale that redefines detriment and externalities in ways that, for example, require remedial action on the part of whole sectors and industries. This, in turn, requires regulators to become more cognisant of the need for, and their ability to, target 'laggard' performers whilst offering light touch regimes to 'leaders'. By doing so, it is a small leap to make the position of vulnerable and disadvantaged groups in society a more central part of a risk-based analysis of the role and work of regulatory bodies.

An important tool in delivering regulatory safeguards for individuals is the extent to which a firm or provider is required to disclose relevant factual information to individuals (or indeed to any organisation that can make use of such data). Such information disclosure can range across a lot of territory and might relate to:

- the past track record of the firm or provider in delivering particular products, services or standards (controlling fully where possible for normal variations in the complexity and circumstances in which some firms and providers operate but others do not);
- the evidence about success or failure in meeting particular performance targets, whether externally imposed by regulators or internally required by management;
- the appropriateness of particular products or services to specific groups or types of customer;
- the extent to which hidden forms of personal risk may obscure the rational decision-making of ordinary well-educated consumers—to say nothing of the handicaps experienced by less well equipped consumers;
- the amount of personal risk exposure that is necessary to balance the operation of market forces and consumer choice on the one hand with the need to protect people in certain vulnerable categories or climates;
- the case for excluding certain consumers from particular products or services where evidence suggests that these barriers are both unjustified and disproportionate; and finally,
- those circumstances in which firms and providers are prevented from accessing or selling to particular groups or in relation to particular products or services where the risks of detriment are overwhelming.

A further innovation might be to require, through innovative use of existing regulatory tools, that firms and providers specifically tailor information to the objectively defined circumstances of individual or groups of consumers. This approach, after all, is already found in relation to the objective fact-finding that accompanies financial advice, whether independent or tied in some way. The basic rationale is that certain factual information about consumers might necessarily preclude consideration of particular financial services or products, the sale of which may prove 'toxic' in particular circumstances. Further, this can also be linked to efforts to learn about and categorise the overall risk appetite of consumers themselves so as to avoid any possibility of mis-selling.

The key question is how far risk disclosure is used as a means to prevent particular consumers from freely operating in particular markets or settings. If the preventative effects are large, then it is important to be able to cite the scale of the likely consumer detriment that is being minimised, if not removed altogether. Such prevention can also be described as a barrier to firms and others who may be offering attractive options. The danger is that regulators can act in such a manner to preclude certain outcomes and may stand accused of acting as self-appointed guardians of selected groups or communities. Such a paternalistic reputation is unlikely to be coveted except in cases where there is reliable evidence of the overt and known limitations of consumers (e.g. mental impairment, so as to protect as the justification for guardianship). But even in these areas, it can be helpful to require the regulator itself to disclose publicly how often and how effective it has been in carrying out such protective intervention in a timely and efficient manner.[12]

Moving forward: exerting regulatory influence and impact

The primary aim of this chapter has been to disentangle current thinking about the role of regulation in shaping general social objectives. It has not sought to focus on the role of the EHRC explicitly, since it is important to first establish a shared understanding of the relationship between equality and regulation. That said, it is worth devoting some space to looking at the general case and role, and how far this might be seen as valuable and timely in shaping the EHRC's mission and brand. There are four closely related avenues that stand out.

The first is producing a culture change among private sector employers. The EHRC might have a useful role to play in addressing and championing the rate of change among private sector employers in relation to performance on equality issues as well as on equal pay.

The aim is to produce greater cultural change among employers, possibly using survey and 'mystery shopping'-style spot checks of the performance of specific employers and firms. This could be via two routes. First, the EHRC could carry out systematic industry- or sector-wide surveys to establish an evidence base about current performance among firms. Such insights might be supplemented by fresh powers to carry out focused studies on particular segments of the private sector that exhibit slowest improvement. This would create a basis for comparison as well as dialogue with individual firms or with employer representative bodies. The case could also be made for further spot checks by firms themselves acting in a self-regulatory capacity, followed up by analysis by the EHRC to assess progress. The main lever, of course, would remain transparency—with the largest incentive being pressure of competition based on reputational strength or damage.

The EHRC could also offer firms of greatest concern the opportunity to work with either itself or with specialists on action plans to improve performance. This would not be a requirement backed by law but it would nevertheless allow the EHRC an opportunity to track take-up rates and the discretion to publish and publicise noticeable gaps in performance and outcome. Such gaps could be linked to public procurement opportunities.

The key point is the case for the EHRC switching its role (and, in due course, its reputation). This would be the upshot of an equalities champion that publicly stated its supportive work with leader firms and those seeking to improve, whilst bearing down on laggard firms by highlighting their poor performance. Such a name-and-shame approach would be a significant departure for the EHRC and allow it to use transparency as a tool for consumers driving change.

The second avenue for the EHRC to pursue is developing and championing risk-based methods for identifying social exclusion priorities. The EHRC has the opportunity to probe the evidential basis upon which mainstream regulators prioritise particular strands of activity over others. For instance, a risk-based spectrum might be used that takes explicit account of the position of vulnerable or disadvantaged groups in society. In relation to financial services, for example, the EHRC may seek from both the regulator and the redress body evidence and reasons to show that such groups are identified adequately and early in their policy-making processes as well as in their direct enforcement interventions.

The third avenue is re-prioritising monitoring activity. The EHRC has some regulatory responsibilities of its own. For instance, all public authorities have now had in excess of five years in which to put in place arrangements to enable them to deliver on all aspects of their general race equality duty (RED). Previously, the CRE, as the legacy body, saw its role as a facilitator and ensured it had robust guidance produced for all public authorities. In addition, it offered considerable individual advice and support work. This was very much seen as the Commission's role and encouraged by government.

The EHRC may wish to see a further step-change in the way in which the RED is monitored and enforced. The monitoring of performance by public bodies requires detailed collection and analysis of data but also robust action against non-compliance, and use of the press and public statements to advertise this. The overarching purpose must be to recognise and reward high performers, isolate and pressure low performers, and, crucially, to continue to assist and support those public bodies that have made some progress but still have a long way to go (fence-sitters, colloquially speaking). The emphasis, in other words, is about moving from inspection and audit against a range of process indicators, to looking in more depth at consequential social outcomes. Clearly the regulatory function of the EHRC has been, and will remain, limited by the legal framework that exists. As such, the separate discussions about a Single Equality Act will be crucial to influencing the regulatory work of the EHRC.

The fourth avenue for the EHRC to pursue is leading the argument for equality in the public interest. Although detailed work needs to be done to flesh out the argument, it is nevertheless possible to sketch out the rudimentary building blocks. These are fourfold:

- *Redefining detriment and externalities.* A modern regulator with a responsibility to regulate to produce market efficiencies that gives regard to externalities for society such as discrimination and persistent inequality.

In practice, this means that unequal patterns of pay are often not the result of unfair pay systems or processes. These patterns are mostly to do with occupational segmentation and segregation in the labour market. In such circumstances, it may be reasonable to expect private sector employers to be required to take actions that seek to compensate or overcome segmentation and segregation patterns that are already embedded. This might take the form of the requirement to engage in outreach initiatives to bring traditionally under-represented groups and communities into greater contact with firms' opportunity structures. Another illustration might be through revision of the Employment Tribunal system, so as to focus on the preventative and educative effects of action, and not just the punitive features at present.

- *Modernising the work and priorities of existing regulators.* As previously noted, this approach involves taking a critical eye to the forward plans of others. This can be most usefully done in relation to examining the emerging challenges that are likely from demographic and technological change. The Office of Fair Trading (OFT) maintains an influential Futures Advisory Board for instance, and this has carried out a path-breaking analysis to assess the future effects and implications of such changes.[13] The EHRC has a role to play by testing both best and worst case scenarios, as well as challenging the OFT to offer greater precision in identifying why and how certain scenarios are best or worst for different sections and interests in society. Clearly, certain scenarios will be particularly challenging for those who are especially immobile, suffer poor health, are inadequately skilled, poorly qualified, inward-facing in their social networks, and experience severe asset (alongside income) poverty. This form of disaggregation is vital if the OFT—and others—are to become better informed about social detriment that is defined not only in consumerist terms.

- *Isolating the biggest risks for society.* A substantial task for the EHRC and for allied organisations is: (a) to show that it can use its own advocated approach to regulation, in order to (b) specify real priorities in addressing settled inequality and disadvantage. This chapter is not an appropriate setting to rehearse the relevant arguments and evidence. However, the EHRC should be able to show how the inequality and lack of opportunity structures experienced in certain communities and groups is recurring and self-sustaining, and the degree to which the costs of such lack of equality and opportunity have accrued to all in society and not just to the groups in question. This involves a simple yet reliable way of showing equality as a positive-sum principle and reality, building for example on areas of existing public understanding and support for childcare and workplace flexibility.

- *A shared definition of the public interest.* The EHRC may be best able to tackle public and social detriment using a public interest test to shape its own and others' interventions. For instance, it is known that in many fields unlawful discrimination persists but its consequences are not just limited to those discriminated against. Such discrimination serves also to diminish social trust and support for important public institutions (e.g. the police or courts) and principles (e.g. equality before the law). The knock-on impacts are partly hidden but are nevertheless substantial for society as whole. For instance, policing and efforts to tackle crime are easily undermined by patchy cooperation among the public with law enforcement agencies. Equally, groups at high risk of sustained social exclusion are less likely to take advantage of opportunity structures that are created or expanded through educational or labour market policies. Their sense of despair and disenchantment thus becomes an even greater barrier to overcome than the actual circumstances might suggest.

Concluding thoughts

The equalities agenda in Britain is deserving of fresh thinking and practice. By observing the work and record of existing mainstream regulatory agencies, much can be learnt about the ways in which change has been delivered, often in the face of entrenched constituencies. The basic purpose of this chapter has been to identify the potentially exciting cross-over point or points between equality and modern regulation, and to link this discussion as specifically as possible to the work of the new Equality and Human Rights Commission.

Bringing about such change also involves a more critical self-examination of the ways in which public bodies charged with fighting discrimination have previously discharged their responsibilities. The legacy bodies that predated the EHRC often acquired a less than flattering reputation for their lack of focus on key priorities, their stand-alone approaches, and their apparent detachment from modern regulation. Each of these areas should be addressed by the EHRC, not least in order to redefine and rebrand the nature of public policy efforts to deliver greater equality and inclusion. The article recommends an approach based on the judicious and tactical use of known regulatory principles and lessons, stemming from the lessons of policing and reforming of complex markets and public services.

Notes

1 This chapter is an abridged version of a longer Occasional Paper commissioned by the Equality and Human Rights Commission in 2008 and to be published in 2009. The views expressed in this chapter are solely those of the author and no inference whatsoever should be drawn about the position of the EHRC.

2 O. James, 'Regulation inside government: public interest justifications and regulatory failures', *Public Administration*, vol. 78, no. 2, 2000, pp. 327–43.

3 See http://www.ofgem.gov.uk/Sustainability/SocAction/Publications/Documents1/Prepayment%20meter%20Customer%20Workshop.pdf

4 *Debt and Disconnection Review: Consumer Research*, Report, December 2007, available at http://www.ofgem.gov.uk/Sustainability/SocAction/Publications/Documents1/Accent%20debt%20disconnection%20final%20report.pdf

5 Home Secretary's speech to the 'New Challenges for Race Equality and Community Cohesion' conference, IPPR, London, 7 July 2004.

6 S. Saggar, 'Ethnic pluralism and social cohesion: strategic challenges for policy', response to the Home Secretary's speech to the 'New Challenges for Race Equality and Community Cohesion' conference, IPPR, London, 7 July 2004.

7 S. Saggar, 'Labour market achievements in Northern Ireland: evidence, lessons and future frameworks for policy', Expert paper, Equality Commission for Northern Ireland, Belfast, 2005.

8 The Puttnam Report: 'Making a good bill better', see http://www.cpbf.org.uk/body.php?doctype=publications&id=257&f=1

9 A. Cangiano, 'Mapping of race and poverty in Birmingham', see http://www.bctrust.org.uk/pdf/Mapping-Birmingham-Report.pdf

10 http://www.bctrust.org.uk/pdf/Cities-Transition-Forum-Report.pdf

11 Transparency as a Regulatory Tool, see http://www.fsa.gov.uk/pubs/discussion/dp08_03.pdf

12 J. Solomon, A. Solomon, S. D. Norton and N. L. Joseph, 'A conceptual framework for corporate risk disclosure emerging from the agenda of corporate governance reform', *The British Accounting Review*, vol. 32, no. 4, 2000, pp. 447–78.

13 http://www.oft.gov.uk/advice_and_resources/resource_base/market-studies/

Gender Analysis of Transfer Policies: Unpicking the Household

FRAN BENNETT

Introduction

THIS CHAPTER puts forward the case for an incoming government to carry out gender analysis of fiscal and social protection (transfer) policies, in particular those concerning benefits and tax credits; and to use the findings of such analysis to promote policies in these areas to advance gender equality and autonomy for both men and women.

This will require more than just gender impact assessment, which may concentrate only on, for example, comparing the number of women and men affected by a benefit or tax credit policy change, or the amounts of resources transferred to women from men. Instead, gender analysis should go beyond this and examine the make-up and labelling of any such transfer between the sexes, and its impact on gender roles and relationships as well as resources.[1] In particular, it is important to consider the impact of policy change on the degree of autonomy enjoyed by men and women, and the way in which within-household inequalities may be affected, both immediately and over the life course.[2]

This entails an attempt to look inside the family at individuals, rather than taking what is sometimes called a 'unitary household' perspective.[3] The article will therefore focus on couples (especially those in male/female relationships, although some issues also apply to same sex couples/civil partnerships). Analysis of the past decade of fiscal and social protection policies demonstrates that such a 'unitary household' perspective has commonly been adopted by the government, despite its commitment to gender awareness and gender equality. This may have been exacerbated by the unusual dominance of the Treasury in domestic social policy over this period. Despite the progress that has been made, this has hindered the development of genuinely targeted policies and gender-sensitive strategies.

As others have argued, 'the more private aspects of welfare and the balance of resources among members of households are too seldom the subject of policy reform'.[4] In the context of current changes in families and public attitudes, more nuanced gender analysis is key for any future government, in order to develop more appropriate and flexible fiscal and social protection policies for men and women. And, as explained below, such policies, which should aim to increase individual autonomy and gender equality, would not undermine families, as is sometimes claimed, but strengthen them.

Major social trends and challenges

Policy-makers designing or redesigning tax and benefits policies today must face up to several major social trends and challenges. The Beveridge social security system was based on a male breadwinner with a dependent wife who looked after the home and family, with 'women expected to achieve social security through their husbands' employment'.[5] But today family fluidity is increasing, meaning that to base individuals' social rights solely or largely on marriage, or even partnership, would be to expose many people (particularly women) to greater risk. This is also true of the 'one and a half breadwinner' model—one partner (usually the man) earning full time, and the other with a part-time job—which several authors have claimed that the UK now has in mind in its current policy mix.

Women can be argued to have chosen to enter paid employment in larger numbers, seeking independence and autonomy. But whilst women are seen as increasingly self-provisioning, they are also seen as the primary carers.[6] This dual role creates immediate policy tensions. Moreover, a recent report by the government's Strategy Unit[7] highlighted the dual care challenge for the UK in the future, with an increasing number of older people as well as children requiring care. It forecast a continued increase in female labour market participation, which it argued is likely to bring about more pressure on work/family life balance and demands for more parent/child time.[8]

But already both mothers and fathers feel squeezed between the intensification of work and parenting in Western European countries. To date, men's lives in Western Europe have not changed as fast as women's.[9] Will this continue to be the case?

There is clear evidence that women and men would like less unequal working hours.[10] Men would also like more participation in caring. What social protection policies would encourage greater sharing of care, both within the family and by society more broadly? How can fiscal and social protection policies be based on the individual, whilst also recognising that individual's interdependence and their caring responsibilities? These are the key policy puzzles to be addressed if autonomy and more flexible gender roles for both men and women are seen as important goals in reforming benefits and tax credits policies.

Public attitudes

Context matters when it comes to gender policies; and similar policies can vary in their effects according to dominant gender cultures.[11] It is therefore important to take account of public attitudes in the UK, as well as recent government measures and positions. The latest British Social Attitudes (BSA) survey[12] finds gender attitudes in the UK changing, but gender roles in practice lagging behind. Only 17 per cent of men surveyed agreed with traditional gender roles for men and women; and only 29 per cent of women (but 41 per cent of men) think that a pre-school child is likely to suffer if his/ her mother engages in paid employment.

This suggests that women's views are changing more than men's. There also seems to be a time-lag in terms of changes in behaviour. Forty-one per cent of women (49 per cent of those working part time) have liberal views about the roles of men and women, but in practice perform a traditional role in the home. This gap between views and reality seems to lead to more stress, according to the BSA report.

This information should lead to the exercise of some caution in policy prescriptions favouring greater autonomy for women and more equality in gender roles. Indeed, one of the problems about the moves towards individualisation in the extensive restructuring of welfare states in the industrialised world over the past decade is that policy-makers' assumptions have sometimes outrun changes in the behaviour of both men and women.[13] The discrepancy between personal beliefs and behaviour displayed in the latest BSA report bears this out. An 'ought' should not be allowed to become an 'is'. In other words, it should not be assumed that women are more economically independent than they in fact are, or that gender roles are more interchangeable than they are in reality.

Policies are needed which take account of the current position whilst moving towards change. It is argued below that it is nonetheless possible to take some steps towards greater gender equality. First, however, it is necessary to analyse the major obstacles which stand in the way of change.

Obstacles to gender awareness in policy analysis

There are several major obstacles to gender awareness in analysis of fiscal and social protection policies. The first is a tendency to focus on households at one point in time, rather than considering the individuals who make up that household and how their position may change over the life-cycle. (This tendency may be exacerbated by the inability of most models used to develop and/or evaluate such policies to take account of behavioural change.)

Secondly, social security benefits and tax credits may be seen in countries such as the UK, with a traditional focus on poverty and means testing, as being primarily intended to meet the needs of households, especially those at risk of poverty.[14] In continental European countries with a firmer tradition of social insurance, on the other hand, the main function of such benefits is more likely to be seen as providing social protection for individuals over the lifetime (albeit often with dependants' additions). And in the Scandinavian countries transfer payments are more likely to be seen as an element of individual citizenship rights. New Labour's policy focus on poverty consolidates the traditional interpretation in the UK. Indeed, Labour MPs are apparently now largely in favour of means testing, whereas Conservative

MPs express strong opposition (according to a survey of 76 MPs carried out by Bochel and Defty from 2004 to 2006).[15]

Thirdly, women may be seen primarily as a conduit for conveying resources to others, rather than as recipients of benefits for their own needs as individuals.[16] Thus, the government can claim, as in 2003, that it was transferring large amounts of money from men to women by means of new tax credits, whilst these resources are in fact largely intended to benefit others (in that case, children).

Underlying at least the first of these perspectives is a view of families as 'unitary households',[17] in which there is one undifferentiated interest and identity, rather than seeing them as made up of different individuals with both common and diverging interests. This, with the UK's narrow view of social security provision, and a limited view of women's role (receiving resources for others), are major obstacles to gender awareness in analysis of fiscal and social protection policies.

For example,[18] the early years of New Labour saw an analysis in which 'work-rich' versus 'work-poor' households figured as a major focus of thinking on poverty and inequality.[19] The increasing presence of women in the labour market was likely to result in more couples becoming 'work-rich' (two-earner) rather than one-earner households. The percentage of non-employed individuals with a partner in work declined from 76 per cent in 1974 to 40 per cent in 1994, and has remained at around that level since then.[20] But analyses which prioritised the existence of 'work-rich' versus 'work-poor' households could be read as being more concerned about households than about individuals. They also failed to note the potential vulnerability of many women in 'work-rich' households in the event of family breakdown (especially when they had only part-time jobs, in 'one and a half breadwinner' model households). In addition, New Labour's policy focus on child poverty included an emphasis on the problem of children living in 'workless households'.[21] This conflated the different positions of lone parents and couple households without paid employment. And this perspective could make it less likely that analysts would focus on developments within a labour market which was still of a gendered nature, a task which many see as essential in order to tackle poverty and inequality successfully.[22]

Another example of the problems of taking a 'unitary household' perspective is the increasing concern, amongst those both in government and outside, about 'in-work poverty'. This phrase frames a policy issue in a particular way. It refers to a situation in which a household contains at least one earner and in which its members live on less than the 'poverty line' income.[23] But there may be any number of people in such a household, from one person (who is also the earner) upwards. And the concept of 'in-work poverty' itself is not as straightforward as it appears. It might be assumed to refer to low pay. But there is a lack of overlap between low-paid work and household poverty: one study found that only 14 per cent of workers with hourly low pay lived in households in poverty.[24] As one author puts it:

... the relationship between low hourly pay and low household income even among working families [sic] is far from close. Likewise, the working poor often do not have a worker in the lowest decile or so of hourly earnings.[25]

Moreover, by labelling a particular household as being in 'in-work poverty', the situation of the earner is automatically foregrounded, and policy solutions are more likely to be privileged which involve improving his/her earnings, and/or supplementing these earnings because they are too low. This may well be the case, of course. But in addition, or instead, the household could be one in which, for example, there is a large number of children, and the poverty of the family unit is primarily due to the inadequacy of the level of state support for children, and the costs of their care rather than to low earnings. Or this could be a couple, in which the adult who is not earning is on maternity leave, but has no (or insufficient) remuneration while they are in that position. Unpacking the situation of the household in this way should lead to consideration of a range of possible solutions in terms of fiscal or social protection policies, depending on their particular circumstances. The labelling of all these possible scenarios as 'in-work poverty', on the other hand, appears once again to collapse the household into one undifferentiated whole, and therefore to be a recipe for the pursuit of untargeted policies.

Treasury documents tend to reveal the 'unitary household' perspective at its clearest.[26] A recent parliamentary answer, for example, reports:

A single earner family with two children on half male average earnings pays no net tax in 2008–09, as tax credits and child benefit more than offset income tax and national insurance liabilities. In 1997–98, their net tax burden was 9.3 per cent of gross income.[27]

This statement ignores the existence of independent taxation, which means that it is not families who pay income tax but individuals—in this case, probably only the single earner. National insurance contributions have always been an individual impost on earnings. Tax credits and child benefit may be being paid to someone else within the family. But none of this is apparent in this answer, which treats the family unit as one undifferentiated whole. Common wording in Treasury documents which betrays a similar blind spot—collapsing the individuals within a household into one—but which refers to earnings rather than taxation, includes phrases about how much or how little a 'family' needs to earn in order to achieve a certain income level, or about how much higher in effect the (individual) minimum wage is, due to the addition of (family-based) tax credits.

Another example is the government's declared ambition of creating a 'family-friendly tax system', which appears to mean the introduction of tax credits which will support one partner in a couple with children staying at home. The intention seems to be to make the financial situation of such families comparable whether they have one earner or two. Despite the introduction of independent taxation in 1990, and the opposition to the idea of transferable tax allowances which lay behind this, tax credits are in effect now fulfilling a similar function for many couples both with and without children, because they include a payment for a second adult and have no rules about what that adult may be doing. This ignores the problems which may arise in terms of one adult's economic dependence on another. And it compares the financial position of one-earner and two-earner families at one point in time, rather than contrasting the differential impact of children on the trajectories of men and women over the life course.

Developments over the past decade

Commentators have argued that New Labour has achieved many positive changes for women over the past decade through its policies on benefits and tax credits, but that other policy goals have often been stronger in this policy area than its commitment to tackling gender inequalities.[28] In addition, some have argued that Labour has produced policies for women, rather than seeking to address and alter existing gender structures and patterns;[29] or that there has been a conflict between the gender sensitivity of the government and its 'workerist' ethic.[30]

This section analyses changes in benefits and tax credits policy from the point of view of their impact on roles and relationships as well as resources, as recommended above, with a particular focus on autonomy and gender roles. However, before doing so it is crucial to acknowledge that the continuing increase of women's employment in the past decade has resulted in access to an independent income for more women, thereby probably bringing about greater autonomy of women within the household and more challenging of traditional gender roles. Between 1997 and 2006 the employment rate of women increased from 67.2 to 70.2 per cent.[31] Lone parents have seen their employment rate increase significantly. The concentration on benefits and tax credits policies in this chapter is not intended to detract from the importance of access to employment as a force for change in gender relations.

Let us now turn to policies on benefits and tax credits. New Labour has increased the resources available to support children, both universal (the rate of child benefit, for the first child) and means-tested (increases in income support for younger children, and then child tax credit). The government claimed that it was transferring £2 billion from men to women[32] as a result of these changes.[33] As women are more likely to be the partner spending household money on children's needs, this is likely to have improved their situation by giving them more resources for this purpose. But these resources were not intended to meet women's own needs.

In terms of gender roles, the decision to pay child tax credit to the partner whom the couple defines as the 'main carer' appears to cement a distinct domestic division of labour. In the vast majority of cases, the main carer turns out to be the woman. This ensures an independent income for women (as well as the greater likelihood that the money will be spent on children, as noted above). But this is double-edged, as it may reinforce domestic norms that money paid to women is for the children—and may also reaffirm ideas that there is a single principal carer.[34]

This may come to matter more on family breakdown, as within-household gender issues often come into focus more sharply when couples split up. Family law recognises shared care, and child support liabilities are reduced if the child spends a certain amount of time with the 'non-resident parent'. But it is not possible to split the payment of child benefit or child tax credit between parents; instead, both will usually be paid to the 'resident' parent, even if the child spends equivalent amounts of time with each parent. Again, it could be argued (and is, by fathers' groups) that this underlines a gendered division of labour, and undermines efforts to encourage genuinely shared parenting. On the other hand, organisations for lone parents and women's groups might argue that because the resident parent incurs most of the costs regardless, and is much more likely to be a woman, and therefore in a disadvantaged position, this justifies the payment of all the benefits for children direct to them.

There have been improvements to maternity pay, in terms of both its amount and the length of paid leave (to 39 weeks, from 2007). Access to maternity allowance, for women who do not qualify for maternity pay, has been made easier by relaxing the rules on contribution conditions (though this does not affect many women). These payments are largely paid direct to women (and several are not means-tested). The same is true of the additional grant to be paid during pregnancy. The government has therefore increased the access of women to income for their own needs in this policy area. But this is perhaps the simplest way in which to do so, because labour market availability and disincentives are not seen as live issues during maternity.

The government has, however, been seen as failing to challenge sufficiently the traditional gendered division of labour in the area of maternity/paternity provision. Paid paternity leave has been introduced for the first time (though only for two weeks); and in future the father will be able to take up to six months of additional leave instead of the mother if she has already returned to work. But the amount of remuneration available makes it unlikely that this will be attractive to many men; and any parental leave after the first year remains unpaid. The one measure which seems to have an impact on the domestic division of caring work in other countries—a 'use it or lose it' period of 'daddy leave'—has not been introduced. And the continuing refusal by the UK to end its opt-out of the Working Time Directive means that the culture of long working hours is not being tackled. The 'choice' agenda seems peculiarly inappropriate to this area of policy, as men's choices may act as constraints on women's.[35]

A real threat to the possibility of an adequate autonomous income for women over the life course follows on from maternity, and is more about its impact on later earning patterns than about income maintenance around the birth. Here the government has also been active, with policies to increase women's labour market security in pregnancy and early motherhood, with a significant fall in the percentage of mothers changing employers on their return to work.[36] The right to request flexible working has been introduced, at first for parents of younger children and disabled children, and now for carers for elderly and disabled people as well. Parents of older children may also be able to apply in future.[37] There has also been substantial investment in childcare, which has been described by the Prime Minister as an additional arm of the welfare state. Both these measures have been praised by commentators, although the government's stance has also been criticised as insufficiently challenging to market imperatives, and overly sympathetic to the 'business case' for greater gender equality. However, these measures are to do with broader social protection rather than with benefits and tax credits; and they tend to be concerned more with enabling paid work to be fitted around caring than with challenging the current division of gender roles between the sexes.

One commentator has argued that 'from 1996 a new model [of the UK welfare system] has emerged based on an activational welfare model with greater emphasis on incentives, support services and conditionality'.[38] Claimants already involved in 'active labour market' measures, for example as long-term unemployed claimants, have seen an intensification of conditionality; and this will be taken further as the changes mooted in the 2008 Green Paper on welfare reform are implemented.[39] Such claimants are more likely to be men. But in terms of the extension of less stringent forms of conditionality to ever more groups of claimants who are seen as 'inactive' rather than unemployed, women (including lone parents, and the partners of claimants of various benefits) have seen, or will see, the greatest changes.

For example, one of the first of New Labour's policies was the introduction of joint claims for jobseeker's allowance for younger childless couples; this was later extended to older childless couples, and, in a modified form, will also apply to some couples with children in future. The partners in childless jobseeker's allowance couples have to fulfil the conditions for benefit receipt in the same way as the claimant; but the couple's benefit is still paid in full only to the claimant. Most such claimants are men. There still seems to be an assumption that it is acceptable for one partner to be dependent on the other.

Claims for tax credits are now also joint claims. This means not only that income and assets are assessed jointly, but also that both members of the couple are jointly responsible for the claim. This seems unlikely to fit well with increasing family fluidity, and has been criticised by some as discouraging committed coupledom among lone parents and by others as undermining individual autonomy.

Moreover, new tax credits have also been evaluated as likely to cause disincentives for second earners: 'a couple with children now faces a relatively stronger incentive, on average, to be a single earner couple, rather than to have two earners or none, than in 1997'.[40] The European Commission has called for reform of means-tested benefits so that each member of a household has an incentive to enter paid work. Whilst the government has recently tried to deal with this problem (and more urgent administrative problems) by increasing the disregard within the tax credits system on additional earnings to £25,000 per year, there is a limit to how much disincentives can be reduced in a means-tested system which is based on joint assessment. The government's focus on the individual in its labour market goals is in tension with its focus on the 'unitary household' in its income redistribution goals, which works against changes in traditional gender roles.

The priority given to in-work support for families over help for individual earners in the government's 'make work pay' strategy has been exposed by the recent debate over the abolition of the 10p income tax rate. Initially, Labour introduced several policies which helped low-paid earners in terms of their individual incomes, by increasing the amount it was possible to earn before paying national insurance contributions and by introducing the 10p income tax rate.[41] But these early reforms have largely been undermined, as allowances were linked to prices rather than earnings, and the 10p tax rate was abolished.[42] This can be seen as an example of the lack of sustained policy attention to fiscal and social protection policies for individuals over their life-time, compared with the consistent emphasis on jointly assessed benefits and tax credits to combat household poverty in the short term.

Another example of this tendency is the fate of national insurance benefits paid to people of working age for interruptions of employment. The government (as noted above) lowered the threshold for qualifying for maternity allowance, the non-means-tested benefit for women ineligible for statutory maternity pay; and low-paid earners can now qualify for national insurance benefits without having paid contributions on a certain slice of earnings. But, in general, it is difficult to describe the last decade as having seen anything other than a continuing decline in working age national insurance benefits. Women were likely to have lost out in particular through the abolition of the non-contributory severe disablement allowance (SDA).[43] Employment and support allowance (ESA), which has been introduced recently, strips out age and dependants' additions from the former incapacity benefit and will thus be paid at a lower rate to many. In addition, in practice those entitled to only the contributory rate of ESA will be worse off than those entitled to the means-tested rate, because they will lose out on various additional benefits. Jobseeker's allowance is still only non-means-tested for six months; and carer's allowance continues to be paid at a lower rate than contributory insurance benefits.

National insurance benefits have the potential to give women an independent income, but have been consistently undermined in recent decades just as women have become more likely to qualify for them via paid employment.[44] The continuation of dependants' allowances in means-tested benefits and tax credits, in contrast to their virtual abolition in national insurance benefits, suggests that what concerns the government is not economic dependence within the household *per se* but the cost of non-means-tested dependants' additions. The latest changes in the Welfare Reform Bill mean that people have to work for longer before qualifying for contributory ESA, and that they only qualify on the basis of more recent work; this is likely to affect more women than men, as they are more likely to have interrupted work histories. The suggestion that those who no longer qualify for the contributory form of ESA can instead claim the means-tested version ignores the likelihood that many women affected in this way will be excluded due to their partners' income level, as in previous reforms.[45] The gender impact assessment of the Green Paper's proposals was inadequate in not drawing attention to these implications.

Any cuts in non-means-tested benefits make it more likely that a couple (or anyone else) will need to claim means-tested benefits. In recent years the Labour government started to uprate (means-tested) pension credit annually in line with earnings increases, but the (non-means-tested) basic state pension only in line with prices. The basic state pension is paid direct to married women, even if they qualify for it on the basis of their husbands' contributions, whereas pension credit is usually claimed by the man on behalf of the couple. So the substitution of pension credit for (part of) the basic state pension meant a transfer of resources from women to men.[46] It is unclear whether many ministers or officials were aware of the implications of this policy, as they did not emphasise issues about which person in a couple received the benefit.

What about the chances of obtaining an adequate autonomous income from future pension provision? The easing of the qualifying conditions for the basic state pension (only 30 years' contributions for those retiring after 2010), and the more favourable treatment of caring, will benefit women in particular— though in fact the Department for Work and Pensions argued recently that most women would soon have qualified for the basic pension on the basis of the current conditions in any case, because of their changing labour market profile. But the state second pension will now become flat rate rather than earnings related by about 2030, rather than 2050. The decision by the government to follow the Pensions Commission's lead and abandon any attempt to deliver an earnings related state pension is likely to result in growing reliance on private income.[47] And the lack of sharing of risks in private pensions relative to state provision means that any women earning above a fairly low level will cease to benefit from the redistribution inherent in the state earnings related scheme, and so will be likely to be left more exposed to risk. Meanwhile, those caught in the pension poverty trap (in which savings bring a lower return, because of the existence of means-tested top-ups for pensioners) are also more likely to be women (because of lower lifetime earnings).

In terms of gender roles, the pensions changes protect carers' rights when caring for a child up to the age of 12. But it has been argued that in general the government does not take sufficient account of the complexity of many women's lives,[48] and the ways in which caring can weave in and out of them. The government did get its fingers burned when it made work focused interviews for those on carer's allowance compulsory, and had to withdraw this provision due to the objections from many carers protesting that they were already fully occupied. An independent review for the government noted that job centres did not know whether claimants have responsibility for children or not, and recommended that this should be taken into account, for both men and women, when their employment position and chances are being considered.[49] It is not clear to what extent this has been done to date.

The government has introduced work focused interviews, in addition to an 'enhanced New Deal', for partners of benefit claimants, with the aim of moving more of them into paid employment. However, the authors of a recent synthesis of evaluation evidence argued that partners often seemed to have very specific needs in terms of hours and flexible working arrangements; that very few couples with children consider formal childcare; and that 'the dynamics of relationships between partners and claimants overlaid all other factors affecting decision making and work related behaviour'.[50] Thus, it appears that domestic responsibilities, and within-household (gender) relations, exert a significant influence on the potential for partners to gain paid work.

This in turn implies that it is not sufficient for the government to pursue a 'unitary household' perspective, even to achieve its own aim of increasing the employment rate—leaving aside the case for more individual autonomy and more flexible gender roles in their own right. It needs to take more account of what goes on inside the household, begin to tackle the gendered division of labour and continue to change the intensely privatised view of the family and of childcare in the UK.[51]

However, most partners were also reported to have found their work focused interview helpful. This may be a pointer to the importance of paying more attention to the 'dependent' partner in a couple on benefits. The latest proposals for changes to benefits and tax credits do pursue this. It has been argued that it is not possible to affect women's labour market participation solely by including women in programmes, without inciting men to take on more domestic responsibilities.[52] The proposal in the 2008 welfare reform Green Paper to treat the partners of benefit claimants in the same way as lone parents may at last bring issues of gendered responsibilities within the household to the fore. Sanctions and compulsion related to labour market participation will be increasing, largely for women. In the meantime, there is not even a clear public discourse about the sharing of care work in order to increase gender equality. Will these welfare reform changes trigger this?

Another proposal in the 2008 welfare reform Green Paper was that disabled people should be given information about the cost of the package of services they currently receive, and individual budgets to spend the same amount as they wish instead. There are argued to be advantages for the disabled (or elderly) person themselves in being enabled to have greater control over the services they require—though the evidence from pilots is in fact mixed.[53] The

110

proposal claims to promise independence, control and personal responsibility for disabled people. These principles do not, however, seem to be applied to the partners of out-of-work benefit claimants, who will not be paid their portion of the benefit they will nonetheless have to fulfil the conditions for (see above).

The findings of research informed by a gender perspective also need to be taken on board if, as appears possible, options include payments made explicitly by the disabled person to their partner. Although it is already the case that benefits may be used to pay another family member for care, research shows that payments from partners or other family members may come with explicit or implicit strings attached. Payment from the state, for example in the form of carer's allowance, may instead give carers more independence. Research carried out for the Gender Equality Network[54] and previous studies indicate that women can find that receipt of a benefit in their own right gives them more say within their couple relationship.[55] Currently, as with labour market participation for partners, there seems little awareness in this policy area either of the possible tensions and conflicts of interest between individuals within couples or of the ways in which different kinds of income can affect these.

Proposed policy focus

A first step towards the sort of gender assessment of fiscal and social protection policies proposed in this chapter is to try to ensure that intra-household analysis is carried out. This has been made more difficult by the cessation (to date) of the Individual Incomes data series which used to be published by the government.[56] Whilst the particular assumptions made in this series about the sharing of income by households, and about ownership of benefits and tax credits, could be challenged, the availability of such data was essential in order to support an analysis which looked inside the 'black box' of the household to try to assess who actually had what income.

It is important not to misinterpret the messages in this chapter. It is not arguing in favour of an atomised individualism. The government's recent Strategy Unit report, whilst noting that more traditional family patterns are receding, also emphasises the continuing importance of the family in individuals' lives. People do still 'clump together'. It is important to take account of individuals' interdependence, as well as their desire for autonomy.[57] Analysis of the impact of policies on within-household distribution of resources, roles and relationships must take fully into account the context within which individuals live and work and care.

And it is possible to put into practice the kind of policy solutions that would promote gender equity alongside, or as part of, individualisation.[58] Such policies would be likely to include progress towards a less gendered labour market and a broader sharing of risks across society, as a background to achieving greater autonomy for women, as well as a determined attempt to tackle the gendered division of paid and unpaid labour.[59] This chapter is focused on arguing for a different way of analysing current developments and potential policies, rather than on setting out a platform of specific solutions. But a policy package which pointed in this direction would be likely to include, first, building on and extending benefits to which people have an individual right (as was done recently for the basic state pension); it would not be likely to favour moves towards more reliance on means testing, which incorporates joint assessment of resources and requirements. There are ways in which means-tested benefits or tax credits can be individualised to some extent.[60] But it is easier to do this in a country, such as Australia, which does not have non-means-tested benefits in addition, as the UK does.

Secondly, faced with a couple or family in a particular position, instead of offering additional support to one partner to support the other with no questions asked (as, for example, in the case of a transferable tax allowance), a government should investigate the situation of the other partner, particularly if they have no income of their own, and develop policy solutions appropriate to their situation. Various ways of supporting gender role sharing more proactively should be found—such as 'daddy months' of paid leave for new fathers following childbirth, which is lost to both parents if it is not taken. Leave for men will only work if it is paid at a realistic level. (Paid) parental leave should be an individual rather than family entitlement if it is to encourage gender equality. Such measures are preferable to long periods of care leave on state benefits, which are usually paid at a low level and do not preserve employment rights. But cash transfers and leave periods are only part of a policy package to encourage autonomy and a fairer division of labour between the sexes; services are also essential, and there is a limit to how much services can be 'cashed out' without adverse consequences for gender equality.[61]

Focusing policies on achieving greater autonomy for individuals and gender equity between men and women does not have to be seen as a threat to family unity and stability. Indeed, it could be argued that not to recognise women's desire for more autonomy would prove the greater danger. Recent research found that individuals often see a measure of personal financial security as necessary in order to take the risk of commitment to a couple relationship; for all but one of the respondents (who were largely women), 'the security of some financial independence was described . . . as providing the necessary security for the relationship to flourish'.[62] Thus policies which focused on steps towards ensuring an independent income for women could also be seen as providing the foundations for successful partnerships.

Less emphasis on means-tested transfers would also mean fewer people (especially women) facing the loss of autonomy consequent on joint assessment of income and assets, and could therefore also encourage (re-)partnering. And 'family-based means testing helps to perpetuate the existing gender division of paid and unpaid work'.[63] Achieving more flexible gender roles within couples would make it more likely that both men and women would be able to find employment—and that women would progress within employment, thereby improving productivity and family security. Fiscal and social protection policies informed by more nuanced gender analysis would thus be more appropriate to the challenges of tomorrow. But they are also—just as importantly—essential to achieving genuine gender equality.

Notes

1 M. Daly and K. Rake, *Gender and the Welfare State: Care, Work and Welfare in Europe and the USA*, Cambridge, Polity Press in association with Blackwell Publishing, 2003.

2 This is the aim behind the research project RES-225-25-2001, project 5 in the Gender Equality Network, which is funded by the Economic and Social Research Council, and in which the author is involved; for details, see www.genet.ac.uk. Co-researchers in this project include Susan Himmelweit, Holly Sutherland, Jerome de Henau and Sirin Sung.

3 G. S. Becker, *A Treatise on the Family*, Cambridge, MA, Harvard University Press, 1991.

4 Daly and Rake, *Gender and the Welfare State*, p. 176.

5 G. Pascall, 'Gender and New Labour: after the male breadwinner model?', in T. Maltby, P. Kennett and K. Rummery, eds., *Social Policy Review 20: Analysis and Debate in Social Policy, 2008*, Bristol, The Policy Press, 2008, pp. 215–39.

6 G. Pascall and J. Lewis, 'Emerging gender regimes and policies for gender equality in a wider Europe', *Journal of Social Policy*, vol. 33, no. 3, 2008, pp. 373–94.

7 Strategy Unit, *Realising Britain's Potential: Future Strategic Challenges for Britain*, London, Cabinet Office, 2008.

8 See also S. Himmelweit and H. Land, *Reducing Gender Inequalities to Create a Sustainable Care System*, Viewpoint, York, Joseph Rowntree Foundation, 2008.

9 R. Lister, F. Williams and A. Anttonen, *Gendering Citizenship in Western Europe*, Bristol, The Policy Press, 2007.

10 Pascall, 'Gender and New Labour'.

11 K. J. Morgan and K. Zippel, 'Paid to care: the origins and effects of care leave policies in Western Europe', *Social Politics*, vol. 10, no. 1, 2003, pp. 49–85.

12 R. Crompton and C. Lyonette, 'Who does the housework? The division of labour within the home', in A. Park et al., eds., *British Social Attitudes: The 24th Report*, London, Sage Publications, 2008.

13 J. Lewis and F. Bennett, 'Introduction' to themed section on individualisation, *Social Policy and Society*, vol. 3, no. 1, 2003, pp. 43–45.

14 There was, in fact, an attempt on the introduction of new tax credits in 2003 to describe them as a mechanism for redistribution over the life-cycle, but this was not continued consistently.

15 R. Lister, 'Review of H. Bochel and A. Defty, *Welfare Policy under New Labour: Views from inside Westminster*, Bristol, The Policy Press, 2007', in *British Politics*, vol. 3, 2008, pp. 263–4.

16 Daly and Rake, *Gender and the Welfare State*.

17 Becker, *A Treatise on the Family*.

18 F. Bennett, 'Gender implications of current social security reforms', *Fiscal Studies*,

vol. 23, no. 4, 2002, pp. 559–84. This chapter updates the analysis first argued in that article.

19 See, for example, R. Dickens, P. Gregg and J. Wadsworth, *The Labour Market under New Labour: The State of Working Britain*, Basingstoke, Palgrave Macmillan, 2004.

20 Pascall, 'Gender and New Labour', citing R. Berthoud and M. Blekesaune, *Persistent Employment Disadvantage, 1974 to 2003*, ISER Working Paper 2006–9, Colchester, Institute for Economic and Social Research, University of Essex, 2006.

21 Dickens et al., *The Labour Market under New Labour*.

22 For example, see Women's Budget Group, *Women's and Children's Poverty: Making the Links*, London, Women's Budget Group, 2005.

23 Whilst the government now uses three measures of child poverty, the most common measure of poverty for children and others is relative low income, which is defined as under 60 per cent of the median disposable household income, adjusted for family size (before or after housing costs).

24 J. Millar and K. Gardiner, *Low Pay, Household Resources and Poverty*, York, Joseph Rowntree Foundation, 2004.

25 P. Gregg, 'Welfare reform 1996 to 2008 and beyond: a personalised and responsive welfare system?', Working Paper 08/196, Centre for Market and Public Organisation, Bristol, University of Bristol, 2008.

26 Unfortunately, analysis of the gender dimensions of Treasury policy by Coates and Oettinger does not focus on this aspect of Treasury thinking, although it does comment on some of the policies analysed in this article. See D. Coates and S. Oettinger, 'Two steps forward, one step back: the gender dimensions of Treasury policy under New Labour', in C. Annesley, F. Gains and K. Rummery, eds., *Women and New Labour: Engendering Politics and Policy?*, Bristol, The Policy Press, 2007, pp. 117–31.

27 House of Commons *Hansard*, Written Answers, 10 July 2008, col. 1781W.

28 K. Clarke, 'New Labour: family policy and gender', in C. Annesley, F. Gains and K. Rummery (eds.), *Women and New Labour: Engendering Politics and Policy?*, Bristol, The Policy Press, 2007, pp. 155–173.

29 C. Annesley and F. Gains, 'Feminising politics and policy: the impact of New Labour', in C. Annesley, F. Gains and K. Rummery (eds.), *Women and New Labour: Engendering Politics and Policy?*, Bristol, The Policy Press, 2007, pp. 3–24.

30 Coates and Oettinger, 'Two steps forward, one step back'.

31 M. Brewer, *Welfare Reform in the UK: 1997–2007*, Working Paper 20/07, London, Institute for Fiscal Studies, 2007.

32 HM Treasury, *Pre-Budget Report*, Cm 6042, London, The Stationery Office, 2003.

33 See Bennett, 'Gender implications', for an explanation of why the situation was in practice more complex, and in fact was likely to result in some women losing out if they lived in a couple on low income with an earner and had received means-tested support themselves through the previous system.

34 Daly and Rake, *Gender and the Welfare State*, p. 121.

35 J. Lewis and S. Giullari, 'The adult worker model family, gender equality and care: the search for new policy principles and the possibilities and problems of a capabilities approach', *Economy and Society*, vol. 34, no. 1, 2005, pp. 76–104.

36 Clarke, 'New Labour'.

37 There have been suggestions that this is less likely to be introduced now because of the recession.

38 Gregg, 'Welfare reform 1996 to 2008 and beyond', p. 1.

39 Department for Work and Pensions, *No-one Written Off: Reforming welfare to reward responsibility*, Green Paper, Cm 7363, London, The Stationery Office, 2008. This is likely to happen whichever party has the majority after a general election since the Conservative opposition welcomed the Green Paper on publication and said it would not oppose it.
40 Brewer, *Welfare Reform in the UK*, p. 14.
41 F. Bennett and J. Millar, 'Making work pay?', *Benefits*, vol. 13, no. 1, 2005, pp. 28–33.
42 Gregg, 'Welfare reform 1996 to 2008 and beyond'.
43 This was replaced by a provision which allows young disabled people to qualify for incapacity benefit (and subsequently the contributory part of employment and support allowance) without having paid contributions; but this did not extend to older women who had been at home and not in paid work, or whose earnings were below the lower earnings limit, who would previously have qualified for SDA.
44 H. Land, *Women and Economic Dependency*, Manchester, Equal Opportunities Commission, 1986.
45 S. Deacon, P. Fitzpatrick, M. Howard and H. Land, *Women and Incapacity Benefits*, London, Child Poverty Action Group in association with Women's Budget Group, 2007.
46 A point which was made cogently by Hilary Land (University of Bristol) amongst others. (Pension credit is often not claimed; when this was the case, there would of course just be loss of income.)
47 D. Price, 'Towards a new pension settlement? Recent pension reform in the UK', in T. Maltby, P. Kennett and K. Rummery, eds., *Social Policy Review 20: Analysis and Debate in Social Policy, 2008*, Bristol, The Policy Press, 2008.
48 Annesley and Gains, 'Feminising politics and policy'.
49 L. Harker, *Delivering on Child Poverty: What would it take?*, Report for Department for Work and Pensions, London, DWP, 2006.
50 N. Coleman and K. Seeds, *Work Focused Interviews for Partners and Enhanced New Deal for Partners Evaluation: Synthesis of Findings*, Department for Work and Pensions Research Report 417, Leeds, Corporate Document Services, 2007; this is from the research summary, p. 2.
51 The authors instead suggest that the current strategy should adopt a 'family focus, providing integrated support for the couple and family as a whole'—though they do acknowledge that joint interviews, which many partners preferred, were seen by many advisers as not suitable for everyone.
52 J. Macleavy, 'Engendering New Labour's workfarist regime: exploring the intersection of welfare state restructuring and labour market policies in the UK', *Gender, Place and Culture: A Journal of Feminist Geography*, vol. 14, no. 6, 2007, pp. 721–43.
53 See, for example, C. Glendinning et al., *Evaluation of the Individual Budgets Pilot Programme: Final Report*, London, Department of Health, 2008.
54 See http://www.genet.ac.uk (project 5) for more information and working papers. This research is funded by the Economic and Social Research Council (RES-225-25-2001).
55 See also J. Goode, C. Callender and R. Lister, *Purse or Wallet? Gender Inequalities and Income Distribution within Families on Benefits*, London, Policy Studies Institute, 1998.
56 Women and Equality Unit, *Individual Incomes of Men and Women 1996/97 to 2002/03*, London, Department of Trade and Industry, 2004.

57 J. Millar, 'Gender, poverty and social exclusion', *Social Policy and Society*, vol. 2, no. 3, 2003, pp. 181–8.
58 B. Hobson, 'The individualised worker, the gender participatory and the gender equity models in Sweden', *Social Policy and Society*, vol. 3, no. 1, 2003, pp. 75–83.
59 Lewis and Bennett, 'Introduction'.
60 J. Millar, 'Squaring the circle? Means testing and individualisation in the UK and Australia', *Social Policy and Society*, vol. 3, no. 1, 2003, pp. 67–74.
61 J. Lewis and S. Giullari, 'The adult worker model family, gender equality and care: the search for new policy principles and the possibilities and problems of a capabilities approach', *Economy and Society*, vol. 34, no. 1, 2005, pp. 76–104.
62 J. Lewis, 'Perceptions of risk in intimate relationships: the implications for social provision', *Journal of Social Policy*, vol. 35, no. 1, 2006, pp. 39–57.
63 Millar, 'Squaring the circle?', p. 69.

Options and the Lack of Options: Healthcare Politics and Policy

SCOTT L. GREER

Constraining divergence and convergence

> The NHS is a remarkable monument to institutional stability and political consensus. The old building has been massively remodelled, but the basic architecture remains intact. (Klein, 2008)

IT SHOULD be no surprise that party politics in Scotland and Wales (let alone Northern Ireland) are different from those in England. And to most observers of devolution, it should be no surprise to find that they have long had distinctive policy communities, different debates, and in general a different 'feel'. Devolution brought the full force of these distinctive party politics and policy debates to bear on policy. Labour politicians could focus on the particular party conflicts of Scotland and Wales while civil servants and policy thinkers could think about policy instead of implementation. The formal autonomy of the devolved governments came with a substantial increase in their legitimacy (Mitchell, 2006) and the start of a slow decoupling of agendas (Jeffery, 2009). That combination of centrifugal politics and a devolution settlement that was both permissive and poorly thought out (Greer, 2004: 200; McLean, 2005; Trench, 2008) created a fragile divergence machine: very effective at creating social policy divergence but vulnerable to many different kinds of malfunction (Greer, 2007).

But that should not obscure natural constraints on the extent to which policies can diverge—both upwards, limiting the amount of difference between health policies, and downwards, limiting the amount of similarity. This chapter reviews their politics and policy decisions, showing both the very divergent policy-making of England, Northern Ireland, Scotland and Wales, and the similar constraints all four systems face.

Constraining health system change

On the one hand, it is always possible to find bits of the NHS systems that look about the same (relative to any other time or place). The structures of health systems, and welfare states, are notoriously difficult to change. Even in the UK, where politicians have a relatively easy time altering policy, health systems employ too many people, serve too many people, cost too much, and are too visible to be easily changed. Wide-ranging reform plans for privatisation or socialisation founder on these rocks, and very few democratic countries seriously change their welfare states. This fact is the basis for the

Published by Blackwell Publishing Ltd, 9600 Garsington Road, Oxford OX4 2DQ, UK and 350 Main Street, Malden, MA 02148, USA

literature on the welfare state today, which repeatedly comments on its stability in the face of both retrenchment (Pierson, 2001) and new demands such as those of an ageing society (Armingeon and Bonoli, 2006).

In real terms, what it means is that health policy is a classic case of path dependency, with structures set in place long ago shaping policy options and outcomes now (Pierson, 2004; Bevan and Robinson, 2005; Oliver and Mossialos, 2005). Two of the systems, Wales and England, conducted major experiments in health reform with strong political support. Both are falling short of the original ideas of the policy-makers. They are falling short because they asked their existing systems to do things that could not be done without more political force and money than the policy-makers could muster. The same trade-offs, between competition and planning, or local accountability and central finance, occur over and over again in all the systems because of decisions made in 1948 (Klein, 2008). The similar (but not identical!) baselines of the systems as they stood in 1997 will shape their possible evolution for a long time to come, even if their variation is impressive within the range of realistic health system change.

The UK has four old houses, built in a row by the same developers with most of the same interior arrangements. While the foundations and outer walls remain the same, every subsequent owner over sixty years has redecorated, expanded or renovated to his or her taste, with especially big renovations in 2000–04, and the cumulative effects are dramatic.

Constraining political change

On the other side, 2007 might reasonably have led us to expect more change than we saw. The UK had four new governments, with the SNP minority government taking office in Scotland, Plaid Cymru entering a coalition with Labour in Wales, reinstated devolution in Northern Ireland led by Ian Paisley and Martin McGuinness, and Gordon Brown replacing Tony Blair as Prime Minister. Until 2007, health policy across the UK was largely Labour policy. New parties in government (and Gordon Brown) might be expected to change many aspects of devolution and health policy.

But was that a reasonable expectation? First, the change in government was not total; Labour is still in coalition in Wales and the SNP is a minority government in Scotland. Second, governments might change overnight but party systems and policy communities do not. The incentive of parties that hope to win is to try to approach the voters who lie on their frontiers with other parties; in other words, to come closer to each other. Furthermore, policy communities do not change quickly. The major figures in health policy in April 2007 were also the major figures in August 2007. Policy communities are based on social institutions and personal networks that change slowly, based as they are in the civil service, the health services and academia. The result is that policies often show continuity between governments, and even before and after devolution (Greer and Jarman, 2008). That is not just because most policy change is incremental; it is also because party competition and slow-changing policy communities constrain the range of options politicians think are politically or practically attractive.

The policies

Expectations of divergence can be confounded by the organisational realities of health system inertia, and expectations of change can be confounded by the powerful pressures keeping systems on a particular trajectory. Devolution was no 'year zero', allowing politicians to design their systems from scratch. Neither was 2007. Change among bureaucracies, voters and policy communities is always slower than change in elections or even institutions. But the trajectories of the four NHS systems remain divergent, and over time we can watch little decisions build up into increasingly different systems in the four systems.

England

It might be the UK government that runs English healthcare, but it unquestionably does so with England in mind. What are the English political traits that make the calculus different for health policy there? There are two obvious ones, easily summarised. The first is the policy community, which has more thinkers on the 'right', more figures with faith in management rather than professionalism, and more devotees of markets as social policy. The second is the party system. England is the only part of the UK where the Conservative party is in a position to win a plurality of votes. This means that its politics, uniquely in the UK, are conducted on a left–right axis. That puts the NHS in a different frame. The NHS is tremendously redistributive because it is funded out of general taxation. Ill health is regressive, affecting the poor more, but progressive taxation hits the rich more. So the NHS and the taxes that fund it, in a sense, are always under threat from parties and voters on the right who perceive that they would do better in a system that involved lower taxes and more private finance. That is why Labour politicians have argued that their mission after 1997 was to 'save the NHS'.

'Saving the NHS' above all meant enormous new funding, especially after 2000. The increase in NHS spending and capacity will be one of the unquestionable legacies of Labour. But that spending, and increasingly worrying perceptions that it did not buy much, led the government to seek reforms that would increase productivity (Stevens, 2004). The first tactic, from about 1999, was 'command and control', i.e. the use of targets backed up by resources and, essentially, the threat of sacking for managers who failed to meet them. There is evidence that the improvement in performance was significant and sometimes quite impressive; what is less well understood are the costs that targetry imposed on morale, honesty or other priorities (Bevan and Hood, 2006; Bevan and Hamblin, 2009).

The political energy required to operate command and control was bound to dissipate and so the government sought some more automatic mechanism to promote quality. The use of competition to attain efficiency, then, gives us the key to English health (and other) policies in recent years (Le Grand, 2007; Hunter, 2008). Competition, above all, is a tool to manage the NHS. The point of both patient choice and private sector engagement is partly to reduce waiting times but is mostly to create 'contestability'. In this reading, one originally born on the New Left, there has long been an NHS monopoly entwined with cartels of doctors. Inefficient NHS managers were left alone because there was no automatic mechanism to discipline them. Their ineffectiveness included letting consultant doctors waste time, which produced waiting lists, which caused patients to go private—and which led to those same doctors making far more money treating them in private practice! There is unquestionably some truth in this reading of the NHS, but it is a sensitive topic. Lord Warner, then a Labour health minister, summarised the logic, and the government's confrontational approach, when he told a gathering of consultants 'you love waiting lists' (Newman, 2005).

How does a government, encumbered with an establishment such as this, drive it to greater efficiency? Management by targets was exhausting and unpopular with many staff. So markets came back, as the government searched for a more automatic disciplinary mechanism. The theory presented now is that, once the worst cases of public sector incompetence had been wiped out by reforms, it became possible to let go and let the healthiest public sector organisations 'earn autonomy' to compete on a level playing field with each other and the private sector (Stevens, 2004; Barber, 2007). Even if this three-stage account is not good historiography, it is excellent politics because it turns the usual mishmash of contradictory policies into a coherent guide for purposes of implementation and further policy development.

Competition restarted with NHS contracts with private or foreign firms for bulk elective and diagnostic procedures and 'choice' policies that allowed patients a choice of hospitals for their procedures. Combined with the reduction of waiting lists, it was bad news for the traditional, high-cost, private sector in England.

But that only works at the margins—choice is something some patients use but most do not demand, and its organisational effects are unpredictable (Fotaki et al., 2008). The key policy in generalising competition, the one that changed the NHS rather than created contestability at the margins, was the rebirth of the classic strategy of Margaret Thatcher. It partly means a programme called 'world class commissioning' that tried to make Primary Care Trusts (PCTs) better buyers. It means a tariff per procedure (called, oddly, Payment by Results) that enhances competition and enables trusts and private firms to compete and benefit when their costs are lower than the tariff. To make NHS providers more competitive—private firms are marginal—the government opted to create Foundation Trusts (FTs). These are NHS trusts that earn a very high degree of independence (higher than most politicians and officials appear to have noticed) and are subject to a very tough and very economic regulator called Monitor. All NHS trusts are to become FTs eventually. Foundation Trust executives have a great deal of autonomy.

The FT policy, along with contracts let to foreign providers, was expected to not just bring competition to bear; it was also expected to unleash the creativity and competitiveness that NHS management had stifled. But failing to balance the budget or having a scandal leads to firings at the top, just as it would with an ordinary trust.

The basic theory is that pushing people out onto very thin ice will make them play hockey. Of course, it does not. Instead of experimentation, the new environment produces very careful management and retention of as much cash as possible in the Foundation Trusts. They use their autonomy to reduce their risk of catastrophe. There was once a 'float' of money that NHS finance directors moved around to keep everything, even the grossly imbalanced, in balance. It is rapidly disappearing from the NHS overall, and reappearing in the books of the FTs and a few other trusts. The receding float of loose money exposes long-standing financial imbalances elsewhere while creating legally protected pools of money in the hands of the FTs. These pools insure the FTs against failure, but are nowhere near enough to fund major capital expenditure (they are also hard to return to purchasers because that would be a price cut, and 'market' as defined for the English NHS does not include price competition).

In an emblematic move, the government has been trying to separate remaining aspects of provision from commissioning (purchasing). In theory, this will also serve contestability. Contestability has driven down the cost of private medicine and cut waiting lists while letting astute PCT managers shape up or put down their worst GP practices. But PCTs still run some services. Disconnecting PCTs from in-house services should extend the benefits and make them permanent, while creating enough little healthcare firms (out of the PCT service provision) to allow competition anywhere.

As ever, the problem is implementation. The theory demands that all units that are currently part of PCTs develop the managerial skills and capital base to compete for health service contracts. It is not clear they will produce either. Nothing in the training of visiting nurses equips or disposes them to run successful small businesses. The NHS already has management problems, so it is not clear where the government expects to find the expertise to produce successful competitors or how much it will cost. Likewise, what happens when the firm made up of an area's visiting nurses loses a contract with the local PCT? They are unlikely to have the scale or capital to survive, and would probably end up as employees of the new provider, but they certainly will have the public support to create problems for local managers and MPs.

Large private sector firms with capital and (it is thought) management skill are part of the answer to this as well as other questions (such as how to get GPs to perform differently). But the political sensitivity of introducing them (as seen with the BMA's furious reaction to the Darzi report of June 2008[1]), the limited profits available, the history of badly written contracts, their inability to compete on price in most cases, their opacity, and their costly disturbance to existing NHS operations all suggest that government will have to work hard to keep them interested. Indeed, the flow of contracts has been small, and under Secretary of State Alan Johnson it has been getting smaller and more local. That is much of the reason why the government is working hard to make NHS commissioning compliant with EU public procurement law. It is only a matter of time before some of the international players lose their patience and sue to recoup their costs on bids for projects that never happened.

Politically, this all might have worked. It has certainly injected a large number of private businesses and their lobbyists into London health policy circles. The Conservatives have endorsed much of what Labour has done, after flirting with private finance during their wilderness years. If nothing else, there is little incentive for the Conservatives to talk about health, given that the topic does not historically win them votes. Better for them to let Labour neutralise it and discuss something else.

As for the tide of policy, we are just past the high water mark (Healthcare Commission and Audit Commission, 2008). Historic amounts of money and political pressure went into creating as much market as exists now, and the government's budget and political power cannot sustain those levels now. There will, in the future, be much more NHS capacity in England and a private sector more contracted by the NHS than parasitic upon it. There will be more contracting, more opacity, and more potential conflicts of interest (Warner, 2007). But it takes tremendous money and political energy to impose these changes, particularly the use of the private sector. In straitened times, it is reasonable for UK ministers to declare victory. They can draw back from expensive contracts with private sector providers and rely on the NHS incumbents, as they are doing. NHS trusts can bank cash and develop their local monopolies, as they are doing. That would certainly fit with the trajectory of English policy since about 1991: introduction of market mechanisms that produce a steady increase in the power of trust management and the Secretary of State for Health.

Scotland

Scotland and England are certainly the two systems that have developed the most worked-out theories, and the best slogans, for what they are doing. When Scottish Cabinet Secretary Nicola Sturgeon said that there was a 'battle of ideas' across the border in health policy, she could refer not just to different policies with regard to the private sector but also to different, well worked out, theories (Triggle, 2008).

Scottish politics underlie the difference in both politics and ideas. England's party system defined the problem as getting value out of the tax-funded and increasingly expensive NHS, and convincing an electorate perceived as likely to vote with their feet twice—first by going private and second by voting Conservative. Scotland, by contrast, has a party system anchored in the left, and with a clear second axis of nationalism and unionism. The swing voters in Scotland are not about to give up on the NHS in the way it is thought they might in England. Scotland also has a very old and impressive set of professional medical elites at the heart of a policy community that has long given Scottish policy a different feel as well as non-trivial differences.

The health policy trajectory of devolved Scotland dates back to the time between the 1997 elections and the election of the first Scottish Parliament. Just after the 1997 election, Labour broke with precedent and created separate White Papers on health for England, Scotland and Wales (Northern Ireland got a Green Paper, which UK government interviewees told me was in the hope that having something to do would induce Northern Ireland politicians to go into office). The Scottish paper, written under medically qualified minister Sam Galbraith, started to unify the system (Scottish Office, 1997). This marked the start of a consistent Scottish approach to organisation that has held ever since, one focused on 'collectivism and collaboration' (or, presently, 'mutualism'), rather than competition (Kerr and Feeley, 2007). The first major reorganisation of the devolved years carried this trajectory to its logical conclusion by abolishing trusts (while the slowness probably eased the transition, the main obstacle was actually the legal difficulty of getting rid of trusts) (Scottish Executive Health Department, 2003). NHS Scotland is now run by fourteen Health Boards with very limited organisational autonomy for their subunits.

The basic Scottish system has been stable ever since (a good thing in its own right—reorganisations are costly). The Scottish approach is also simpler because it is more likely to endorse existing professional organisation than it is to develop tools to change it in the English manner. There are fourteen large Health Boards that are responsible for management and planning. Their size and distance means that they are more strategic and less engaged in performance management, and in practice that means less tough performance management. In other words, the Scottish NHS has a light managerial touch by design. Scottish policy-makers have fewer tools to control managers, and Scottish managers have fewer tools to control their staff. In theory, this liberates clinical networks to organise care around patients and mobilise professional values. It might also align professionals with health policy by giving them more collective responsibility for decisions. It has not produced obvious improvements in efficiency, relative to 1997 or to the much increased health budget.

There was a failure of nerve around 2005, triggered by improvements in key English indicators, motionless Scottish indicators, and the very bad press given to devolved health systems in the 2005 general election (Labour ran a UK campaign boasting about health in England, something that made life difficult for Scottish and Welsh MPs, many of whom were very eager to complain to the media about what they saw as devolved incompetence). This had a predictable effect: a change of minister. It also led the Scottish coalition to adopt some unexpected ideas, such as an English-style independent treatment centre and some openness to private primary care (Scotland was already a major user of PFI for capital investment).

These borrowings cut against the grain. Scotland did not apply the intense political pressure that the English applied to force independent sector participation into the system. Without that, what might have been a bit of English-style 'contestability' merely became one more case of the Scottish NHS buying in some extra private capacity. Neither Scottish politics nor the direction of travel of the Scottish NHS allowed the initiatives to work. So they withered, and the basic reliance on professional networks continued to be the core of Scottish health policy.

The most remarkable sign of consensus about Scotland's trajectory is probably the reception of the report commissioned from Professor David Kerr (a Scot at Oxford) on the Scottish health service (Scottish Executive, 2005). The report, which said not a word about finance, was a Labour–Lib Dem government's report and could have been pilloried by the opposition. But when it came out the SNP endorsed it and framed their health policy arguments in terms of its correct interpretation. That might look like a sign of consensus. It was. Much of what the SNP did in office after 2007 was what Labour had at one time or another said it would do, such as improve health promotion's connection with communities policy, and its first major health policy document was framed, including during the consultation, in terms set by the Kerr report (Scottish Government, 2007). As a policy document the Kerr report is old, but as an indicator of consensus it was impressive.

The arrival of the SNP in power also brought a government that had appeared to benefit from public discontent with NHS management decisions (especially facility closures). Since they entered government, the SNP has put more emphasis on diluting provider power with public consultations and community involvement. In other words, the Scottish government is responding to discontent with service planning by trying to increase voice rather than the English exit options. That same interest in improving responsiveness—and stopping unpopular closures—without using market mechanisms leads to the principal legislative proposal. This is a pledge to institute direct elections for the Health Boards. (The SNP committed itself to review a small number of reconfigurations, and did so. Contrary to what is often reported, they did *not* oppose all closings.) This is their solution to the problem of improving NHS effectiveness and accountability—democracy where England tried patient choice. The policy is being watered down because directly elected health boards would create a series of imponderables long familiar in NHS systems. If they are elected but not responsible for revenue, for example, all their incentive is to blame Scottish government stinginess for their problems. If they are elected on low turnout, they might easily become captured by NHS staff or special interest groups. The problem—a small version of the big problem created by UK devolution finance—is in the concept, and that makes implementation hard. Boards can at best help balance professional power. The explicit dependence on professionals is precisely what makes Scottish health policy so politically stable despite ample ammunition for those who would criticise its efficiency or outcomes.

Wales

Wales, like England, is a case of a distinctive political project with high ambitions constrained by the basic characteristics of its NHS system. But the difference is that while England's politics drove its government to embrace competition, Welsh politics drove its health ministers to embrace localism and equality. And just as English policies are hobbled by the costs of converting the NHS into a market, Welsh policies are hobbled by the intrinsic difficulties of making it local or a solution to health inequalities.

The first fact about Wales is a political diversity almost incredible for its size. As John Davies wrote, the problem of Wales is 'not so much too many mountains as too many plains' (Davies, 1993: 97–8). Each of the plains nurtures a distinctive political culture and set of cleavages. The ones in South Wales are most important because they have the bulk of the population, but the different politics of Welsh-speaking Wales nurtured Plaid Cymru and give it a base from which to compete with Labour. Liberal Democrats and Conservatives also have their local bases and can venture out. The result is a complex four-party politics that belie ideas that Wales is an Old Labour fortress—even before we investigate the internal diversity of Welsh Labour. The Welsh party system, then, is complex but broadly left-wing. While the stances of the Welsh Conservatives have changed greatly from one election to the next, all four parties tend to affirm their leftism and differentiation from England.

Welsh fragmentation and local communitarianism also mean that it cannot adopt some of the ideas that a health policy technocrat might suggest, such as unified service planning with services centred in Cardiff. At the same time, that communitarianism means that health inequalities are a major issue and there is pressure to resolve them (health inequalities, broadly, refers to the inequalities of illness, avoidable death and poor quality medical care, which almost always correlate with social class and race). Therefore Wales long sustained a community-oriented, leftish, public health network of considerable influence (Michael and Tanner, 2007). Add in the power of local government in Welsh Labour and politics, and it is possible to understand the immediate post-devolution policy direction.

The key decision in Wales was to focus on public health (reduction of health inequalities) as a policy goal, and use a reorganisation of NHS services to enable that focus by promoting local joined-up action (Drakeford, 2006). All four governments talk about reducing inequalities, but insofar as it is possible to rank commitment, the Welsh were by some distance the most committed. The focus on inequalities meant rewriting the spending allocation formula and developing a range of strategies. The reorganisation meant organising commissioning and primary care functions into Local Health Boards that were coterminous and tightly linked with local government. A former special advisor to First Minister Rhodri Morgan explains that this 'created the . . . potential for the management of care networks which include GP services, locally commissioned hospital services, pharmacists, social services, schools, housing and leisure services' (Griffiths, 2007–8: 30). In theory, joining up at the local level would improve health and save money, both by keeping people from getting sick (with pre-natal classes, early years interventions or visiting nursing) and by treating the less acute problems in primary care or community settings. But this is very hard; reducing inequalities is a 'wicked problem' that requires the collaboration of people with different resources, worldviews, responsibilities and accountabilities (Blackman et al., 2006).

In practice, it meant a large and disruptive reorganisation that Wales could not afford. Finding the managerial staff for 22 new LHBs was difficult, given that the obvious centre of power in the Welsh NHS would be the hospital trusts. Meanwhile, it did not solve the problem of health inequalities. Health inequalities often come from social inequalities. Health ministers are poorly placed to address those—the chief policies are tax and benefits (which are reserved), and, in the long term, education, transport and economic regeneration. So a 'wider determinants' strategy tends to produce advice for everybody but the health minister (National Assembly for Wales, 2001). Reorganising to capture what was possible—joint working with local government—incurred a high cost in NHS organisation while not producing much reduction in health inequalities. If anything, reorganising made some problems worse by distracting managers from problems such as decaying primary care in the Valleys and pockets of low quality that predated devolution.

The organisational problems, and the difficulty of fulfilling the health inequalities goals, would have made 2005 a bad year for Welsh policymakers even if there had not been a general election. Arguably, it was even worse for them than it was for their Scottish counterparts, since the Welsh public consumes more English media and the Welsh Labour MPs were more publicly unhappy with devolved deeds. Dismal statistics of all sorts did not help. *Only 31 per cent* of the top managers of the Welsh health service would have wanted themselves or their loved ones to be treated in Wales (Longley and Beddow, 2005).

Like Scotland, Wales changed health minister and made a few feints towards English policy (promising choice of provider to patients who waited too long). The change of minister meant a shift from strategy without tactics to tactics without strategy. A new guiding document was written and managers told to stabilise finances and waiting lists, or else. This produced a wave of contentious reconfigurations, perfectly timed to make enemies for Labour in the 2007 Welsh elections. If local hospital battles were not the cause of Labour's poor showing, they at least contributed to the electorate's bad mood.

The current Welsh coalition promised, in its agreement, to 'eliminate the internal market' (ten years after the 1997 Labour manifesto promised it for England). Saying that, in 2007, sums up the leftwards tug and distinctiveness of Wales compared to England, where in policy documents the 'internal market' has given way to the market, full stop. Health minister Edwina Hart announced on 16 July 2008 that the Welsh Assembly government would create seven unified health organisations to manage all provision in given areas, including a single board for north Wales. That means the new Welsh solution would look much like Scotland. The reorganisation, under consultation at the time of writing, will probably solve many of the administrative problems of NHS Wales. The loss of the internal market might be taken to mark a loss of competitive discipline, but there has never been any real evidence of competitive discipline in the Welsh system. It also marks a retreat from the focus on local joint working, and is another indicator of the weakness of any policy that hopes to address health inequalities from a health department. English markets and Welsh localist egalitarianism are both falling prey to the way NHS systems work. Path dependency—above all from decisions made in 1948—matters.

Northern Ireland

The glacial nature of Northern Ireland's health services (slow and melting) fits with the inattentiveness and ineffectiveness of its political leadership over decades. The Northern Ireland party system and the Northern Ireland health policy community are both shaped by the conflict that has shaped the whole society. Constitutional and sectarian issues overwhelm policy, including health policy. There is intense interest in health in Northern Ireland, but at elections it gets swept aside by the demands of the largely sectarian party system, in which several Unionist and two nationalist parties each compete to be the best representative of 'their community'. Healthcare does not appear to win votes, but between elections it does cause the minister significant grief. Of course, Northern Ireland politicians have not been in charge for most of recent Northern Ireland history; instead health, like other services, was run by 'direct rule' junior ministers from London who would handle large portfolios on one or two days a week. They had no electoral accountability to Northern Ireland at all, but had the responsibility (and an incentive to avoid it along with the grief).

The result was a political leadership vacuum in a highly political area. Managers filled it. The Northern Ireland health policy community is largely made up of those managers, who require thick skin, great tolerance for high-level administrative irrationality, and willingness to operate without political leadership or cover (Greer, 2004: 159–94). It also meant that there was little policy change; by design, there are decisions that managers and civil servants cannot make in a democracy.

Devolution did not change this situation much. The Blair government, when in charge of Northern Ireland, initially made a point of not making policy in order to give Northern Ireland politicians the opportunity to do it. This was apparently a weak incentive when devolution was suspended, and the Northern Ireland Executive did not take up the opportunity when devolution was operational. So reviews of services and proposed reconfigurations ground on with no resolution.

Finally, in 2004–5, the UK government changed tactics with regard to public services, and began making decisions. This achieved two objectives. It put a new kind of pressure on Northern Ireland politicians by imposing decisions they did not like; and it satisfied the Treasury, which was increasingly irritable about the high cost, high share of employment and low productivity of the public sector in Northern Ireland. One of the first decisions was on the siting of a new hospital that would replace two inadequate ones in Omagh and Enniskillen. This led to a moment of cross-community amity in County Tyrone, which elected a doctor on a save-the-hospital platform after the direct rule minister decided on Enniskillen. But the next decision was to reorganise the health services, eliminating a quango-heavy structure of boards and trusts that had given Northern Ireland many more managerial units than it needed. There had been a report on management commissioned by the direct rule ministers (Appleby, 2005) and there had also been extensive consultations on organisation, spurred by the larger review of public administration, and the civil servants had supplied a plan that the Executive could adopt (Birrell, 2008). It adopted the plan for reorganisation and set out to hire (new) managers for the new organisations.

But then devolution was restored, in May 2007. Change, whether of hospitals or of organisations, ground to a halt, with a new consultation and the legislation being debated in the Assembly only in late 2008. And so it was possible, in late 2007, to schedule amicable dinners in Belfast attended by chief executives who were waiting for the months-overdue abolition of their jobs, and other chief executives waiting for the months-overdue creation of their new jobs leading the replacement organisations. The future and the past could dine in a sort of eternal present, exchanging tips on how to motivate staff under such circumstances. The possibility of such events shows how well the Northern Ireland health service has adapted to its policy-making process. Northern Irish health policy is a story of the failure of elected politics, above all.

Options and the lack of options

There are two kinds of lessons these stories can teach us about health policy options. The first is about the role of the Department of Health (DH) and UK government in health. The DH is a very thin rim around the edge of a very large health system, and always tends to turn into the Department of the English NHS. It is also a department with little internal memory, few career civil servants and a strong focus on delivery (Jarman and Greer, forthcoming). Those are not helpful attributes for intergovernmental relations. The first, small-scale, and almost absurdly do-able, advice to a UK government is to pay more attention to institutionalising those parts of the DH that deal with devolved systems. This would be easily enough done, perhaps by reinstating something like its old Constitution Unit, and perhaps by assigning clear responsibilities for coordinating cross-border issues. Plenary or policy Joint Ministerial Councils should also send clear messages to officials that devolution matters (Greer and Trench, 2008). This would deal with the inescapable but manageable problems that come from divergence, such as problems in workforce planning and cross-border patient mobility.

Beyond that, the question is whether health policy should be part of a larger UK government strategy for the Union, in the manner suggested by Gordon Brown's constant invocation of 'the NHS' as a key element of Britishness. It is not very promising. The extent of devolution in health is already quite considerable, and it would definitely break the divergence machine (and possibly the whole settlement) if the UK government were to declare itself a guardian of standards in health. If there are questions about what common UK citizenship means today, constitutional law makes it clear that the answer does not include common health standards. Only with exceptional luck and political skill could a government in current circumstances even state a shared set of NHS values, rather than touch off a firestorm.

The second kind of lesson is for health policy. Devolution, like history, teaches us about what NHS systems, as a family, can and cannot do. This set of lessons is mostly negative, and mostly taught by the English and Welsh experiences. They are about the key facts of the NHS systems, which are simple to state, hard to change and easy to ignore.

NHS systems are tax financed by democratic governments. That means that accountability sticks to ministers. As Wales is showing, and Scotland might presently show, more local accountability falls foul of the fact that finance is not local, so few pay attention to the local decision-makers. It also means that competition—which necessitates the threat of failure and waste—will forever fit badly with the efficiency and high capacity utilisation we demand of tax-financed services, as we see with the stalling of much competition policy in England.

NHS systems are a series of local monopolies with large payrolls and local infrastructures. That means that they are everywhere dominant actors in healthcare. Replacing them is usually just not an option. Introducing competition or reconfiguring services involves creating direct costs for local hospitals, doctors and nurses, all of whom are more popular than ministers and managers, as all the systems have found. It also means that keeping them accountable by any means, be it patient choice or local democracy, is difficult and often fails to produce satisfaction (Pickard, 2007).

NHS systems ultimately depend on professionals who are difficult to manage. Policies that are not aligned with their incentives or worldviews tend to fail. The most interesting thing about Scotland, and a source of its relative stability, is that its politics lead it to align policies with professional values. That is, of course, a political judgement: there are obvious costs to aligning public services with the preferences of even their most admirable employees, and obvious difficulties for politicians who try to control them.

NHS systems are public, and one of the key facts about public administration is that the key component of success is avoiding public failure. Neither direct election, nor local government participation, nor Foundation Trust status changes that.

NHS systems are about healthcare, and (despite the name) departments of health are about the vast NHS systems that they oversee. That means that asking them to promote health, as against healthcare, is always difficult; their policy tools allow them to treat the sick, not tutor the healthy (or, less still, reduce inequality, improve workplace safety or reduce social exclusion). Probably their biggest contribution will be what it always has been—doctors nagging patients to eat or smoke less, treatment enabling people to participate in society, and the health minister nagging colleagues to regulate smoking. The Welsh tried hardest to go further, and are back at bus-stop advertisements about the hazards of smoking.

But that does not mean we should stop arguing about policies. It just means that an incoming government should be more sensitive to the damage imposed by reorganisation and less prone to the lure of organisational fixes that have failed across the border or across the water. There is scope still for learning and intellectual provocation, but, more importantly, there is still scope for challenges—on grounds of accountability, efficiency and quality—to those who do and organise the day-to-day work in the NHS systems. Effectiveness, quality, transparency and accountability are more likely to come from good management and professionalism than from high-level reorganisation. And citing examples across the border or across the water, appealing to pride even, might help those challenges improve that work.

Note

1. Their anger was because the seemingly harmless proposal for big 'polyclinics' would be well suited to bids by outside providers who would compete with them. Given the limited success of outside bidders, and the equally limited success of polyclinics over the seventy or eighty years that they have been repeatedly tried, this anger is a better indicator of GP morale than of real policy change.

References

Appleby, J., *Independent Review of Health and Social Care Services in Northern Ireland*, Belfast, Department of Health, Social Services and Public Safety Northern Ireland, 2005.

Armingeon, K. and G. Bonoli, eds., *The Politics of Post-Industrial Welfare States: Adapting Post-War Social Policies to New Social Risks*, London, Routledge, 2006.

Barber, M., *Instruction to Deliver: Tony Blair, the Public Services, and the Challenge of Delivery*, London, Politico's, 2007.

Bevan, G. and R. Hamblin, 'Hitting and missing targets by ambulance services for emergency calls: impacts of different systems of performance measurement within the UK', *Journal of the Royal Statistical Society*, vol. 172, 2009, pp. 1–30.

Bevan, G. and C. Hood, 'Have targets improved performance in the English NHS?' *British Medical Journal*, vol. 332, 2006, pp. 419–22.

Bevan, G. and R. Robinson, 'The interplay between economic and political logics: path dependency and health care in England', *Journal of Health Politics, Policy, and Law*, vol. 30, 2005, pp. 53–78.

Birrell, D., 'The final outcomes of the review of public administration in Northern Ireland. Tensions and compatibility with devolution, parity and modernization', *Public Administration*, vol. 86, 2008, pp. 779–93.

Blackman, T., A. Greene, D. J. Hunter, L. McKee, E. Elliott, et al., 'Performance assessment and wicked problems: the case of health inequalities', *Public Policy and Administration*, vol. 21, 2006, pp. 66–80.

Davies J., *A History of Wales*, London, Penguin, 1993.

Drakeford, M., 'Health policy in Wales: making a difference in conditions of difficulty', *Critical Social Policy*, vol. 26, 2006, pp. 543–61.

Fotaki, M., M. Roland, A. Boyd, R. McDonald, R. Scheaff and L. Smith, 'What benefits will choice bring to patients? Literature review and assessment of implications', *Journal of Health Services Research and Policy*, vol. 13, 2008, pp. 178–84.

Greer, S. L., *Territorial Politics and Health Policy: UK Health Policy in Comparative Perspective*, Manchester, Manchester University Press, 2004.

Greer, S. L.. 'The fragile divergence machine: citizenship, policy divergence, and intergovernmental relations', in A. Trench, ed., *Devolution and Power in the United Kingdom*, Manchester, Manchester University Press, 2007, pp. 136–59.

Greer, S. L. and H. Jarman, 'Devolution and policy styles', in A. Trench, ed., *State of the Nations 2009*, Exeter, Imprint Academic, 2008, pp. 161–97.

Greer, S. L. and A. Trench, *Health and Intergovernmental Relations in the Devolved United Kingdom*, London, The Nuffield Trust, 2008.

Griffiths, P., 'Social policy—the Welsh way', *Agenda*, 2007–8, pp. 29–32.

Healthcare Commission and Audit Commission, *Is the Treatment Working? Progress with the NHS System Reforms*, London, Healthcare Commission and Audit Commission, 2008.

Hunter, D. J., *The Health Debate*, Bristol, Policy Press, 2008.

Jarman, H. and S. L. Greer, 'In the eye of the storm: civil servants and managers in the Department of Health', *Social Policy and Administration*, forthcoming.

Jeffery, C., 'Devolution, public attitudes and social citizenship', in S. L. Greer, ed., *Devolution and Social Citizenship in the United Kingdom*, Bristol, Policy Press, 2009, pp. 73–96.

Kerr, D. and D. Feeley, 'Values in NHS Scotland: a tale of two C-words', in S. L. Greer, ed., *Devolving Policy, Diverging Values?: The Values of the National Health Services*, London, The Nuffield Trust, 2007, pp. 29–36.

Klein, R., 'Editorial: What does the future hold for the NHS at 60?', *British Medical Journal*, vol. 337, 2008, p. 549.

Le Grand, J., *The Other Invisible Hand: Delivering Public Services through Choice and Competition*, Princeton, NJ, Princeton University Press, 2007.

Longley, M. and T. Beddow, *NHS Wales Barometer 2004*, Pontypridd, Welsh Institute of Health and Social Care, University of Glamorgan, 2005.

McLean, I., *The Fiscal Crisis of the United Kingdom*, Basingstoke, Palgrave Macmillan, 2005.

Michael, P. and D. Tanner, 'Values versus policy in NHS Wales', in S. L. Greer, ed., *Devolving Policy, Diverging Values?: The Values of the UK's National Health Services*, London, The Nuffield Trust, 2007, pp. 37–54.

Mitchell, J., 'Devolution's unfinished business', *Political Quarterly*, vol. 77, 2006, pp. 465–74.

National Assembly for Wales, *Improving Health in Wales: A Plan for the NHS with its Partners*, Cardiff, National Assembly of Wales, 2001.

Newman, M., 'You love waiting lists', *Hospital Doctor*, 28 April 2005, p. 1.

Oliver, A. and E. Mossialos, 'European health systems reforms: looking backward to see forward?', *Journal of Health Politics, Policy, and Law*, vol. 30, 2005, pp. 7–28.

Pickard, S., 'Choice, voice, and the structures of accountability in the new NHS', in A. Hann, ed., *Health Policy and Politics*, Aldershot, Ashgate, 2007, pp. 75–86.

Pierson, P., ed., *The New Politics of the Welfare State*, Oxford, Oxford University Press, 2001.

Pierson, P., *Politics in Time: History, Institutions and Social Analysis*, Princeton, NJ, Princeton University Press, 2004.

Scottish Executive, *A National Framework for Service Change in the NHS in Scotland: Building a Health Service Fit for the Future*, Edinburgh, TSO, 2005.

Scottish Executive Health Department, *Partnership for Care: Scotland's Health White Paper*, Edinburgh, HMSO, 2003.

Scottish Government, *Better Health, Better Care: Action Plan*, Edinburgh, Scottish Government, 2007.

Scottish Office, *Designed to Care: Renewing the National Health Service in Scotland*, Edinburgh, HMSO, 1997.

Stevens, S., 'Reform strategies for the English NHS', *Health Affairs*, vol. 23, 2004, pp. 37–44.

Trench, A., 'Devolution in Scotland and Wales: muddled thinking and unintended results', in P. Facey, B. Rigby and A. Runswick, eds., *Unlocking Democracy: Twenty Years of Charter 88*, London, Politico's in association with Unlock Democracy, 2008.

Triggle, N., 'Private firms face Scots GP block', *BBC News Online*, 8 July 2008.

Warner, C. M., *The Best System Money Can Buy: Corruption in the European Union*, Ithaca, NY, Cornell University Press, 2007.

Entrepreneurship and Innovation Policy: Retrospect and Prospect

ALAN HUGHES

Introduction

THE UK has experimented for over twenty-five years with a wide range of enterprise and innovation promotion policies. In its most recent manifestation this experimentation has included a major overhaul of science innovation and small business support policy. It is not possible within the confines of a short chapter to analyse all of the changes in policy affecting innovation and small and medium-size enterprises, but it is possible to give a broad overview of the changes that have occurred prior to the financial crash in 2008–9. Although small and medium-sized enterprise (SME)/entrepreneurship policy can be separated conceptually from innovation policy, in practice there has been considerable overlap in these areas. For a more general critique of the basis of UK policy in this area and in particular in relation to innovation and spin-offs, see Hughes (2008), and for an analysis of developments in the financial crisis period 2008–9, see Cosh et al. (2009).

The chapter begins with an overview of the significance of SMEs in the UK economy both in terms of their share of activity and in terms of their innovative activity. It then provides a brief overview of the way in which current government policy is designed to encourage enterprise and innovation. This is followed by a brief outline of the case for small business support policy and an overview of the range of small business support policies and innovation support policies which has been put in place. This includes a discussion of the estimated cost of the support provided for SMEs.

In order to assess impacts, we first provide a broad overview of changes in the stock of SMEs, the survival rates of new firms and other broad structural features reflecting the health of the SME sector. The chapter then switches to a more detailed disaggregated approach using the biennial enterprises surveys carried out by the Centre for Business Research (CBR). These have been carried out since 1991 and provide a unique series of snapshots of developments on a wide range of criteria by which the performance of SMEs may be gauged over the last decade and a half.

The next section of the chapter looks at one aspect of the innovation agenda which has assumed increasing significance. This is the nature of and extent to which business–university links affect innovative activity and have been enhanced by a variety of policy initiatives designed to increase the rate at which ideas arising from the science base are commercialised. The chapter concludes with a broad assessment of the impact of the introduction of the ten

Published by Blackwell Publishing Ltd, 9600 Garsington Road, Oxford OX4 2DQ, UK and 350 Main Street, Malden, MA 02148, USA

year science and innovation investment framework and raises some broad questions about the challenges facing the UK in the area of raising R&D expenditures.

The significance of the SME sector

It is helpful in discussing SME policy to keep a sense of proportion about their role. At one level SMEs are clearly a highly significant part of the economy. In 2007 there were 4.7 million enterprises in the UK economy. Of these, however, 3.5 million employed no one. These sole proprietors or individuals otherwise working for themselves accounted for around 17 per cent of UK employment, but only 8 per cent of turnover. A further 1 million SMEs employed 1–9 people, the vast majority of which employed fewer than 5. In total 1.2 million enterprises employed between 1 and 499 workers, whilst only 2,920 employed 500 or more. These 2,920 larger enterprises, however, accounted for 44 per cent of all employment and 41 per cent of all turnover. In contrast, the 1.2 million SMEs who employed 1–499 workers accounted for 43 per cent of turnover and 40 per cent of employees (BERR, 2008).

It is also possible to describe the role of SMEs in innovation activity. Here the data allows us, in particular, to distinguish between the innovative activity of businesses employing fewer than 250 workers and those employing 250 workers or more. If we first of all focus on the R&D undertaken by independent SMEs, it appears that in 2005 the former accounted for £454 million worth of R&D activity which is 3.3 per cent of total UK business enterprise research and development expenditure which was over £13 billion in that year. In 2006 the amount was £356 million (Office of National Statistics, 2008, table 26). The total amount of R&D expenditure undertaken by independent SMEs is probably understated because of problems of data collection and because many high technology small firms do R&D on a contract basis rather than on their own account, but this is still a very minor contribution to R&D expenditures. It is important to note, but far less easy to measure, the important role that small firms may nonetheless play in the area of research and development and engineering consultancies, which contribute substantially to the innovative process in other firms through the supply of variety of design, contract research and other innovation-related support activities. I return to the issue of contract R&D in the discussion of innovation policy later in this chapter.

Another way of assessing the relative importance in SMEs in relation to innovation activity is to look at the incidence of product and process innovation in firms employing fewer than 250 employees compared with the incidence of such innovation in firms employing 250 employees or more. Product innovation and process innovation on this basis are substantially higher in the larger than in the smaller firms. Thus in 2002–4, 23 per cent of businesses employing fewer than 250 employees reported having introduced a product innovation and 14 per cent reported having introduced a process innovation. By contrast, 39 per cent of those firms employing 250 employees or more reported a product innovation process (DTI, 2006). Of course, the total stock of businesses in these size categories means that there are many more small innovating enterprises than there are larger innovating enterprises. However, when the results are weighted by shares of activity, then once again it is clear that larger firms are dominant in terms of innovation activity. This might not seem surprising and yet it belies much of the common rhetoric on the role of smaller firms in the innovation process.

Why are SMEs of policy interest?

Given the statistical dimension discussed in the previous section, it might seem surprising that so much emphasis has been placed on the importance of the SME sector. Just over thirty years ago there was concern in the UK about what was seen as a precipitous decline in the role of the small business sector. By the early 1990s, however, interest in the SME sector in the UK was on an upward trend. SMEs were argued to be the engine of employment generation. In the UK and elsewhere, evidence pointed to a recovery in the shares of small business activity. This led to a prolonged debate about the role of small businesses in employment generation, the outcome of which was not that small firms in general were responsible for employment generation, but that a relatively few relatively fast growers accounted for the bulk of new jobs in the small business sector and, as we shall see, that these were concentrated in particular sectors of the economy. In the course of the 1990s in particular, the employment generation argument was replaced by the view that entrepreneurship and small business formation and growth should be regarded as being in the vanguard of technological innovation and part of a key set of links between the science base and the commercialisation of new scientific ideas and the growth of productivity (BERR, 2007).

Figure 1 sets out the most recent government view of the links between enterprise, innovation and productivity. In the framework shown in the figure, enterprise is enabled by a mixture of factors including entrepreneurial culture, the knowledge and skills base, the opportunity to innovate, access to finance and the regulatory framework. Taken together these enablers produce enterprise which along with key drivers of productivity in the economy, including skills, investment, competition and overall innovative activity, drive productivity and hence wider social benefits. There are clearly some circularities in this model in that innovation possibilities both enable enterprising new ventures to develop and, alongside innovation enterprise, themselves become a driver of productivity. Similarly knowledge and skills which are essential enablers of enterprise are seen alongside enterprise itself as a driver of productivity. The linear interpretation given by the chart is therefore clearly to be seen as subject to non-linear feedback loops. Figure 1 is nonetheless useful in that it indicates the range of areas in which enterprise support policy and innovation policy might operate in relation to the small and medium-sized business sector.

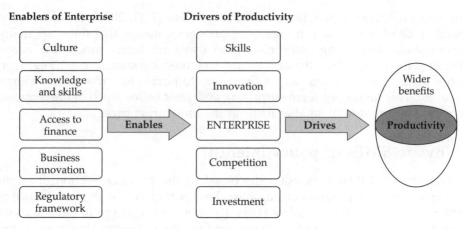

Figure 1: Enterprise enablers and productivity
Source: Adapted from HM Treasury and BERR (2008), p. 17

The case for business support policy

In practice, the pressure to support the SME sector has been based on a number of key propositions. (There is a large literature on the rationale for small business support policy in the UK and the particular issues of training, access to finance and innovative ability; see, for example, Hughes and Storey, 1994; Storey, 1994; Bank of England, 2001; Cosh et al., 2003; HM Treasury, 2003; Parker, 2004; National Audit Office, 2006; HM Treasury and BERR, 2008.)

The first of these is that the knowledge and skills for effective developments of SMEs requires both information about and access to adequate levels of skills and managerial training. The case for government information here is usually made on standard market failure terms. Because the benefits of training cannot always be captured entirely by the funder of the training, less training than is optimal will be done. In the case of SMEs this is supported by various arguments of a less convincing kind that they are unaware of the benefits that training will give or the schemes that are available.

A second argument has been the need to reduce taxation on the small business sector. This has either taken the form of an argument that because SMEs are inherently risky (and in particular those involved in high technology sectors), there is a need to reduce rates of taxation to encourage risk taking. Equally it has been argued that, at the margin, small business enterprise founders are choosing between employment and business formation and that there should be some standardisation of tax rates at the lower end. This has been associated for example with a lowering of small business corporation tax rates to 20 per cent.

The most significant area for policy experimentation has been in relation to capital market failures in the provision of both equity and loan finance. Once again, the arguments here are in conventional market failure terms in relation to the inability of banks to efficiently identify and price for risk using interest rates. Access to finance is thus limited to those with established past histories of performance and sufficient assets to form collateral for loans. The provision of equity capital, it is argued, is hindered by indivisibilities in the market for the supply of equity. Smaller businesses have less information commercially available about them, because of the relative cost of obtaining such information and indivisibilities in the costs of meeting listing and other requirements limiting access to the stock exchange. Again, a range of policy initiatives have been developed to promote a variety of junior stock markets and to promote equity risk-taking by the reduction of taxation associated with capital gains and with the costs of investing and returns from investing in high technology businesses in particular.

Finally, in relation to innovation, policy has focused not only on the risk side of the innovative process facing small firms, but also on the potential benefits claimed to be derived from the development of, usually locally grouped, so-called clusters of businesses. 'Cluster' policy has formed part of the response to a general concern to improve the extent to which smaller businesses may act collaboratively both with each other and with major suppliers and customers and, in particular, may have improved access to the science base. Again a range of policy instruments have been developed here to promote small firm interaction, for example with universities through the introduction of standardised IP contracts and the involvement of regional development agencies in a range of small business initiatives through the Higher Education Innovation Fund (HEIF) and other expenditure streams.

Capital market interventions include the Small Firms Loan Guarantee Scheme, the introduction of zero and reduced rates of corporation tax, VAT exemption and payment relief to ease the burden of the VAT tax system on smaller businesses, export credit guarantees, community investment tax relief, early growth funds, enterprise capital funds, late payment legislation designed to reduce the burdens on smaller firms imposed by bad practices of larger firms in this respect, regional venture capital funds, support for community development finance initiatives, plus a wide range of advice and brokerage programmes including various experimentations in form and structure with the Business Link initiative in England, with a great variety of services delivered mainly locally and regionally. Subsidies to investors in every stage of high technology ventures are produced through the Enterprise Investment Scheme (EIS) and venture capital trusts plus reduced capital gains tax.

Innovation-relevant support programmes have included the Grant for R&D, formerly the Small Firms Merit Award for Research and Technology (SMART), Grant for Investigating an Innovative Idea (now defunct), small firm R&D tax credits, and the Small Business Research Initiative (SBRI), which in various forms has sought largely unsuccessfully so far to stimulate an effective public sector R&D procurement programme in the UK. A variety of initiatives have sought to enhance enterprise and stimulate commercialisation across the university–industry boundary. These have included the Science Enterprise Challenge Scheme to develop excellence in enterprise teaching and enterprise business formation in universities, which was subsequently subsumed into an enhanced and formula-based HEIF in an attempt to add a regular formula-based stream of funding to support so-called 'third' stream activities in addition to the dual funding structure in support of teaching and research.

As a result of the 2003 Innovation Report and further reviews of science and innovation policy in 2007 and 2008 (Sainsbury, 2007; DIUS, 2008), a wide range of innovation policy support programmes have been rationalised under the auspices of the Technology Strategy Board (TSB). TSB now functions as an executive agency separate from the Department for Innovation, Universities and Skills (DIUS) with responsibility for delivering a range of innovation policy (products). These include collaborative R&D, Knowledge Transfer Networks (formerly Faraday Partnerships), which currently cover twenty-four sectors of the UK economy and are designed to promote interaction between sectoral innovation players including large and small firms and the research base, and Knowledge Transfer Partnerships (formerly Teaching Company Scheme), which is designed to encourage the placement of university postgraduate students in businesses to help address specific business-related problems with a research content.

The costs of this burgeoning support for enterprise and innovation was not well documented until 2006. The outcome of this analysis is shown in Table 1. The top half of the table shows central and regional government programme budgets across departments. The lower half estimates the cost of tax incentives granted to support the small business and innovation endeavour. The combined cost is approximately £8 billion in 2003–4, or roughly £220 per person of working age in the UK. What the table does not reveal is that central government alone was operating 267 separate service programmes, over 50 of which were innovation and design focused (PACEC, 2006), and in total there were over 3,000 national, regional and local support programmes (NAO, 2006).

The largest single element is tax breaks (£3.6 billion per annum) of which the 20 per cent corporation tax rate is a major element. Around £0.5 billion is spent in support of high technology activities through the SME R&D tax credit and the EIS and VCT schemes. The second biggest individual expenditure arises in relation to skills and training through the Learning and Skills Councils which in 2003–4 accounted for £1.7 billion. It is noticeable that the then DTI (now BERR and DIUS) had a relatively modest budget of £425 million in direct support of small businesses and innovation. Finally, it is important to note that European Commission structural funds and the European Investment Bank also supply a substantial source of support for UK small businesses. Shifting trends in that expenditure can have important implications especially at regional level.

138

Table 1: Support for small businesses in 2003–04 (£m)

Learning and Skills Council (National) incl. Vocational Qualifications	1,672
Department for Trade & Industry	425
RDA/Local Authority	360
Department for Culture, Media and Sport	336
Department for Work & Pensions/Job Centre Plus	331
Department for Environment, Food and Rural Affairs (excl. CAP)	297
European Commission (Structural Funds)/European Investment Bank	276
Small Business Service	271
Department for Education and Skills	126
UK Trade International	81
Others	62
Office of Science and Innovation	49
TOTAL	**4,286**
Corporation Tax (20% Rate)	2,300
VAT Small Traders	450
Corporation Tax (Zero Rate)	350
SME & R&D Tax Credit	260
Enterprise Investment Scheme/Venture Capital Trusts/EMI	255
TOTAL	**3,615**
COMBINED TOTAL	**7,901**

Note: Data are not available for Inland Revenue or HM Customs & Excise and the table excludes CAP subsidies amounting to £2,398 million.
Source: PACEC (2006).

Is it worth it?

It is possible to address the question of the impact of enterprise support in general aggregate terms and in relation to specific programmes. There is not the space here to look in detail at specific programmes. It is possible, however, to comment on general trends in the enterprise sector in terms of its overall scale. In addition, the disaggregated survey-based data collected by the Centre for Business Research at Cambridge on a regular basis since 1991 answers a number of questions about changes in SME birth rates, likelihood to train or export, innovative activity, overall growth rates and collaborative activity with the science base. It is also possible to analyse changes in the reported views of these businesses on the constraints they face in meeting their business objectives.

Figure 2 provides a long-run picture of changes in the stock of all UK enterprises registered for VAT. The numbers are driven overwhelmingly by changes in the SME population. The data provides a rough comparison

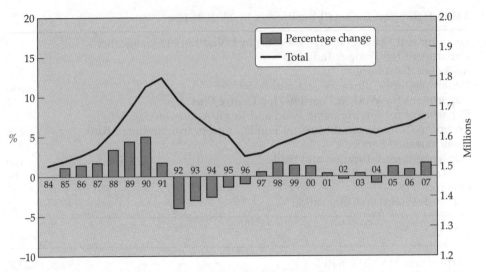

Figure 2: Levels and changes in the stock of UK VAT-based enterprises, 1984–2007
Source: www.statistics.gov.uk

because of breaks in the series due to changes in the VAT threshold. It nonetheless represents a robust picture of broad trends in the stock of UK SMEs which, as we have seen, dominates the overall stock of businesses in terms of numbers.

The picture that emerges is a dramatic one. In the credit-inspired boom which lasted from the mid-1980s to the early 1990s, the enterprise stock expanded dramatically. There was then a substantial decline in the numbers of enterprises through to the mid-1990s and even a decade of relatively stable and sustained growth since then has failed to restore the stock of enterprises to the levels achieved at the end of the 1980s. It is likely that the massive expansion fuelled by the Lawson boom led to an unsustainable expansion in the business stock. This was aided and abetted by a range of policies focused on encouraging business start-ups as a solution to unemployment problems, including for instance the Enterprise Allowance Scheme. The crash hit businesses good and bad with remarkable severity and led to a major debate about the way banks managed their relationships with smaller businesses. The extensive use of overdraft and other short-term financing meant that major financial pressures were exerted on the small business population as monetary conditions tightened.

The picture described in Figure 2 conceals a more fundamental change. Figure 3 makes it clear that the most significant increase in numbers of businesses since the 1980s right through to 2007 has been a sustained expansion in finance, property and business services sectors. The overall growth in enterprise numbers is driven by a structural shift away to the

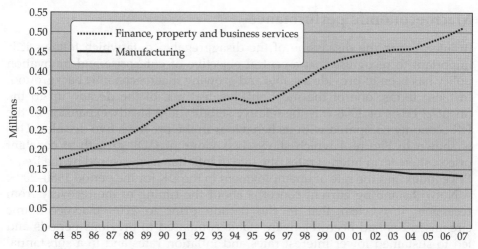

Figure 3: The stock of UK VAT-based enterprises in manufacturing and finance, property and business services, 1984–2007
Source: www.statistics.gov.uk

business services sector. It is also clear that expansion has been at the micro end. The share of micro-firms (employing fewer than ten) in the total number of enterprises has risen from 79.7 per cent in 1993 to 83.5 per cent by 2004, and their share in turnover has arisen from 13.7 per cent to 15.7 per cent. Firms above that size have shown stable or falling shares of activity.

Finally, it is worth noting a significantly improved rate of business survival. The three-year survival rate in 1995 was 65.6 per cent. This had risen to 71.3 per cent by 2002 (www.sbs.gov.uk\survival).

A more disaggregated approach

We can now turn to the evidence from the CBR surveys. This section draws heavily on joint work with my colleague Andy Cosh and is more fully described in Cosh and Hughes (2007). The results reported here are based on comparing a sample of firms drawn from a series of CBR surveys that are matched in terms of size, age and broad industrial sector. The sample as a whole consists of 3,387 firms of which 1,165 each are drawn from the 1991, 1997 and 2004 CBR surveys. The CBR surveys do not cover the whole economy, but focus on manufacturing and business services. The emphasis on business services reflects the increased importance of this sector in the period in which the surveys have been carried out and the desire to be able to compare them with developments in the manufacturing sector.

Macroeconomic performance

In interpreting the discussion of the disaggregated data which follows it is important to recognise that a central objective of enterprise and innovation policy has been to provide a stable and growing macroeconomic background. In these terms, one of the most striking features of the decade up to the financial crisis of 2008 was the relative stability and steady expansion of the UK economy compared with its behaviour in the previous two decades. This is shown in Figure 4 which shows behaviour of GDP growth at constant prices, short-term interest rates, the rate of inflation as measured by the Retail Price Index and the rate of unemployment in the UK for the period 1980–2008.

Notwithstanding current concerns about the timing of the recovery from recession, it is clear that in the decade prior to 2008 macroeconomic circumstances had been relatively stable compared to previous periods and led to sustained lower interest rates and inflation rates and to a substantial decline in the rates of unemployment. The economy had also been clearly much less unstable in this period. Other things being equal, this by itself should have enhanced the prospects for new firm formation and survival and investment in innovation, irrespective of more supply-side focused intervention.

It is important to bear in mind this improvement in macroeconomic performance in the last decade compared with the two preceding decades in interpreting the brief selection of results which follow. As Figure 4 clearly shows, the first survey took place in the midst of a major recession with high interest rates and rates of inflation and that, as we have discussed, the

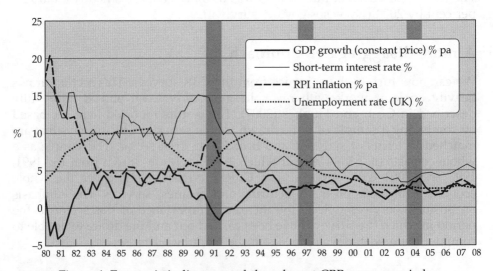

Figure 4: Economic indicators and the relevant CBR survey periods
Source: Cosh and Hughes (2007).

financial position of smaller businesses in particular was severely hampered by prevailing macroeconomic conditions. The 1997 survey occurred in more favourable circumstances with a more stable macroeconomic environment and the same is true for 2004, although there was some concern for low levels of demand particularly in the manufacturing context. The impact of these macroeconomic conditions on responses of firms, for instance to the terms on which they can access capital, will have an important bearing on the answers they provide. This must be borne in mind in interpreting the data as representing the impact of policy in a broad sense.

Start-ups

On the basis of their matched sample comparisons of manufacturing and business services, Cosh and Hughes (2007) show that new start-ups as a form of business foundation have fallen in significance over the period from 67.5 per cent to 51.4 per cent. Spin-offs have risen in importance from 19.3 per cent to 30.0 per cent. Thus the overall impact of business policy as reflected in this data has not been to produce, other things being equal, a higher rate of business formation, even though economic conditions have improved significantly since the 1991 survey took place.

Growth objectives

Figure 5 provides an analysis of the annual percentage employment growth of survey firms at the date of the three surveys. Since the growth of firms is related to their age, the figure shows median growth rates for firms grouped by age. The downward gradient from left to right of the curves for each of the

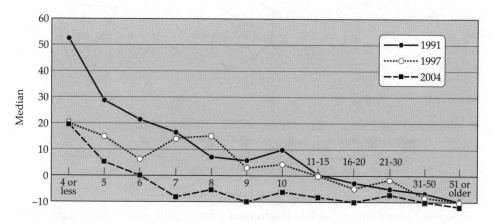

Figure 5: Annual percentage employment growth: 1991, 1997, 2004 surveys
Source: Cosh and Hughes (2007).

survey periods shows that, in general, younger firms grow faster. What is most compelling about the figure, however, is that in successive survey periods, despite the improvement in macro growth conditions, the actual recorded growth rates of firms are in general lower in the latest period than they have been previously, although the first period will include some echoes of the buoyant conditions before the 1990–91 decline.

Constraints on meeting business objectives

If we focus on the factors that firms report constrain their ability to grow, an interesting picture emerges. This is shown in Figure 6, which shows for three size classes of small and medium-sized firms the proportion of firms that reported a significant constraint arising from each of seven different factors. It is clear from the figure that some constraints have lessened in importance over time and some have increased and that the pattern varies by size of firm. If we focus on market demand constraints, constraints arising from internal business skills and constraints arising from access to finance, we find that these were the most highly rated barriers in each year. As we might expect, given the financial conditions in 1991, the availability and cost of overdraft finance and the availability and cost of finance for expansion were the most highly rated constraints for each size class of firms, though clearly more biting for the micro group. By 2004, however, it is clear that there has been a major reduction in the significance of financial constraints as a barrier to growth. It

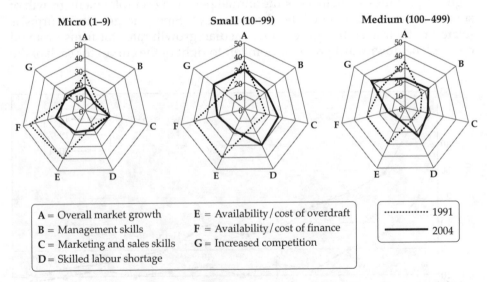

Figure 6: Factors limiting ability to grow for micro, small and medium-sized firms, 1991–2004
Source: Cosh and Hughes (2007).

is, however, difficult to disentangle the extent to which this reflects an overall improvement in credit market and economic conditions or the impact of the major expenditures on attacking capital market problems that enterprise support policy has induced in the last decade. The robustness of the system in the face of the current financial crisis sheds some light on the extent to which the enterprise support system in relation to financial markets has ameliorated the worst aspects of the small business capital market that blighted the early 1990s. Thus SME surveys carried out by the author and his colleagues in the midst of the crisis in 2008–9 reveal that financial constraints *per se* were less dominant concerns than in the recession of the early 1990s (Cosh et al., 2009).

We noted earlier the major expenditure of enterprise policy in the area of training and skills. Figure 6 shows that, for small and medium-sized firms within the SME group, barriers arising from management skills, marketing skills and skilled labour were, despite these major expenditures, higher in 2004 than they were in 1991. The small SMEs felt most constrained by these factors in each year. It thus appears that for this size class of firm, management and training skills are a particularly significant constraint on growth prospects. In all size classes of firm within the SME category, barriers from competition were more important in 2004 than in 1991, especially for the small and medium-sized firms within the group. This is also associated with increased international trading pressures facing these firms.

Innovation, training, exporting

If we turn now to actual patterns of innovation patterns, training and exporting, which have been major areas of policy support, we find in Figure 7 that there has been little change in the proportion of firms carrying

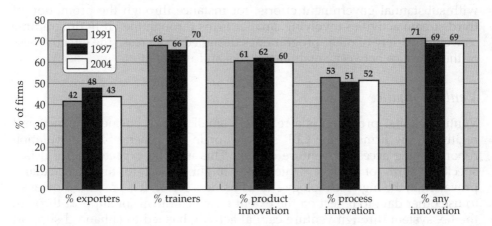

Figure 7: Innovation, training and exporting (% of firms)
Source: Cosh and Hughes (2007).

out any of these activities between 1991 and 2004. In the case of exports, there was some increase in the proportion of exporting between 1991 and 1997, but the proportion then fell back by 2004. There is very little sign of any change in innovative activity or training over the period despite the massive policy effort which has been put in.

Cosh and Hughes (2007) probe a little further into R&D activity by looking at the proportion of staff in SMEs involved in full- or part-time R&D activity. They show a small increase for the SME group as a whole from 5.7 per cent to 6.5 per cent. For micro firms employing fewer than ten people, the share rose rapidly from 16.7 per cent to 25 per cent between 1991 and 1997 and then stayed constant. In interpreting this data, Cosh and Hughes note that the percentages of staff involved in R&D can change quite dramatically in micro businesses simply because adding one person in a five-person firm has a significant impact on the percentage of staff.

Collaborative activity

The emphasis on policy in promoting collaborative activities has been associated with an increase in collaboration by small and medium-sized firms since 1991. Cosh and Hughes (2007) show that by 2004, 44 per cent of the sample firms reported a collaborative arrangement with another organisation. These were most frequently with customers and suppliers (52 per cent and 53 per cent, respectively, in 2004). Collaborative arrangements with higher education institutions were substantially less than those with business, but had risen from 12 per cent in 1991 to 22 per cent in 2004. The outcome of these changes is that, whereas in 1991 collaborative activities with suppliers were over three times more frequent than those with higher education institutions, by 2004 they were just over twice as frequent. This represents a substantial change in collaborative behaviour by SMEs which has coincided with substantial government efforts, for instance through the promotion of third stream activities involving smaller firms through the HEIF programme as well as variety of other programmes designed to increase the effectiveness of the interface between small businesses and universities.

Venture finance

Venture capital provision is a relatively small part of business finance and relatively few firms in the CBR samples or in the general SME population report having access to venture capital. This is to be expected since it is a specialist form of finance which one might expect to find particularly prevalent in the high technology small business sector. It is possible, however, to use other data to reflect on the extent to which the major support through the tax system through venture capital activity has led to enhanced support for the high technology small business sector in the UK. In 2004 UK venture capital investment was £9.7 billion, of which 66 per cent was raised in the

USA and 45 per cent of which went overseas. The market for venture capital is clearly an international one. This raises the important question of why, if the potential supply of UK high technology businesses is good, substantial inward flows are not attracted. The answer may be that in fact formal venture capital invests relatively little in high technology small businesses in either the UK or the USA. Thus, of the total UK venture capital investment of £9.7 billion, £5.3 billion was invested in UK businesses, but only 6 per cent was for start-ups and early-stage businesses, 14 per cent was for expansion and later-stage deals, and 80 per cent was for large-scale management buyouts (Hughes, 2008). Whilst not wishing to underestimate the potential importance of private equity involvement in large-scale management reorganisations, it is difficult to paint a picture of a tax system driving a substantial proportion of formal high risk venture capital towards small-scale early-stage high technology business activity in the UK.

Conclusion on the aggregate trends in SME support

There is bad news and good news arising from this overall survey of changes in the small business sector. New start-up rates appear to have fallen over the period and the business population is still significantly below the levels reached in 1991. SMEs have grown less fast in recent years despite better macroeconomic circumstances. This may reflect increasing constraints arising from management skills and from skilled labour of all kinds which reinforces the need for a careful assessment of the skill requirements of businesses and the nature of current training support provision. There is little evidence of a significant change in the proportion of employees involved in R&D in the small business sector and little evidence of any change in innovative activity, training or exporting. Venture capital finance is focused away from start-up and smaller firms. On the other hand, there is good news too. Survival rates have improved and the constraints arising from the availability of finance for expansion and overdrafts fell significantly in the period 1991–2004. The jury is still out on whether this represents an impact of policy or of macroeconomic conditions. The final outcome of the current financial crisis and in particular the future structure of the banking sector as government attempts to break up some of the current big players will be important here. Finally, collaborative activity appears to have risen steadily, especially with higher educational institutions. The question which arises in relation to these is their quality and the extent to which they will have value for both parties concerned. (For a critique here, see Cosh et al., 2006.)

SME policy rationalisation and the innovation agenda

An increasingly important aspect of SME support has been a focus on policy. This has been accompanied by a major restructuring of innovation support programmes following the 2004 DTI review of the UK innovation system.

Subsequent reviews, including the recent Innovation Nation White Paper, have led to attempts to further rationalise the executive administration of these programmes and to use them effectively in a strategic and linked way in the recent reorganisation of the Technology Strategy Board with important implications for the role of small business in the innovation system.

The reorganisation of the DTI and DfES in July 2007 has led to the creation of two new departments: the Department for Business, Enterprise and Regulatory Reform (BERR) and the Department for Innovation, Universities and Skills (DIUS) with the intention of separating and clarifying the functional purposes of each. The Small Business Service has been reorganised into an enterprise directorate within the Department for Business, Enterprise and Regulatory Reform. In relation to small business support in general, a major consultation on programme rationalisation was launched in July 2007 with the target of reducing 3,000 support programmes to a target of around 100.

The split of small business activity in general from the innovation agenda and the potential link, for instance between regulatory activity and innovation, may raise coordination problems between the two departments which will need to be addressed as their roles are clarified. The Department for Children, Schools and Families is the third department which has emerged out of this amalgamation and restructuring of activities, and there have been further structural changes to skills support following the Leitch Report which are beyond the scope of this chapter to pursue. In the coming decade the key challenges will be policy rationalisation and a need to focus on effective delivery rather than new policy initiatives.

In relation to innovation policy and SMEs, it is useful to take a somewhat broader policy view and discuss developments and options within the long-term science and innovation investment framework announced in 2004. Within this framework private sector business R&D expenditure is a key driver. In 2004 private sector R&D represented 1.24 per cent of GDP compared to total science base expenditures of 0.35 per cent and other government R&D of 0.31 per cent.

The ten-year Science and Innovation Investment Framework covering the period 2004–14 was announced in 2004. It represents an explicit attempt to commit the government to a substantial increase in its own R&D expenditures. They are committed to rise faster than the real rate of growth of GDP. Taken together with a desired growth of private sector R&D from 1.24 per cent to 1.7 per cent of GDP, this would result in meeting an overall framework target of R&D set at 2.5 per cent of GDP by 2014. These figures are shown in Table 2. This was an ambitious target and there are major challenges in relying on the private sector and in particular small firms to play their part.

Ten-year framework performance

The year-on-year growth in public science spend has been substantial. This has been a major positive commitment to the science and research base in the

Table 2: Ten-year framework R&D target

	R&D investment as percentage of GDP	
	2004	2014
Science base	0.35	0.5
Other government R&D	0.31	0.3
Private sector	1.24	1.7
UK total	1.90	2.5

Source: Science and Innvoation Investment Framework 2004/14, HM Treasurey, DTI, DfES July 2004.

UK. Moreover, it has been combined with a number of fundamental reforms to the nature of university funding of which two in particular are worth comment. The first is the introduction of full economic costing of university research projects to help maintain the infrastructure in the science base. The practice of underpricing research contracts by charging marginal cost and failing to recover full overheads was clearly unsustainable. The commitment to full economic costing has, however, meant a substantial increase in the price of university research to potential users with concomitant responses from the business community about the changing international competitiveness of the provision of such services. Nonetheless, there has been a substantial increase in third stream funding activity in the UK university sector. In addition, the gradual embedding of third stream funding through the HEIF initiative and its conversion to a formula basis has meant a clearer ability of universities to use such funding to build capacity and adopt a more strategic approach to commercialisation activities.

A further important change has been the attempt to rationalise the innovation policy portfolio and to strengthen the role of the Technology Strategy Board (TSB) so that the various innovation policy products may be used in a more strategic fashion. Over the years 2008–11, the TSB will have over £1 billion to support innovative activities in selective areas of emerging technologies in the UK. Its overall remit is to encourage a restructuring of the UK economy towards high value knowledge-based manufacturing and services and higher levels of inward investments in the fields of emerging technologies. It is also leading pilot studies of innovative procurement policies by government departments with defence and health first on the agenda (Connell, 2007). The opportunity to use the grant for collaborative R&D, knowledge transfer network and knowledge transfer partnership schemes in tandem, and in particular the development of innovation platforms in response to key innovation challenges, represents an attempt to be more selective and coherent in the application of policy. In each of these areas a key challenge for the TSB is to ensure effective engagement with SMEs. The

TSB has, moreover, been given responsibility for a much wider range of elements of the current innovation system support products, and it remains to be seen how effectively they can focus their activities given the very wide range of responsibilities they have inherited.

The most recent reforms to the innovation policy approach in the UK are important in two respects. First, they represent an attempt to be more focused and strategic in the allocation of support resources and to see SMEs as part of larger sectoral systems based around technology platforms. Secondly, through the TSB they have begun to represent a more sectorally focused approach with the potential of the application of policy support mechanisms, such as the knowledge transfer partnership and knowledge transfer network programmes, with collaborative R&D as part of the more systemic view of the innovation process. Whilst the notion of innovation as a system has become embedded both in the language of successive innovation reviews and in the latest discussion of how to evaluate the impact of innovation support policies, the justification of policies in terms of system failure rather than market failure remains relatively underdeveloped.

Whilst it is clear that R&D expenditure is a relatively small part of the forces driving effective innovative behaviour, it is nonetheless an important one. It is worth reflecting finally on the potential risks and opportunities for SMEs which are arising from the current conjunction of increased de-risking and outsourcing of R&D activities by larger businesses. To the extent that larger businesses seek to close down their own high risk R&D commitments in favour of outsourcing from a variety of sources, then the possibility of effectively contracting for such R&D opportunities increases the opportunities for small firms in the UK to enhance their growth prospects. A key challenge here, however, is whether the SME sector in the UK has sufficient resources in terms of skilled employees and management talent, and sufficient contract research capacity to meet this demand. A policy focus on this aspect of high technology business compared with business doing R&D on their own account is required.

In relation to universities, the direction of their research and the commercialisation opportunities for small firms, a rather different set of challenges emerges. Businesses value universities precisely because they are doing research that is different from the kind of research that they do, and universities can therefore be used as a window onto a different range of possibilities. There is a danger, however, that as larger businesses reduce their own R&D expenditures, they will nonetheless attempt to influence the direction in which university research is pursued. This may be combined with concomitant pressures on research councils and other funding bodies to fund areas of research which are deemed to have commercial applicability. Whilst this raises obvious opportunities for universities to attract research funding, it also runs the danger of eroding the Haldane principle that has governed much of the allocation of research expenditure patterns in the UK. The Haldane principle, by which it is left to the scientific community through peer review to establish the direction of basic research, has important benefits in terms of separating out essentially commercial driven lines of activity from those which are deemed to be of scientific interest in themselves.

The potential erosion of the principle clearly raises questions of a loss of diversity in the spread of research funding across different activities insofar as a single commercial imperative comes to be more influential in determining the direction of research. Equally it is clear that in innovation policy there needs to be strategic focus in the allocation of scarce public resources to the overall science and technology effort (Council for Science and Technology, 2007). In this connection it is important to bear in mind an important distinction between inventive activity close to the science base and innovative commercialisation, which is primarily a later stage in the interactive process by which new ideas are translated into commercial reality. It is on the boundaries between innovation and invention that the most difficult questions lie in allocating resources both for basic research activities and those which are of a more user inspired variety. Whilst it has always been the case that there have been close links between basic research driven by questions of fundamental understanding and applied research driven by considerations of use (Stokes, 1997), the balance of expenditures between each is a fundamental policy question which will remain at the centre of the innovation and SME policy debate in the coming decade.

References

Bank of England, *The Financing of Technology-based Small Firms*, London, February 2001.

BERR, *Productivity in the UK: Securing long-term prosperity*, London, HMSO, November 2007.

BERR, SME Statistics, 2008, at http://stats.berr.gov.uk/ed/sme

Connell, D., '"Secrets" of the world's largest seed capital fund: How the United States uses its small business innovation research programme and procurement budget to support small technology firms', Centre for Business Research, University of Cambridge, 2007.

Cosh, A. D. and A. Hughes, eds, *British Enterprise: Thriving or Surviving?* Centre for Business Research, University of Cambridge, 2007.

Cosh, A. D., A. Hughes and R. K. Lester, *UK plc: Just How Innovative are We?* Cambridge/MIT Institute (CMI), Cambridge, 2006.

Cosh, A. D. and A. Hughes, with A. Bullock and M. Potton, *The Relationship between Training and Business Performance*, Research Report No. 454, London, HMSO, 2003.

Cosh, A. D. and A. Hughes, with A. Bullock and I. Milner, *SME Finance and Innovation in the Current Economic Crisis*, Centre for Business Research, Cambridge, 2009, available at http://www.cbr.cam.ac.uk/pdf/CrCr_EconCrisis.pdf

Council for Science and Technology, *Strategic Decision-Taking for Technology Policy Making*, London, CST, November 2007.

DIUS, *Innovation Nation*, London, Department for Innovation, Universities and Skills, March, CM 7345, 2008.

DTI, *Innovation in the UK: Indicators and Insights*, DTI Occasional Paper No. 6, London, July 2006.

HM Treasury, *Bridging the Finance Gap: Next Steps in Improving Access to Growth Capital for Small Business*, London, December 2003.

HM Treasury and BERR, *Enterprise: Unlocking the UK's Talent*, London, HM Treasury, 2008.

Hughes, A., 'Innovation policy as cargo cult: myth and reality in knowledge-led productivity growth', in J. Bessant and T. Venables, eds., *Creating Wealth from Knowledge. Meeting the Innovation Challenge*, Cheltenham, Edward Elgar, 2008, pp. 80–104.

Hughes, A. and D. J. Storey, eds., 'Introduction: financing small firms', in A. Hughes and D. J. Storey, eds., *Financing Small Firms*, London, Routledge, 1994.

National Audit Office, 'Supporting small business', report by the Comptroller and Auditor General, HC 962, Session 2005-6, May 2006.

Office of National Statistics, 'Research and development in UK businesses 2006', MAI14, London, ONS, 2008.

PACEC, *Mapping of Government Services for Small Firms: Final Report*, London, Small Business Service, 2006.

Parker, S. C., *The Economics of Self-Employment and Entrepreneurship*, Cambridge, Cambridge University Press, 2004.

Sainsbury, *Lord Sainsbury of Turville: The Race to the Top: A Review of Government's Science and Innovation Policies*, London, HMSO, October 2007.

Stokes, D. E., *Pasteur's Quadrant*, Washington, DC, Brookings Institution, 1997.

Storey, D. J., *Understanding the Small Business Sector*, London, Routledge, 1994.

Information Exchange between Government and Citizens

HELEN MARGETTS

Introduction

THIS CHAPTER looks at how information exchange between the British government and citizens has changed in the last ten years, as use of the internet has become widespread. Information exchange includes government dissemination of information to citizens; citizens looking for and finding information about government; government collection of information about citizens; and the storage and safeguarding of that information. This article is divided into four sections, the first of which looks at the last decade in terms of how the information environment and citizens' information-seeking habits have changed as a result of the internet. The second section covers the government's policy initiatives on using the internet to exchange information with citizens during the decade. The third section examines the impact of these policy initiatives on three types of information flow between citizens and government. Finally, some policy recommendations are made which show how governmental organisations could do more to maximise the potential of the internet to enhance information flows and enrich government–citizen relationships.

The last decade: a transformation of the information environment

The last ten years have seen radical changes in the information environment for both governments and citizens, particularly in terms of how citizens seek information about anything they want to know about, including government. Between 1998 and 2008, internet penetration in the UK rose from around 10 per cent to over two-thirds of the population, and appears to be still rising.[1] By the end of the decade, 85 per cent of internet users had a broadband internet connection at home, meaning that they had constant unlimited access to the internet, and thereby an almost infinite variety of information sources. In the early days of societal use of the internet, there was a shortage of useful information and people with internet access to make it worth organisations providing it. But once a 'critical mass' of producers and consumers had accumulated, websites proliferated exponentially. In these early years, it could be difficult to actually find information; some commentators at the time described the internet as the virtual equivalent of a huge library with no

Published by Blackwell Publishing Ltd, 9600 Garsington Road, Oxford OX4 2DQ, UK and 350 Main Street, Malden, MA 02148, USA

cataloguing system. But during the early 2000s, the experience of internet users was revolutionised by the arrival of increasingly sophisticated search engines, the most widely used of which is Google, which made it easy to find virtually anything on the internet and meant it was no longer necessary to remember or bookmark internet addresses.

From its origins as a restricted technical academic network for geeks, the internet has become a major social innovation. As well as doing things they used to do offline, people use the internet to do things they did not do before. Early entrants to the online world were the online bookstore with no offline presence, Amazon and the online auction site, eBay, which has involved millions of people who had never visited an auction room in buying and selling on a regular basis, some even making it a key source of income. Midway through the decade, video and photo sharing sites such as YouTube and Flickr rapidly acquired millions of UK users. And online social networking became extremely popular during the period, meaning that many internet users acquired vast virtual networks of friends and contacts. By 2008 the social networking site Facebook had 8.5 million UK users, MySpace had 5 million and Bebo (aimed at schoolchildren) had 4.1 million UK users.[2] These sites can be seen as one aspect of a phenomenon that characterised internet development in the later 2000s, that is the rise of so-called 'Web 2.0' technologies, which allow users themselves to generate content (rather than just reading what the site's owners have placed on a website). Other examples include the online encyclopaedia Wikipedia, with millions of contributors, or the 'blog' phenomenon, where 'bloggers' can write their own online diaries and other users can post responses and comments.

It would not be too strong to say that widespread use of the internet has transformed many people's information-seeking behaviour. Evidence from the Oxford Internet Survey in 2007 suggests that 84 per cent of internet users have used the internet to make travel plans, 69 per cent to look for news, 68 per cent to look for health or medical care information and 48 per cent to look for a job. A growing percentage of the population claim that they 'would go to the internet' first to find information on a whole range of issues. When respondents to the survey in 2007 were asked to choose from the internet, telephone, a personal visit or book or directory as their first port of call for finding out about something, 54 per cent of people (77 per cent of internet users) would go to the internet first to plan a trip, 40 per cent (55 per cent of internet users) to look for information about a local school, and 46 per cent (64 per cent of internet users) to look for the name of the local MP if they didn't know it. These figures have all risen substantively since the previous survey in 2005.

So if government wants to disseminate information to internet-using citizens—or such citizens want to find out about government—the internet is likely to be the cheapest and easiest channel for both parties. Indeed, the data suggests that for a significant proportion of internet users, the electronic 'face' of government is their preferred access point for government, perhaps the only part of government with which they interact. For those citizens that do not use the internet, of course other channels have to be kept available. But even for these citizens, there is evidence to suggest that a significant proportion have indirect access to internet-based resources, because they can find an intermediary to use the internet for them. In 2007, the Oxford Internet Survey asked respondents 'If you needed to use the internet to send an email or something now, do you know someone who could do this for you?'; 73 per cent of non-users and 88 per cent of ex-users responded that they 'probably' or 'definitely' could.

Policy interventions

So how has the UK government responded to this changed environment? Certainly the decade has seen many policy initiatives in this area and substantial dedication of resources to what during the decade came to be termed electronic government or 'e-government'. E-government may be defined as the use by government of the internet and related information technologies internally and to interact with citizens, firms, voluntary organisations and other governments. Defined in this way, e-government has been around since the 1950s, when large mainframe computer systems first entered the largest transaction processing departments of UK and US governments. From that time, nearly all governmental organisations have become increasingly dependent for both operations and policy innovation on computer-based information systems. It was the advent of the internet, though, that gave e-government real potential to make a difference to governments' relationship with citizens. Earlier information technologies were largely internally facing, used almost exclusively for internal processes and were mostly invisible to citizens, except perhaps when they received an automatically generated letter or were told by an official that 'the computer won't let me do that'. But the internet is used by many citizens, as noted above, so it allows real potential for government–citizen interactions to take place electronically, just as it facilitates online shopping and banking.

Essentially, in the internet era e-government has two 'ends'. The 'front-end' is government's online presence in terms of government websites and the placing of government information and facilities on other sites, the part of government citizens can see online and with which they can interact. This part of e-government has grown from almost nothing to millions of web pages in the last decade. The 'back-end' consists of the complex network of information technology systems internal to government. These systems have been developed, modified and maintained during the last six decades, in response to developments in information technology, the most recent of which are web-based technologies and the internet. By 2008, all government departments and agencies are heavily reliant on networks of information systems which involve a mixture of new and old technologies. It is often assumed that these two 'ends' of e-government are heavily intertwined, and sometimes this is the case. When a citizen renews their road tax online (see below), for example, databases of insurance companies, MOT registrations and the DVLA's own internal databases will be accessed during the interaction. But there are far more examples where the 'front-end' is attached to little internal information, but rather is a broadcasting of content especially devised for the purpose. Indeed, there are cases where information received via a website is printed off and rekeyed into internal information systems.

Central government attention to the issue of e-government has followed the same 'boom-and-bust' pattern of electronic commerce a couple of years earlier, although developments have lagged behind and been rather less dramatic than in the commercial sector. In 1999, UK government policy was more or less to let a thousand flowers (or nettles) bloom, with little attempt from the centre to guide or encourage the online strategies of departments. There was a small policy unit, the Central Information Technology Unit (CITU), in the Cabinet Office with only twenty-nine staff and a tiny budget of only £5 million. A central website, www.open.gov.uk, offered links to the main websites of departments and agencies but little else. The CITU commissioned a consultancy to undertake focus group work on citizens' views on government websites and found that 'the existing pattern of sites was confusing for many users, with a jungle of different styles for navigating sites and information organised more in line with insider knowledge than citizens' needs'.[3] These characteristics of the UK government's online presence were probably one explanation for why usage of government websites was very low at the time, in comparison with the burgeoning usage rates for e-commerce. In autumn 1997 Tony Blair used his Labour conference speech to pledge that by 2002 at least 25 per cent of all government interactions with citizens would be 'electronic' (although there was some confusion over what electronic meant, with some governmental claims that it should include faxes, for example) and this modest target was replaced in 2000 with a target that all services be available online by 2005.

The early 2000s were the 'boom' period for e-government in the UK and many other countries. At this time the governments of almost all developed nations embarked on some kind of e-government initiative and many introduced targets for the percentage of governmental transactions that were to take place online. In the UK, the Office of the e-Envoy (OeE) was set up to play the lead role in a wider drive to 'get the UK online', and in September 2000 CITU was absorbed into the OeE. The OeE had core policy objectives to make the UK the best environment in the world for e-commerce by 2002; to ensure that everyone who wants it has access to the internet by 2005; and to achieve a target for electronic service delivery of making all government services (a further revision of the 50 per cent target) available electronically by 2005. The Office was headed up by an e-Envoy who reported directly to the Prime Minister and grew rapidly to nearly 250 staff by October 2001 with annual running costs of £22 million. The Office was frequently visited by policy officials from overseas, keen to see what the UK government was doing with this cornucopia of resources. A new portal was set up in 2001 to replace open.gov.uk, called www.ukonline.gov.uk, whose usage figures were disappointing in comparison with similar portal sites in the United States, Australia and the Netherlands, in spite of far higher levels of investment. Rankings of e-government proliferated, produced by international organisations such as the UN and the World Bank, the European Commission and the largest private sector consultancies (particularly Accenture, who produced reports annually from 2002). The UK tended to score as a mid-ranking country on these rankings, with the United States, Canada, Australia and Singapore generally amongst the leaders. But departmental initiatives were considerably more developed than in 1999 and usage of departmental sites was growing steadily.

During the second half of the 2000s, central attention to e-government diminished and central agency operations were scaled down. The Office of the e-Envoy was closed and the 'target' for 100 per cent electronic service delivery quietly disappeared from view shortly before it was due to have been achieved. In fact, there are many examples of interactions which even by 2009 still could not be carried out electronically; applying for most benefits delivered for the Department of Work and Pensions, for example. By the mid-2000s the general theme of central government policy was that e-government had already been achieved and the emphasis was on 'transformation', an approach put forward in the strategy paper *Transformational Government: Enabled by Technology*, published by the Cabinet Office in November 2005. A foreword by Tony Blair claimed that he personally had asked for a strategy on 'how we can use technology to transform government services'. The report gave a new and much smaller e-government unit in the Cabinet Office responsibility for IT systems across the government and the IT profession as a whole, but less of an emphasis on the front-end of e-government. The new unit was later renamed and packaged up with some other units to form the Delivery and Transformation Group. Although departments had all progressed with e-government initiatives, there were few signs of innovation. The National Audit Office report *Government on the Internet* in 2007 found hardly any examples of 'Web 2.0' technologies being used by government organisation, in spite of the huge rise in their use in other sectors noted above. At the same time, the government embarked on a radical centralisation strategy around another new portal or cross-governmental website for citizens, www.direct.gov.uk, and a similar site for firms, www.businesslink. gov.uk. The plan was to radically reduce the number of central government websites (of which there were at the time around 2,500 in central government alone) by moving main service delivery and related information provision onto these two 'super sites'.

The *Transformational Government* report is high on rhetoric for how technology can transform relationships with citizens, but contains some confessions of failure regarding the infrastructure of information systems at the 'back-end' of government: 'virtually every public service depends upon large scale processes and technology, particularly the large and complex transactional systems that support individual front-line public service . . . Yet many of these systems are also old and custom built, use obsolete technologies, are relatively costly to maintain by modern standards and hence stretch the capability of the whole technology industry when it comes to amending or replacing them.' These confessions point to a larger phenomenon within the history of UK e-government; the propensity of large-scale IT modernisation projects to fail, meaning that many information systems are not replaced as planned. Examples during the last decade include the complete failure of the Passport Agency in September 1999 due to the failure of a new computer system (hundreds of people missed holidays and the Home Office paid millions in compensation and staff overtime) and cancellation of a £1 billion contract between the government, the Post Office and Fujitsu to build a system to administer social security benefits using a smart card at post offices (the project eventually collapsed completely when it proved too complicated to integrate the new systems into Benefits Agency computers). In 2003, the Child Support Agency's new system was labelled as a '£456 million fiasco', and even by 2005 the agency's annual report revealed that computer problems were leading to mistakes in one out of four cases, an administrative cost per case of around £200 and with 12,000 new cases being processed by hand. By 2008, it was evident that the £12 billion project 'Connecting for Health', to modernise IT across the health service in England was running into severe difficulties, with major contractors pulling out, deadlines continually missed and major cost over-runs of up to 700 per cent. In 2006, a seven country study of e-government in seven countries concluded that 'the UK is apparently a world leader in ineffective IT schemes for government'.[4]

The impact of policy interventions

By 2007, UK government certainly had an extensive presence online, with over one million pages on the Web for central government departments[5] alone. Some of these sites are widely and repeatedly used and rated reasonably well by their users, with improvements from an earlier National Audit Office study in 2002. Some online innovations have been really popular. For example, it is now possible for the European Health Identification Card to be applied for entirely online; users complete a short form on the website, and by 2006 the mix of applications was 56 per cent online, 25 per cent postal and 19 per cent by telephone, suggesting that, where applications are successful, people are willing to use them.[6] At the same time, the 'back-end' of e-government has continued to grow and modernise. Resources devoted to e-government throughout the period remained substantial; the government admits to spending about £14 billion a year on new and existing information technology and related services, directly employing about 50,000 IT professionals.[7]

So how have these policy initiatives impacted upon different kinds of information exchange between government and citizens? First, with respect to citizens finding information from and about government, there is some evidence to suggest that UK government still does not maximise the potential of the internet and the new information environment. Usage of electronic government, including information seeking, in the UK has lagged behind other sectors and other countries. There has been no governmental equivalent of the huge success online of social networking sites such as Facebook and MySpace, or the video sharing site YouTube or the online encyclopaedia Wikipedia. Figures from the European survey Eurostat suggested that in 2005, only 24 per cent of UK citizens had used an internet site to look for government information or interact with government services in the last three months, compared with over 50 per cent in some Scandinavian countries. UK figures present a particularly stark contrast with those for the United States, where, in 2007, 78 per cent of internet users had visited government websites. In the United States, 65 per cent of internet users said that they had contacted the government in 2007, compared with 36 per cent of those who do not use the internet. In Canada, 30 per cent of all government transactions were electronic.

Comparatively low levels of online information exchange between citizens and governments in the UK cannot be attributed to a more general reluctance among UK citizens to exchange information on the internet. Within the UK, while 84 per cent of internet users had used the internet in the last year to make travel plans, 90 per cent to look for or buy goods or services and 53 per cent of users used their bank's online services, only 46 per cent had used it to undertake any sort of interaction with government, including information seeking. The figures for any kind of civic participation were even smaller, with only 2 per cent using it to contact a politician and 1 per cent to join a civic organisation or association. In total, only 9 per cent of users had used the internet to undertake any kind of civic interaction, while 36 per cent of users had undertaken such an activity offline.[8]

With respect to government collecting information from citizens, some of the disappointments of government policy interventions arise from the problems of the 'back-end' infrastructure of e-government noted above and hinted at in the *Transformational Government* report. In the UK, transactions where government actually collects information from citizens—as opposed to providing it—in order to receive a payment or pay a benefit for example, rely on some secure kind of interaction with internal information systems and the sharing of information across systems, often developed and maintained by different agencies and departments. Again, the UK government seems to have been slower than firms or other governments in building the type of authentication mechanisms required to make such interactions possible. By 2007, while 48 per cent of internet users had used the internet to pay a bill, only 12 per cent had used it to pay for a government tax, fine, rent or service online.[9] Again, these figures contrast strongly with the United States, where even by 2004, 65 per cent of tax returns were filed electronically. These figures point to a marked difference in UK citizens' propensity to transact with government online, in comparison with firms and with citizens in other countries. There are exceptions, however. For example, there has been a successful, complex IT project to computerise MOT registration and facilitate the paying of road tax online, which involved computerising 20,000 MOT testing stations, making links to car insurers' databases and producing an online facility for re-registration. The project has been hailed as a success by many and as evidence that public sector IT projects 'really can work' by the British Computer Society.

With regard to the storing and processing of information about citizens by government, there have also been some problems. During the latter years of the decade, the UK government has shown itself to be a rather incompetent guardian of citizens' data. In 2007, the Revenue and Customs department had to admit to losing two disks containing the details of the 25 million UK citizens who claim and receive child benefit. The disks were lost during a National Audit Office investigation, when an official in the tax department sent to the NAO the unencrypted disks which contained details of names, addresses, dates of birth, national insurance numbers and bank and building society account details, although the NAO had only asked for national insurance numbers. In 2008, 600,000 people's details were lost on a Navy officer's stolen laptop, six laptops holding 20,000 patients' details were stolen from a hospital and the Home Office lost a memory stick containing details about 10,000 prolific offenders as well as names, dates of birth and some release dates of all 84,000 prisoners in England and Wales and 33,000 records from the police national computer. All these incidents involving data loss suggest that officials place little value on the intimate personal information habitually held by government departments and agencies. Such events inevitably erode trust between citizens and government.

Policy options for the future

In spite of the dedication of attention and resources outlined above, there is some evidence to suggest that neither citizens nor governments are receiving all the benefits they might from the new information environment. Regardless of who wins the next election, the next UK government should take care to confront the possibilities that the internet and related digital technologies offer for really enriching citizen–government relationships. The internet is not some passing societal fad, as some policy-makers and officials seemed originally to hope. It is intertwined with a high proportion of activities that constitute most people's daily lives. The potential for innovation and benefits through embedding internet interactions at the heart of the citizen–government relationship will only increase.

The recommendations below relate to three key forms of information exchange between government and citizens. The first is concerned with enhancing the ways that citizens can find information from government and government can disseminate information to citizens. The second is concerned with what government might do to enhance its ability to collect information from citizens. The third is concerned with how governments store and process citizens' data.

Maximising the visibility of government information on the internet

The increasing amount of time that most citizens spend using the internet provides a great opportunity for government to disseminate information. But to realise this opportunity, citizens have to find government—or the information that they wish to disseminate—when pursuing their normal information-seeking behaviour. Research has shown that this behaviour involves using search engines—usually Google—and rarely looking beyond the top ten results. So if governments want citizens to find their online presence, they must make sure that they are there in the top ten results. In fact, government could find its ability to disseminate information to citizens actually reducing in the online world. The internet creates new kinds of competition for citizen attention; information can be obtained from many sources and many of these are much better than government at ensuring that they appear in the top ten. Experimental research into how citizens look for government-related information online suggests that over half of sources eventually used to answer frequently asked questions are non-governmental.[10] While there is no intrinsic problem with people getting information from other sources, it means that the chance for a government agency to create a channel of communication with citizens is lost, not easily revoked when the need arises. And search engines, particularly Google, have emerged as major new players, crucial intermediaries in the citizen–government relationship and gatekeepers in the competition for who gains the attention of citizens.

Collecting information: realising the potential for using citizen inputs

The key way that government collects information from citizens is through developing online transactions with citizens, in which individual and personal data is securely transferred, and they have had some successes in this field, although there are many high volume transactions that remain offline. Lack of a secure system of authentication for such transactions has been identified as the key barrier to further development. Yet government has proved remarkably lax at collecting other sorts of information which do not need the same levels of authentication but could have real value in the enhancement of public services. One key policy potential is for the use of Web 2.0 technologies to obtain user generated content about public services and allow citizens' voices to play a role in service delivery and improvement. As noted above, such technologies became widespread in other sectors, but are hardly used by government. Meanwhile, a number of (non-governmental) organisations have started to develop such applications in the public sector context. For example, the social enterprise site www.patientopinion.org allows people who have received healthcare to rate and post comments on treatment they have received, while the private sector site www.ratemy teacher.com (based in the United States but with nearly a million UK users) collects feedback from school pupils and their parents. The UK NHS has now contracted a citizen-facing site called www.nhschoices.org which includes an attempt to emulate these resources. But it lacks prominence on the site, so usage is low and most healthcare organisations have low levels of comments. There is massive potential for an expansion of such applications by government, which would give agencies an opportunity to fine tune their services in response to high volume complaints or negative ratings—as well as providing the information that citizens need if they are indeed to make informed choices in public services.

Another way to collect data about citizens, particularly those who do not use the internet, is to recognise the importance of intermediaries. As noted above, those that don't use the internet often have available individuals (such as friends or family) or organisations (such as Citizens Advice Bureau, NGOs and community organisations) who could use it on their behalf. But departments have been reluctant to formalise channels with intermediaries; there is no dedicated online presence for tax consultants, for example, and various non-governmental organisations have complained that there is no formalised route for them to contact benefits agencies on behalf of their customers. Yet dedicated tracks for organisational intermediaries could be a key way to increase efficiencies in provision of information and services. Likewise, allowing information exchange to take place online, via e-mail for example (which several UK departments do not), could be a way for internet-savvy friends and family to help non-internet users find out about services and benefits or to provide information or documentation.

Realising the value of anonymised information to understand citizens

The future of e-government—just as for e-commerce—depends crucially on understanding how citizens behave online. Any economist will tell you that the key benefits of the internet and related technologies for firms is the ability to understand their customers and to treat them differently. It should be the same for government organisations, but currently a major supermarket is likely to know far more about its customers, through analysis of anonymised transactional data, than any government department. UK government departments have been very slow to realise the valuable information that their websites and information systems provide, through the analysis of usage statistics and transactional data, for example, which can be used to improve services around citizens' needs and feed information back into policy-making. A National Audit Office study in 2007 illustrated how many departments and agencies still had only weak information on the usage of their sites, in spite of a 2002 Public Accounts Committee recommendation that 'all central government organisations should have excellent information on who is using their online services and why'. The danger of the current strategy to centralise web-based provision via the Directgov 'supersite', outlined above, is that individual agencies will not see such information as being at the core of their interactions with citizens. They will only receive usage statistics indirectly via the Directgov team and there could be an abdicating of responsibility, as agencies are encouraged to think of it being done somewhere else. There are notable exceptions, which could provide an example to other parts of government. Transport for London, for example, has been extremely innovative in using the data generated by the Oyster card ticketing system and visits to their own website to redesign their online presence to better suit passengers' needs and to use anonymised information about passengers and journeys to feed back into policy-making.

The kind of data that might be used in these ways can be anonymous, in contrast to the highly personalised and intimate data with which government agencies have shown themselves to be so careless in the past decade. Again, search engines emerge as important players here, as they hold even more information about citizens' behaviour and interactions than government itself. Much of this data is not available for analysis, and companies like Google and Yahoo do not even publish results of their own analyses. Government might be more imaginative in persuading, coercing or collaborating with the major search engines to gain access to insight from this data, in return for their almost complete freedom from regulation.

Conclusion

The policy suggestions made here involve realising the value of information. During the last decade, the UK government has devoted substantial resources and attention to the development of information systems and websites that make up e-government, but has consistently failed to value the information they provide in three key ways. First, the value of government's online presence (the front-end of e-government) in terms of disseminating information to internet-using citizens has been underplayed, in spite of the clear willingness of UK citizens to look for information online; the UK government lags behind other countries and other sectors in terms of online interactions with citizens. Government could also be more innovative in using its 'front-end' online presence to collect new sorts of information; that is, what citizens think about public services, healthcare and even public policy developments (and feed such information back to other citizens). Second, key types of information about how citizens behave—anonymised transactional and website usage data—which could be used to improve public services and policy-making more generally, are often under-valued or even ignored completely.[11] Third, the information stored in the 'back-end' of e-government has been under-valued and carelessly handled. It requires managing and safeguarding in a careful, consistent and co-ordinated way—using an account management approach in dealings with citizens, in the same way that banks and shops can do. Future policy in this area should involve closer attention to the potential value of information that the internet and e-government provides for both government and citizens.

Notes

1 The data on use of the internet reported in this and subsequent sections are from the biannual Oxford Internet Survey; for more data, see W. Dutton and E. Helsper, *The Internet in Britain 2007*, Oxford Internet Institute, University of Oxford. It is available online at www.oii.ox.ac.uk.

2 *The Guardian*, 21 February 2008.

3 The National Audit Office has produced three key reports on the state of UK government on the internet during the decade; National Audit Office, *Government on the Web*, HC 87 Session 1999–2000, London, The Stationery Office, 1999; National Audit Office, *Government on the Web II*, HC764 Session 2001–2002, London, The Stationery Office, 2002; *Government on the Internet*, HC 529, Session 2006–2007, London, The Stationery Office, 2007. The author co-directed the team that researched and wrote these reports, which are referred to throughout this article and are available for download at www.governmentontheweb.org.

4 There are many other examples of IT disasters in the UK government over the past decade; see P. Dunleavy, H. Margetts, S. Bastow and J. Tinkler, *Digital-Era Governance: IT Corporations, E-government and the State*, Oxford University Press, 2006, for other examples and a full discussion of causal factors.

5 *Government on the Internet*.

6 Ibid.

7 Ibid.

8 Dutton and Helsper, *The Internet in Britain 2007*.

9 Ibid.

10 See H. Margetts and T. Escher, 'Understanding governments and citizens on-line: learning from E-commerce', paper presented at the Annual Meeting of the American Political Science Association (APSA) in Chicago, 30 August–2 September 2007, available at www.governmentontheweb.org.

11 *Government on the Internet*.

Options for Britain: Europe

PATRICK DIAMOND and ROGER LIDDLE

Introduction

THIS CHAPTER discusses how Britain's European policy might develop in the period to 2020; it is neither taxonomic nor purely speculative but, instead, charts three realistic policy paths, based on historical precedent, the implications of the UK's current political climate, and likely trends in European integration, which will set the context for UK policy-makers. This development could be channelled through one of three scenarios. This chapter will debate the policies that would dominate in each of those scenarios and the factors that will determine the likelihood of particular outcomes. Within each, there is of course a spectrum of possibilities which will also be elaborated.

The first scenario is a *'unsteady as she goes'* conditional Europeanism. This is the scenario that best characterises government policy since 1997, though some recent straws in the wind suggest the possibility of a more positive approach, as indicated by the Government's commitment to the EU climate change agenda, its relatively untroubled ratification of the Lisbon treaty and the leadership role played in Europe by Gordon Brown during the October 2008 global financial crisis.

The second scenario is one of *'stand-off, stalemate and possible crisis'*. Under a Cameron government, this direction is most obviously a risk for pro-Europeans and an opportunity for anti-Europeans that might lead to a temporary withering of the EU's effectiveness. This occurred at the time of Margaret Thatcher's row with our then EC partners over the Community's budget in the early 1980s. Alternatively, it may provoke an existential political crisis in Britain's relations with the EU.

The third possible scenario is the development of a *'more committed pro-Europeanism'*. This scenario would flow from a reassessment of Britain's role in the world; it would result in a conclusive settlement of our EU membership as the best available means for Britain to project its values and interests in a global age.[1] It might in time lead to a higher priority for European defence and foreign policy-making and a reconsideration of whether it is in Britain's interests to join the Euro.

Published by Blackwell Publishing Ltd, 9600 Garsington Road, Oxford OX4 2DQ, UK and 350 Main Street, Malden, MA 02148, USA

And yet it moves: how the changing course of European integration might influence European policy development in Britain

One clear complication in making a firm assessment about the direction of Britain's European policy is that it is contingent on and cannot be isolated from the direction of the EU project itself. This remains notoriously unfinished business. European integration has no generally accepted final destination, which is why it arouses such fears for the future of national sovereignty and stokes such strong suspicion and opposition among many Britons.[2] Moreover, the EU's history has consistently been marked by crisis and uncertainty, with successive 'one step backs' interrupting the 'two steps forward'. While the momentum of and appetite for European integration has ebbed and flowed, many eminent observers have succumbed to the temptation of writing Europe off altogether.[3]

The British view of European integration has historically been characterised by a presumed tension between Britain's 'pragmatic' and 'nation state' view, on the one hand, and the 'United States of Europe' ambitions of traditional pro-European federalists for 'ever closer union', on the other. Whether or not this was ever how other member states really saw their future in Europe—though there has always been an influential body of opinion on the Continent that did—few objective observers doubt that the high point of European federalism was reached in the run-up to the Maastricht Treaty in 1992. The decline of traditional European-state building integrationism has been entrenched by the enlargement to a Union of 27 diverse member states. Most European policy-makers now perceive the European Union as a 'hybrid' of intergovernmentalism and supranationalism. For many, the failed Constitutional Treaty and its Lisbon successor are seen as embodying that hybridity for the foreseeable future. For all the furore these texts aroused in some UK circles, on the Continent they were perceived as marking a decisive shift to an 'Anglo Saxon' view of Europe's future.[4]

In addition, the conventional wisdom of this contemporary juncture is that the EU has to find a new rationale, now that the old one of ending war and division in Europe has been achieved with such conspicuous success. Globalisation is widely perceived as providing the obvious basis for this new rationale. In a world of emerging industrial nations, where the balance of world economic power has decisively tilted to Asia, the EU provides a natural framework for cooperation between member states whose relative power is in decline,[5] yet where global issues have become central to domestic politics. This applies to a varying degree across a wide range of fields: trade and international economics, energy and climate change, international development aid and peacekeeping, immigration and security. At one level these developments are good news for Britain, certainly for 'the traditional Foreign Office view' that recognises the political constraints on Britain's commitment to European integration, but forewarns of the enormous risks to Britain of ending up being left out.[6] On these grounds, Britain should find it easier to live with the concept of 'Global Europe' providing the likely framework and impetus for European integration in the years ahead.[7]

Yet the surface logic of the argument that 'Global Europe' eases British participation in European integration is not as compelling at a deeper level. Outcomes that appear logical are often dismissed for a variety of reasons and prejudices as politically unrealistic or impossible to achieve. Cooperative action on these global issues intrudes on sensitive matters of national sovereignty, far more than EU regulations such as those, for example, to control lawnmower noise, or determine what is meant by chocolate, which characterised the earlier construction of the Single Market. This led to complaints that Europe was, in Douglas Hurd's memorable phrase, reaching into 'the nooks and crannies' of ordinary daily life.[8] But sovereignty pooling over these larger issues raises questions of legitimacy about political decision-making at EU level to which there is no simple or unambiguous answer.

Angst about these deeper questions is no longer confined to the UK. The 'no' votes in the constitutional referenda in France and the Netherlands, two of the founding six, no less, were a huge shock in Brussels. Two 'no' votes in the Irish Republic against the Nice and Lisbon Treaties have also demonstrated the weakness of the European idea in a country that has arguably seen its position transformed as a result of EU membership.[9] In many member states populism on both the left and the right is on the march—politically united by a dislike of the European Union. There is a distinct possibility that the reaction to globalisation in many member states will not take the form of demands for a stronger role for the EU, but instead, could lead to a lurch towards protectionist and anti-immigrant legislation, as in Austria and Berlusconi's Italy. While enlargement has therefore increased the EU's weight in the world, the increased diversification of its culture, demography and civic society triggered by this process could be a huge obstacle to further integration.

These issues can no longer easily be set aside by national elites committed to European integration as they were in the immediate postwar decades. This is not because national elites have lost the power to impose their own priorities on their countries in the face of public scepticism, as British participation in the war in Iraq bears witness. But there is a structural problem with the legitimacy of the European Union, inherent in its present institutional status quo. Member states see their membership of the European Union as an extension of their ability to promote their own national interest. They like to win 'victories' in Brussels and take the credit for themselves for what they perceive to be good about the Union; indeed, in our experience a conscious effort was always made to present EU Council decisions in terms of 'red lines' and the British national interest.[10] Member states also tend to blame the EU for policies that are unpopular at home, for example Commission decisions on competition questions in France or the flaws of the Common

Agricultural Policy in the UK, even when in Brussels they signed them off in the Council of Ministers despite the fact that many key decisions still require unanimity and the practical threshold for qualified majority voting (QMV) is a high one.[11] This habit of demonstrating one's commitment to Europe by aggressively and noisily standing up for so-called national interests used to be a British speciality but it has unfortunately been copied by others—and it makes it increasingly difficult, if not impossible, to pool sovereignty gradually, the favoured approach of the postwar governing class in Britain.

However, it is important not to overestimate the EU's weaknesses. The populists chip away at support for Europe, but they are rarely in power in EU countries. Populism leans in one direction, but objective national interest in another. Poland is a good example of this dissonance. Its leaders can strike poses, but its economic and social future is inextricably bound up with the neighbouring German economy and the continuation of Structural Fund transfers from the richer member states.[12] This applies to Central and Eastern Europe as a whole, where the relationship with Germany is historically complex *and* fundamentally dependent. In the South, Spain's remarkable catch-up from economic backwardness has not been matched by increased weight in global institutions: it needs a stronger EU to give modern Spain the clout it deserves, if necessary at the expense of the national positions of the more established member states. For all Berlusconi's maverick behaviour, it is an article of faith among many Italians that they would be better run by Brussels than their own discredited political class.[13] While it is true that the Nordics were never enthusiasts and the Benelux bloc is no longer solidly integrationist, the dream that some Conservatives harbour that out of the modern European Union, a British government could construct a reliable Eurosceptic, anti-integrationist bloc is almost certainly a chimera. Of course, there are coalitions in which the British can play a key part, such as the 'northern liberals' on trade and budget reform. But the Central and Eastern Europeans, who are misleadingly seen as closet 'Anglo Saxons' in their view of Europe, would, for example, disagree with Britain on these issues: witness, for example, the bitterness with which Poland reacted to Britain's attempts in the 2005 budget negotiations to hold on to its 'rebate'.

What is manifestly obvious is that the Franco-German 'motor' is no longer as strong as it once was. Even when the 'two' act together, they do not have the clout to determine policy outcomes that they once had. The EU of 27 will no longer accept a Franco-German agreement as a 'fait accompli', as was shown in their failed attempt to impose Guy Verhofstadt as Commission President in 2004. Yet if Britain wants the EU to be a key global player, its only option is not to try to construct coalitions against the French and Germans, but to work with them intensively to maximise European influence.

Britain's ability to work with France and Germany in recent years has been helped by the change of leadership from Chirac to Sarkozy and from Schroeder to Merkel. Yet from a European perspective, it is arguable that the bigger problem for the EU is when together 'the two' fail to form a common view of where they wish to advance the European project, which has up to now at least been particularly true of issues surrounding economic governance since the establishment of the euro. In early 2009, a key uncertainty for the future was how Franco-German policy will develop in the light of the global financial crisis. Were Franco-German proposals to emerge for a highly centralised European Financial Services Authority or a common European seat in a reformed set of international financial institutions, this might cause problems for some in the UK governing class.

Constraints on British policy

There is a paradox about British policy over the last decade. The high hopes of pro-Europeans in 1997 have been disappointed. When Tony Blair took office in 1997, he was widely seen as the most pro-European Prime Minister since Edward Heath. Yet, though Blair insisted that he wanted a 'step change' in UK relations with the EU, putting Britain at the heart of Europe and securing EMU membership, it never quite materialised and the mooted elimination of anti-Europeanism remained just that: a moot point. There has been no transformation in the EU relationship; the old ambivalence and semi-detachedness has not been set aside. The moment of existential choice for the British people that commentators like Hugo Young yearned for[14] never materialised. Tony Blair made many fine speeches about Europe—most notably in French to the National Assembly in Paris in 1998 and in June 2005 to the European Parliament at the start of his second EU presidency—through which a passionate commitment shone, and there is no doubt this was a deep and genuine instinct on his part. He had a strong distaste of Europe bashing. Indeed, the only occasion he succumbed to it was instructive: when in March 2003 Downing St heaped blame on President Chirac's so-called 'veto' for Britain's failure to secure a second UN resolution to authorise military action in Iraq. When it came to high politics, other priorities than Europe were shown to matter more—and this proved also true in Blair's acceptance of the negative euro assessment in 2003 and the decision to call for a referendum on the Constitutional Treaty in April 2004. It may be a harsh judgement that when it came to the crunch, Europe was sidelined rather than his premiership put at risk, but there is a grain of truth in this assessment. From a pro-European perspective Tony Blair made up for it during the second British presidency and his final year of office, in settling the EU budget (and surrendering part of Britain's rebate despite vociferous Treasury protests); taking a bold lead on energy and climate change; and ensuring a version of the Lisbon Treaty was agreed that Britain could sign up for.

However, Britain still remains deeply ambivalent and divided about Europe. The number of people who think Britain's membership of the EU is 'a good thing' hovers a little above 30 per cent. Half the UK poll (50 per cent) believes that the UK had not benefited (this is the highest European figure, with the sole exception of Hungary at 53 per cent). Those who believe

Britain has benefited tend to be younger, better educated (63 per cent), managers (56 per cent), the self-employed (46 per cent) and white-collar workers (47 per cent). By contrast, only 24 per cent of manual workers, 27 per cent of the retired and 29 per cent of the unemployed believe that the UK has benefited from membership. Similarly there is evidence of a strong North–South divide: 47 per cent of Londoners, 41 per cent of those in the South-East and 40 per cent of people in the South-West believe membership has brought benefits; in comparison just 27 per cent of those in the North-East, 28 per cent of Yorkshire/Humber and 29 per cent of the East Midlands.[15] Labour's 'core vote' remains largely sceptical of EU membership, despite the preferences of the party's current generation of leaders. This may explain why Labour campaign strategists have consistently argued that in general elections, the party needs to 'neutralise' the opposition's ability to use Europe as a 'wedge' issue, for instance by promising referenda on Britain's membership of the Euro and the failed Constitutional Treaty.

But this scepticism does not mean that there is public support for withdrawal or indeed that the electorate regard Europe as a major issue facing the country. The latest comparative polling conducted in the autumn of 2008, on behalf of the Bertelsmann Foundation, suggests that while the proportion of the British population favouring withdrawal (32 per cent) is double that of any other significant member state (the figure stands at only 5 per cent in Ireland despite their referendum rejection of the Lisbon Treaty), a solid 57 per cent in the UK oppose withdrawal.[16] In polls of the most important issues facing Britain, Europe was deemed as such by only 3 per cent of respondents in August 2008. This was down from 19 per cent in June 2005; and has been less than 5 per cent since December 2007.[17]

Both the Labour and Conservative parties today claim they want to make a success of British membership, according at least to their own leaderships' perceptions of what organisational form the EU should take.[18] This apparent consensus is certainly fragile, but it is in marked contrast to much of the period of Britain's EU membership. Labour opposed the original terms of entry and the party itself (though not a majority of the Labour Cabinet) officially supported a no vote in the 1975 referendum. In 1983 its manifesto argued for withdrawal, before the party gradually moved to a pro-European position under Neil Kinnock's leadership. The high point of Labour pro-Europeanism was in the parliamentary debate on the Maastricht Treaty when John Smith criticised the British 'opt-outs' that John Major had negotiated. But after 1994, this criticism of 'opt-outs' was dropped and Labour's support for the single currency became highly conditional and subsequently defined by the now infamous 'five tests'.

The Conservative party became significantly more hostile to the EU in the late 1980s. The high point of Thatcherite commitment to the European project was the Prime Minister's decision in 1985 to sign up for the Single European Act that enabled the Cockfield/Delors plan for the creation of a European Single Market to be implemented. From then on her opposition to Delors integrationist plans for a single currency and Social Europe became steadily more vocal. Margaret Thatcher was removed from office by Conservative backbenchers largely as a result of discontent over domestic policy, especially the poll tax. However, strong pro-Europeans such as Michael Heseltine, Geoffrey Howe and Kenneth Clarke all played key roles in her ejection from office. After the debacle of British withdrawal from the ERM two years later, Thatcherism became identified with visceral anti-Europeanism rather than the radical economic and industrial relations policies of the 1980s which Heseltine, Howe and Clarke had all enthusiastically supported. Disunity over Europe contributed to the massive scale of the Conservatives' 1997 general election defeat. The obsessive anti-European tone of the Conservative campaigns of 2001 and 2005 did little to improve the party's prospects.

Nevertheless, despite this latent, albeit weak, agreement between the major parties that Britain should remain a committed member of the EU, Euroscepticism remains rife in the UK. The present Labour government has been much more successful at pressing a classically British view of Europe in Brussels than it has at selling Europe to the British people at home. The 2004 and 2007 enlargements were triumphs of traditional British policy, irreversibly increasing the EU's diversity and at the same time strengthening its Atlanticism. The Foreign and Commonwealth Office's nightmare that a 'United States of Europe' might emerge in some form that would both stretch the limits of political integration that British ministers could be brought to accept, and force Britain to choose between America and a united Europe, holds fewer terrors now. The Treaties of Amsterdam, Nice and Lisbon, as well as the failed Constitutional Treaty, have all been heavily scored with Britain's numerous 'red lines' and 'opt-outs', though anti-Europeans still remain outraged at the steady erosion of national sovereignty that they believe these Treaties represent. The British economic consensus supported Gordon Brown's decision to stay out of the euro in 2003 on the basis that membership would have forced Britain to adopt the European Central Bank's lower interest rates, thereby increasing the risk of a property price and consumer debt bubble. After that bubble finally burst in 2008, it was argued by some pro-Europeans that if Britain had joined the euro in 2003, financial regulation would have had to be strengthened at a far earlier stage and a tighter fiscal policy would be used to offset lower interest rates—though Britain would not have had the flexibility to allow sterling to depreciate as part of the necessary rebalancing of the UK domestic economy.

Yet despite the failure to sell Europe to the British people, in the last ten years Britain has imperceptibly become more of a 'European country'. Its economy has become more integrated with the EU, with the City of London strengthening its position as the largest financial centre of Europe's expanding Single Market. Seventy per cent of all eurobonds are traded in London, while 53 per cent of the global foreign equity market and over 80 per cent of the $24bn EU Emissions Trading Scheme is based in the Square Mile.[19] We have seen huge increases in migration, both of British citizens emigrating to live and retire in other parts of the EU, as well as continentals seeking work in the UK whether as East European migrants looking for a job or well-educated continentals wanting to work in the European 'global city' that London has become. It is estimated that 665,000 Eastern Europeans, including Bulgarians and Romanians, are currently resident in the UK[20]—many employed in the London labour market. Meanwhile, approximately 1.5 million Britons—of which a significant number are pensioners—have emigrated to France, Spain, Cyprus, Germany and Ireland.[21] The British social model has moved closer to the norms of the 'European social model' through an increase in public service investment, the relief of child and pensioner poverty, the acceptance of the provisions in the Social Chapter, and anti-discrimination legislation. The impact of fundamental rights legislation and European Court of Justice (ECJ) jurisprudence is becoming more pervasive within the British legal system. European legislation is driving Britain's 'green' agenda, particularly the massive expansion of renewables as a result of the 2007 European climate package.

At the same time, Gordon Brown's vision of a 'Global Europe' that looks outward is making progress against the inward-looking, institutionalist focus of the EU's first fifty years. Economic openness has so far been broadly sustained in the face of protectionist pressures throughout much of Europe. Internally, economic integration has been driven forward with British support. The liberal reforming impetus of the Single Market, that Margaret Thatcher grudgingly judged to be in Britain's national interests when she signed the Single Act in 1985, has been sustained by the Commission and the ECJ. In part this reflects the impact of the EU liberalisation agenda in Europeanising big business, increasing the scale of cross-border mergers and takeovers, and weakening national champion policies. Capital mobility within the EU has shifted the balance of power between labour and capital with a general decline of the trade unions Europe-wide (except in Nordic countries)—all achieved 'without a Thatcher'. At the same time, step-by-step, welfare, labour market and tax reforms, the reduction in corporate taxes and the non-wage cost burden on employment, the shift to active labour market policies and pension reforms has led to a surge in employment growth on the continent.

So why do Britain's relations with the EU remain so problematic if the reality is policy convergence and a more Anglo-Saxon EU? The Blair experience shows the difficulties within the British political system of pursuing well-intentioned pro-Europeanism. The roots of Euroscepticism are multi-layered. Some observers attribute most of the blame to a hostile British press. Seventy-five per cent of newspaper readers are subjected to a steady 'drip-drip' of anti-European stories.[22] These newspapers have no compunction about publishing untruths about the European Union: no one challenges their right to do so. Ambitious politicians shy away from being identified as pro-European because they fear the press will turn on them: the chequered careers since 1997 of Robin Cook, Peter Mandelson, Stephen Byers and Charles Clarke are seen as evidence of these dangers by younger 'up and coming' politicians. Proprietors such as Rupert Murdoch are alleged to exercise undue influence over government policy. Yet when a British government clearly decides to implement a pro-European policy, come what may, as Tony Blair did over European defence in 2000 and Gordon Brown did on the ratification of the Lisbon Treaty in 2007–8, the power of the press has emerged as something of a paper tiger.

Rather, our view is that the root of UK scepticism is more profound. The media and the political class share in common a passionate belief in the virtues of the British polity. Among politicians there is a deep attachment to sovereignty in Westminster politics on both right and left. There is also the strength of Anglo-American ideology in Britain's political class, which manifests itself as a military and strategic alliance, a capitalist model, a model of governance, a set of doctrines and ideas, as well as a popular culture.[23] These convictions run deep. In addition, the party politics of Europe is complicated. The European issue has always played a bigger role in intra-party politics, both in the Conservative party prior to 1997 and during the Blair premiership, than in electoral competition. However, politicians cannot ignore the growth of populism in the British electorate which links Europe to other emotive issues such as migration, crime and terrorism, loss of national identity, and the growth of Englishness. There are also real unanswered problems of legitimacy about the EU given its present unsatisfactory hybrid existence between intergovernmentalism and federalism. In the light of these constraints, we go on to examine the likely future scenarios for British European policy in the decade ahead.

Scenario one: *'unsteady as she goes'*: a weak consensus behind conditional British pro-Europeanism

This scenario would, in essence, amount to a continuation of the Labour government's European policy of the past decade. Government policy towards the EU would remain one of cautious support, but with awkward and even confrontational engagement at times, as the EU continues to develop haltingly on its present 'hybrid' course. Britain increasingly relies on the EU to achieve its global policy objectives in areas such as trade, international economics and climate change, but big policy tensions remain over areas such as financial regulation, tax policy and the EU budget, not to mention the relationship with the United States and the EU's future institutional development.

In many respects, a weak pro-European consensus is typical of the shift in British politics from 'position' to 'valence' issues highlighted by Vernon Bogdanor. British politics is now dominated by agreement on fundamental aims—for instance, an effective NHS, or better schools, or in this context, EU membership—and disagreement, meanwhile, is confined to the issue of which party is best placed to achieve them.[24]

Our view is that the natural instinct of the leaders of both the major political parties in the UK, whoever wins the next general election, will be to maintain this weak pro-EU consensus. Gordon Brown may not be an instinctive pro-European, but he is certainly not 'anti' as his robustness on the Lisbon Treaty has proved. As for David Cameron, if one takes the view that his leadership represents a reversion to a more traditional Conservative statecraft on the model of Stanley Baldwin and Harold Macmillan, his first instinct will be to take a pragmatic non-ideological approach to Europe within the constraints imposed by party management and maintaining his hold on power. Indeed, Jim Bulpitt's statecraft argument is particularly applicable to Cameron's European policy. Bulpitt argues that British governance amounts to one long electoral campaign, albeit of varying degrees of intensity, and to the interaction of a number of 'court interests'. Anti-Europeanism is a strong 'court interest' within the Conservative party which Cameron has to placate, as demonstrated by the Conservative Party's withdrawal from the mainstream centre-right grouping in the European Parliament, the EPP. The reality of this constraint means that as Prime Minister he would pragmatically accept certain anti-European arguments for the sake of party unity.[25] Whether this pragmatism would prove politically sustainable will be discussed below, but for the moment let us assume it will be.

In this scenario under both Brown and Cameron, a provisional assessment of the central features of this consensus would be as follows:

– *Global issues*: Britain will use its EU membership to maximise its limited leverage on global issues in key international negotiations. This will apply across a wide agenda where the UK would have little influence if it simply acted alone: reform of global economic institutions in the wake of the global financial crisis; trade and the resumption of negotiations for a new global trading agreement under the Doha Round; the UNCCC process on climate change, the next stage of which is a push for global agreement on what will replace Kyoto at Copenhagen in 2009; international aid questions and monitoring progress towards the UN Millennium Development Goals. On all of these issues, the relationship between the British Prime Minister, the French President and the German Chancellor are crucial. Britain is well positioned to have a decisive say—though there will be some differences of emphasis, as with the French on trade—provided the politics of Europe are manageable and do not allow other issues to sour the necessary close tripartite relationship if European influence is to be maximised.

– *Enlargement*: Britain will continue to be the strongest advocate of enlargement to the Western Balkans, Turkey and possibly Ukraine on geopolitical grounds. 'First past the post' politics in Britain make it unlikely that British policy will be overcome by populist pressures on this issue, because none of the main parties would succumb to anti-enlargement pressures. This is unlike France, where the 'two round' system gives a voice to political parties and emotions charged mainly by fear of Muslim immigration. However, if Britain wants to get its way on enlargement, it is likely to have to pay a price in areas such as immigration control, British budget contributions and further institutional/constitutional reform.

- *Foreign policy and defence*: sovereignist objections to pooling diplomatic and defence resources may be weakened as a result of domestic public spending pressures on the defence and overseas aid budgets. Nevertheless, British support is uncertain for the development of the EU External Action Service, stronger EU coordination of national aid budgets, and the development of a European defence identity with its own military headquarters and pooled equipment. The US view of these developments—more positive under President Obama—is likely to be decisive.

- *Energy and climate change*: Britain will stick to its present strong commitment to a tough climate change and energy package with a more comprehensive, tighter EU emissions trading scheme, ambitious renewable targets set at EU level, and the attempt to develop a common energy policy. But this policy will come under pressure from Eastern Europe where coal is essential to energy security against Russia; energy intensive industry lobbies who will point to carbon leakage and the drift of jobs to other parts of the world; corporate national energy champions who want to do their own deals with Russian oil and gas interests; and electoral resistance to the higher energy prices that low carbon strategies imply. It may lead to further disillusion with the EU if our partners are seen to fail to deliver on their commitments. So making the EU policy stick will require increased transfer payments through the Structural Funds to weaker economies, new budgetary commitments to promote low carbon jobs and help poorer energy customers, and possibly trade sanctions against imports from countries that are seen to be free-riding on their climate change commitments. The politics of climate change are wide ranging, complex and potentially more integrationist than is commonly perceived.

- *Economics and the Single Market*: as Gordon Brown has argued in the teeth of economic recession, Britain will mount pressure for further Single Market and trade liberalisation, but it could find itself in an awkward minority in the wake of the global economic crisis on Single Market issues such as pressure for stronger EU level regulation of financial services and corporate governance as well as tax coordination to prevent tax competition putting further strain on weakened fiscal positions and national budgets. There could also be renewed pressure for social legislation to strengthen employee rights to retraining and flexible working, given a likely swing away from labour market deregulation. Traditional British positions on these issues have lost intellectual and moral authority as a result of the obvious excesses of Anglo-American capitalism in bringing about the global financial crisis.

- *EU budget*: the promised mid-term review of the EU budget in 2010 will open up once again the question of the British 'rebate' as a major divisive issue in British–EU relations. It may be possible to build an EU consensus around a comprehensive reform agenda that further reforms the CAP and Structural Funds, while developing new policies to meet the EU's low carbon, knowledge economy and social modernisation challenges. But this would require a degree of imagination about future policy that the UK has not so far shown.

Within each of these British priorities for Europe, there are both potential tensions with our partners and clear stumbling blocks, unless the UK is prepared to concede more integrationist steps than might be its first preference under the weak pro-EU consensus. For the harsh truth about this consensus is that its scale of ambition outreaches its likelihood of achievement, unless the need for potential trade-offs with our partners and the existence of some inherent contradictions is honestly addressed. Still less confronted are the institutional implications of the policies the UK is keen to espouse. Can the UK's climate change ambitions, for instance, be achieved without a strong European Commission willing to take enforcement action against recalcitrant member states and an activist European Court of Justice willing to back up the Commission's powers? Questions of institutions cannot be separated from policies—as all too often the weak pro-European consensus in the UK imagines.

A bigger set of doubts concerns whether this conditional pro-Europeanism will prove robust in the face of internal political pressures, particularly in the Conservative party, and whether major external shocks will require its fundamental reassessment. These are developments that could, depending on the political circumstances, favour either of the other two scenarios tentatively outlined in the introduction to this chapter.

Scenario two: 'standoff, stalemate and possible crisis'

The second scenario is one of *political crisis* in Britain's relationship with the EU, almost certainly occasioned by a major institutional clash. This might occur relatively quickly if the Conservatives came to power at the next election and the Lisbon Treaty had not been fully ratified by every other member state, or very recently so. This is a distinct possibility if the Czechs are not to complete their own national ratification process following the Irish referendum. Alternatively, the ratification might be so recent that a new Conservative government would be under enormous pressure in some way to re-open the British position. At present Conservative policy is that if the Treaty has not been ratified fully elsewhere by the time they come to office, they will call a UK referendum on ratification. If it has been ratified, William Hague, the Shadow Foreign Secretary, insists that they 'will not let matters rest there'.[26] This is, of course, deliberately ambiguous and, at the time of writing, the Conservatives refuse to be drawn further.

What we do know is that the Conservatives want to re-instate the British Maastricht opt-out from the Social Chapter. This, of course, is not as simple as it sounds, assuming—a big assumption—that our partners were willing to agree. If Lisbon is ratified there is no longer a Social Chapter to opt out from. 'Social' provisions are scattered through the Treaty, including in the statement of the EU's objectives. EU 'social' legislation derives from a variety of legal bases under the Treaty. For example, the controversial Working Time Directive was never subject to the British opt-out because it derived from the health and safety provisions of the Treaty, which it is inconceivable that a UK government could opt out from.

The Conservative leadership presumably believes this ambiguity is helpful; in party management terms, it partly satisfies the anti-Europeans without being clear what is precisely proposed. But on the assumption that on political grounds an incoming Conservative government would be obliged to do something, there is potential here for an ill-defined and escalating row with our partners that would distract from the wider objectives of British EU policy. Our EU partners are unlikely to be willing to grant the UK what they will see as an unfair competitive advantage that strikes at the heart of European values of social solidarity, least of all at a time when Britain is seen to enjoy the advantage of competitive devaluation as long as sterling remains outside the euro. This row would then feed into further deep aggravation with our partners over the mid-term EU budget review. A Conservative government would experience the reality that using the EU to extend British influence in the world is incompatible with being seen to be 'bad Europeans' when it comes to the internal policies of the Union.

If Lisbon is not ratified, it is inconceivable that our more integrationist partners would be satisfied. David Cameron may, of course, believe that he can establish a Eurosceptic bloc in the European Council, taking advantage of present political trends on the continent, and including not just some of the Central European new member states, but possibly for different reasons, countries such as Austria, Italy and Sweden. Failure of Lisbon may therefore lead to a prolonged stalemate. But there is a risk that this would result at some stage in a determination by France, Germany and other continental partners to develop some form of 'inner core' EU that marginalises Britain. The Foreign Office nightmare would return.

There is also the possibility that, for internal party management reasons of its own, a Cameron government would choose to hold a referendum on Europe, the outcome of which might put British membership in question. Pressure for this could occur if domestically the new government runs into early unpopularity as a result of putting up taxes and cutting sensitive areas of public spending. Right-wing populists within the party, such as the new generation followers of Lord Tebbit, would then argue that the government should seek to restore its popularity by taking strong positions on issues such as immigration and Europe. Indeed, Tebbit recently argued to the right-wing anti-European Bruges Group—established to honour Margaret Thatcher's infamous 1988 speech—that a David Cameron premiership should seek to re-negotiate the terms of British EU membership before a holding a referendum in which 'the British people would decide whether to accept what was on offer—or simply to leave the Union.'[27] One can be pretty sure that Cameron would not want this: the question is whether he would be driven to it in order to hang on to the leadership and to ensure the survival of his premiership.

These outcomes are highly speculative. But it is legitimate to speculate as long as the Conservative leadership refuses to make a clear commitment to work constructively with our partners to make a success of Britain's EU membership.

Scenario three: 'a more committed pro-Europeanism'

The third path is one of *positive Europeanism*. In response to the economic, social, environmental and security challenges of globalisation, EU integration discovers a new momentum and acquires a new legitimacy. At the same time Britain itself comes to realise the necessity of the EU in the global world. This permits a transformation of political attitudes towards sovereignty pooling that allows Britain to shape Europe's renewed integrationist momentum in accord with British interests and values. From the perspective of social democrats who believe in the necessity of a stronger European Union to help shape a more inclusive and sustainable globalisation, this is the most desirable policy option though it is the least likely. For such an outcome to occur, current British attitudes would require profound change.

What is the probability of a major external shock that would fundamentally change the picture for UK–EU relations? Will British governments be forced in the next ten years to reassess fundamentally Britain's role in the world as the Macmillan government did post-Suez? There are three possibilities that could precipitate this reassessment:

1. President Obama believes the United States must win friends and allies in the rest of the world in order to achieve its geostrategic objectives. Part of this could involve a new determination on the part of the United States to form a 'special relationship' with the EU—*not* Britain alone. In order to forge a new multilateral and multipolar world order, Britain will be forced to accept that in order to retain influence in Washington, it must be strong in Europe and unambiguous about its European commitment.[28]
2. Economic turbulence, recession and the weak position of sterling convinces the UK government of the need to get closer to Europe and possibly seek the security of euro membership. Wolfgang Münchau argues that the financial crisis will seemingly 'accelerate the enlargement of both the EU and the eurozone'. The expansion and further integration of the eurozone is especially significant, given that countries that seemed likely to stay out indefinitely—for instance, Denmark and Sweden—are now reported to be actively reconsidering their position.[29] Yet, the financial crisis has created a

new economic phenomenon, one where, as Buiter and Sibert argue, small countries with independent currencies have banking sectors that are too extensive to be rescued by national authorities.[30] Moreover, in combination with the transnationalism of European financial services, this heightens the attractiveness of euro membership. Although this set of criteria is not fully applicable to the UK, thanks in large part to our residual reserve currency status, it may precipitate the return of the euro debate to British politics.

3. A new impetus emerges on the continent for integration either towards a stronger foreign policy and defence union, or a more integrated inner core based on the euro area, from which the British government feels in the national interest it cannot be excluded.

For this scenario to become a reality, the view that the Anglo-American form of capitalism is vastly superior to the 'European social model' would have to undergo sharp modification, as would the lingering attachment of the British political class to the idea of a unique special relationship with the United States. Given this change of mindset, British membership of the euro could be considered afresh on its merits, given the failure of the post-ERM macroeconomic regime and Bank of England independence to guarantee stability and end 'boom and bust'. Britain would then be able to contemplate institutional and democratic solutions to the EU's 'legitimacy problem' through a new political lens.

Conclusion

At the time of writing, the prospect of this pro-European reassessment remains weak and the much larger risk is of stalemate or political crisis in Britain's relations with the EU, were the Conservatives to win the next election. But, as in the past, the European issue will retain its capacity to surprise.

Acknowledgements

The authors would like to thank Simon Latham at Policy Network for the diligent research and comments that he contributed to this paper. We would also like to thank Dr Varun Uberoi in the Department of Politics and International Relations, Oxford University, for his comments.

Notes

1 For further explanation of this argument, see P. Diamond, 'Introduction', in *Shifting Alliances: Europe, America, and the Future of Britain's Global Strategy*, London, Politico's, 2008.

2 For a contemporary account of how the British media accentuate these fears, see C. Grant, 'Why is Britain Eurosceptic?', Centre for European Reform essay, December 2008.

3 See, e.g., John Major's article in *The Economist*, 25 September 1993, pp. 27–9, in which he wrote that 'I hope my fellow heads of government will resist the temptation to recite the mantra of full economic and monetary union as if nothing had changed. If they do recite it, it will have all the quaintness of a rain dance and about the same potency.'

4 See 'The Europe that died', *The Economist*, 2 June 2005.

5 See, e.g., J. M. Barroso, 'More Europe where it matters!', speech to the European Parliament, Strasbourg, 15 March 2006. Barroso argues that 'In a globalised world, no Member State can go it alone. This is not the time for economic nationalism'. See also P. Mandelson, *The European Union in the Global Age*, London, Policy Network, 2007.

6 What we term the 'traditional Foreign Office' view on Europe is illustrated in chapter 9 of S. Wall, *A Stranger in Europe: Britain and the EU from Thatcher to Blair*, Oxford, Oxford University Press, 2008.

7 For further explanation of this argument, see A. Giddens, P. Diamond and R. Liddle, *Global Europe, Social Europe*, Cambridge, Polity, 2006, and D. Miliband, 'Europe 2030: model power not superpower', speech to the College of Europe, Bruges, 15 November 2007.

8 Douglas Hurd, BBC On the Record interview, 22 June 1994.

9 The Irish Business and Employers Confederation (IBEC) claims that one million new jobs have been created in Ireland since its accession to the EU in 1973, and that Ireland has received €58 billion of EU funding in transfer payments. For more information, see http://www.ibeclisbon.ie/Sectors/Lisbon/LisbonTreaty.nsf/wvPages/eu+membership+benefits+benefits+of+eu+membership?OpenDocument

10 Mark Mardell wrote in his online blog on 6 July 2007 that government officials had privately admitted to him that the notion of 'red lines' were 'purely presentational' (http://www.bbc.co.uk/blogs/thereporters/markmardell/2007/07/brussels_and_babies_bottoms.html), while Gordon Brown claimed in a recent House of Commons statement after a European Council summit that Britain's 'national interest is, and remains, a strong Britain in a strong European Union' (Statement on EU Council, 24 June 2008—http://www.number10.gov.uk/Page16131).

11 At present the Nice Treaty requires two criteria to be fulfilled in order to pass a vote in the European Council in the absence of consensus. It must be supported by a majority and in some cases two-thirds of member states and 73.9 per cent of the overall votes cast. This means that it is relatively easy to create a blocking minority, especially in contentious areas. The proposed Lisbon Treaty will reduce this threshold to a 55 or 72 per cent majority of member states, which represent 65 per cent of the EU population. And if the condition to block (at least four member states against a vote or 35 per cent of the population plus one member state where measures are not applicable to all EU members) that a measure will also pass. For a more detailed analysis, see http://europa.eu/scadplus/constitution/double majority_en.htm

12 A. Banjonovic, 'Improving Poland's transport infrastructure', *Euromonitor International* (http://www.euromonitor.com/Improving_Polands_transport_infrastructure) shows that Poland will receive 4 per cent of its GDP in EU aid between 2007 and 2013. Poland will receive approximately €90 billion, of which nearly 40 per cent is being allocated to finance regional development and infrastructure.

13 A recent Eurobarometer survey shows that levels in trust in Italy towards the EU

institutions are significantly higher than national institutions: between 43 and 51 per cent of Italians trust the various EU institutions, while only 16 per cent of Italians trust their national parliament and only 15 per cent trust their government. See *Eurobarometer 69*, July 2008, National Report: Italy—Executive Summary, pp. 4–5. A total of 1,022 interviews were conducted from 25 March to 26 April 2008.

14 See, e.g., H. Young, 'A tight Treasury fist still grips our European future', *The Guardian*, 10 June 2003.

15 *Standard Eurobarometer 69*, Spring 2008. The UK fieldwork was undertaken from 1–24 April, 2008.

16 D. Hierlemann, 'Lessons from the treaty fatigue', Bertelsmann Stiftung, Spotlight Europe, 2008/14 December 2008, p. 2.

17 IpsosMORI, 'The most important issues facing Britain today', 16 July 2008. http://www.ipsos-mori.com/content/turnout/the-most-important-issues-facing-britain-today.ashx

18 The Conservative party's website states that the party believes 'in an open, flexible Europe in which countries work together to achieve shared goals, not the ever greater centralisation of power in Brussels'. But that if the Lisbon Treaty is ratified and the EU therefore lacks democratic legitimacy, they will 'not let matters rest there'. (http://www.conservatives.com/Policy/Where_we_stand/Foreign_Affairs_and_Europe.aspx). Gordon Brown argued recently that 'Our national interest is, and remains, a strong Britain in a strong European Union' (Statement on EU Council, 24 June 2008—http://www.number10.gov.uk/Page16131).

19 City of London, http://www.cityoflondon.gov.uk/Corporation/media_centre/keyfacts.htm

20 N. Pollard, M. Latorre and D. Sriskandarajah, 'Floodgates or turnstiles? Post-EU enlargement migration flows to (and from) the UK', Institute for Public Policy Research (IPPR), April 2008.

21 D. Sriskandarajah and C. Drew, 'Brits abroad: mapping the scale and nature of British emigration', IPPR, December 2006.

22 Grant, 'Why is Britain Eurosceptic?'.

23 See A. Gamble, *Between Europe and America: The Future of British Politics*, Basingstoke, Palgrave, 2003. There is an extensive discussion on 'Anglo America' in Chapter 5.

24 V. Bogdanor, 'The rise and fall of the political party', *New Statesman*, 23 October 2006.

25 J. Bulpitt, 'The European question: rules, national modernisation and the ambiguities of *Primat der Innenpolitik*', in D. Marquand and A. Seldon, eds., *The Ideas that Shaped Post-War Britain*, London, Fontana Press, 1996, pp. 225–6.

26 'We would hold referendum even after EU treaty is ratified, William Hague suggests', *The Times*, 13 November 2007.

27 Lord Tebbit, speech to the Bruges Group, 20th Anniversary Dinner, 27 October 2008.

28 In the 'Barack Obama and Joe Biden: a stronger partnership with Europe for a safer America' briefing paper (http://www.barackobama.com/pdf/Fact_Sheet_Europe_FINAL.pdf), Obama and Biden argue in favour of a 'strong US partnership with the European Union. The Bush administration's policy of "divide and rule", splitting Europe into those who were "with us or against us", has been counterproductive. The United States has an interest in a strong, united and

peaceful Europe as a partner in global affairs. Barack Obama and Joe Biden will continue to support European Union enlargement'.

29 W. Münchau, 'Now they see the benefits of the Eurozone', *Financial Times*, 2 November 2008.
30 W. Buiter and A. Sibert, 'The Icelandic banking crisis and what to do about it', CEPR Policy Insight No. 26.

Global Poverty and Inequality: A Brief Retrospective and Prospective Analysis

MICHAEL WOOLCOCK

THIS OVERVIEW essay on policy responses to global poverty and inequality over the last ten years is structured around four themes. First, drawing on the most recent empirical data, it provides some stylised facts on recent trends in poverty and inequality in developing countries. Second, it considers the distinctive ways in which the UK government in particular has responded to these challenges over the last decade, in the context of the broader global policy effort in which it is embedded. Third, it provides a critique of these responses, finding much to both commend and about which to be concerned. On the basis of this assessment, the fourth section considers some options for the next decade, some quite modest and others more ambitious. The final section concludes.

Some stylised facts

Present trends in global poverty and inequality need to be understood in their broader historical context. For the economic historian Robert Fogel (2004), the world is currently at the beginning of the fourth century of a 400-year process of unparalleled economic transformation, which began[1] in roughly 1700 and will continue through 2100, during which the world's population will go from being overwhelmingly poor to predominantly rich. The significance of this cannot be overstated, given that most people for most of history have lived a Hobbesian existence, one famously characterised for being 'poor, nasty, brutish and short'. While it is always dangerous to extrapolate from the past, not least because qualitatively new challenges such as global warming loom large, past trends do suggest that it is likely that within the current century this historical norm of human existence will indeed itself be made history. Put differently, one empirical challenge is to explain the origins and spread of broad-based living standards above poverty levels, since it is this—not the persistence of poverty—that is novel. (The issue of inequality is somewhat different, but this is addressed below.)

Cheery conclusions drawn about the impending eradication of global poverty, however, mask real and present concerns (Collier, 2007). Some of these are conceptual and methodological—what exactly is 'poverty', how does one measure it, and how does one make valid and reliable comparisons across time and space?[2] While there are real policy and political implications associated with adopting one set of criteria over another, the general consensus among researchers is that, since about 1980 (when broadly compar-

Published by Blackwell Publishing Ltd, 9600 Garsington Road, Oxford OX4 2DQ, UK and 350 Main Street, Malden, MA 02148, USA

able global data began to be collected), the global poverty rate, i.e. the percentage of the developing world's population living in poverty (as currently measured at income of less than $1.25 per day in 2005 prices) has declined (from about 50 per cent to 25 per cent) while absolute numbers have stayed about the same (about 1.4 billion people) (see Ravallion and Chen, 2007; Chen and Ravallion, 2008).[3] If there is some disagreement on whether global poverty targets as embodied in the Millennium Development Goals will be met,[4] few dispute that the global poverty rate has been trending downwards.

These global numbers, however, mask huge regional variations. In India and China, for example, both poverty rates and absolute poverty have plummeted; in Latin America and Eastern Europe little has changed; in Africa, however, relative poverty has modestly declined while absolute numbers have increased significantly. Within these regions, individual countries show great diversity—in Africa, for example, Botswana has made significant progress, while Zimbabwe has regressed—and even within countries there is also high variance: in India, the state of Kerala has largely achieved first-world standards of public health while Orissa lags far behind even their own national average. Wide variation in poverty outcomes is also to be found in rich countries such as Great Britain (Palmer et al., 2007), with Glasgow and the northwest of England having poverty measures—in particular, health outcomes—significantly worse than those found elsewhere.

These differences matter politically, since practitioners of, and advocates for, poverty reduction are heavily influenced by absolute poverty numbers in the short run (Kanbur, 2001). Put most starkly, those who run soup kitchens for the poor will derive little comfort from being told that the national poverty rate is declining while 100 people continue to show up on their door every week to be fed. More specifically, poverty reduction advocacy is driven to a large extent by single-issue campaigns, and if the particular constituency (e.g., the homeless, those with HIV-AIDS) of an influential group remains the same size (or increases), claims that aggregate, long-term, relative poverty trends are moving downwards will be, even if factually true, a tough sell.

Measured inequality trends also depend on the definition and methodology chosen. Researchers generally distinguish between three types of inequality: (a) global inequality, which is a measure of the dispersion in income at the individual level, with the world's 6 billion people lined up from the richest to poorest; (b) within-country inequality, which considers the variance of income among the citizens of a particular country; and (c) between-country inequality, which considers the variance in average incomes among the world's nations.[5] In general, the results show that global inequality has been rising, and that although within-country inequality has risen in many cases (see Bourguignon and Morrisson, 2002),[6] the real driver of rising global inequality has been the rise in between-country inequality—that is, that many countries, including the richest, have continued to get richer, while many of the poorest countries have stayed poor (World Bank, 2005).

As with poverty, these aggregate measures of inequality mask considerable regional, national and sub-national differences—that is, inequality has been rising in most (but not all) places, but at much faster rates in some countries and regions than others. Various explanations have been put forward for this, including the advent in the late twentieth century of 'skill-biased technical change', in which the returns to education have increased disproportionately. Some cite the declining influence of labour unions, who for much of the twentieth century, it is said, were sufficiently large and powerful to negotiate larger wage increases for workers than they have recently gained; others (e.g. Paul Krugman) have argued that a cultural shift has occurred in which tolerance for large salary differentials between those at the top and bottom of the corporation has increased; another line of argument (see Ravallion, 2003) is that increasing global economic integration is producing, in effect, a 'regression to the mean', with increasing inequality occurring in countries where it was previously 'artificially low' (e.g. as a result of decades of communist rule) and decreasing inequality occurring in countries (e.g. Brazil) where it was initially 'artificially high'. Identifying more precisely the specific factors underlying the increase (or decrease) in inequality in particular contexts remains an issue at the forefront of social and economic research. Whatever the ultimate explanation(s), most researchers now agree that high inequality is itself an impediment to economic growth and poverty reduction (World Bank, 2005), even as differences endure as to what exactly can be done, and by whom, to reduce inequality.

The policy response: what is distinctive about the last eleven years?

Just as global poverty and inequality trends need to be understood historically and contextually, so too does the UK government's policy response need to be considered within the broader ambit of the responses made by the international community. Seen in this light, there is little doubt that in the past decade the UK has increasingly been a leader, even as the international community itself—through civil society campaigns (e.g. Make Poverty History) and multilateral commitments (the Millennium Development Goals)—has accorded global poverty reduction unprecedented attention. While it is hard to formally attribute positive (or negative) outcomes to specific UK government initiatives,[7] it is instructive to document some of the changes that have occurred over the last decade or so, many of which one would not have anticipated in the mid-1990s.

First, the UK government now has a separate Cabinet-level position for development issues: the Department for International Development (DFID). The UK is one of only a handful of countries to accord 'development' this high political status.[8]

Second, the UK government has matched this administrative initiative with the allocation of significantly increased resources, which have raised the UK's

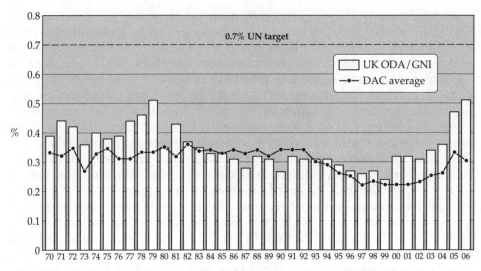

Figure 1: The evolution of British foreign aid, 1970–2006
Source: DFID website, http://www.dfid.gov.uk/pubs/files/sid2007/section2.asp

position in the league table of development donors. In 1998, DFID's budget was £2.3 billion; by 2007, it had increased to £5.3 billion. The UK's expenditure on development aid rose from 0.27 per cent of GNI in 1997 to 0.47 per cent of GNI in 2006[9] (see Figure 1), and the government is committed to reaching 0.53 per cent of GNI by 2010–11 and 0.7 per cent (the UN target for donors) by 2013. Only six countries currently exceed the UK's aid spending relative to GNI, and of these, the top five have already met the UN target (see Figure 2). One of the highest-profile of the UK's commitments has been to the International Development Association (IDA), a branch of the World Bank that provides grants and interest-free loans to the world's poorest countries. In 2007, the UK became the largest donor to IDA. Financially as well as institutionally, the UK government has thus increasingly become an international leader in the promotion of development. In its most recent 'Commitment to Development' survey, the Center for Global Development, a Washington think tank, rated the UK 9th in the world for its contributions to development in general, and third in its contributions to Africa (the world's poorest region) in particular (Roodman, 2008). This measure considers, albeit imperfectly, not only the volume of aid, but a country's policies on immigration, the environment, trade, and peacekeeping. The UK scored especially well on its levels of investment in Africa (on which it ranks first) and contributions to peacekeeping and security (ranked second).[10]

Third, the UK government has substantially expanded its financial commitments to scholarly research on development. As a host of recent publications have noted,[11] much of the policy-making in development occurs in something of an empirical vacuum,[12] and efforts to rectify this are sorely needed. The

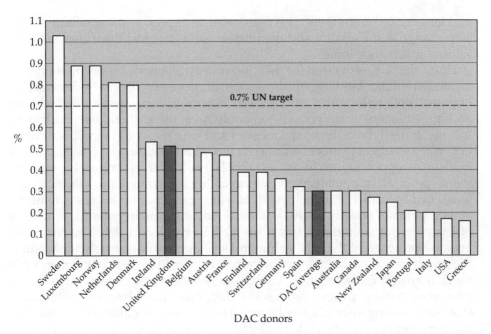

Figure 2: Wealthy countries' contributions to development assistance, 2006
Source: DFID website, http://www.dfid.gov.uk/pubs/files/sid2007/section2.asp

expanded research programmes sponsored by DFID (often in partnership with the Economic and Social Research Council) have been characterised not only by their scale, but also by their focus on building and rewarding interdisciplinarity, partnerships across UK universities (especially with southern research groups), and policy impact. Substantively, it has chosen to invest in a small number of large research centres (as opposed to making larger numbers of smaller grants to individuals or teams) and to focus on key thematic issues, such as chronic poverty, immigration and pro-poor growth.

Fourth, the UK, through DFID, has become a high-profile leader on the complex issue of governance. Now widely recognised as a key development issue in its own right (after many years of skittishness about discussing 'political' issues such as corruption, legal reform and human rights)[13] and, more instrumentally, as a driver of economic growth and poverty reduction (Kraay, 2006), DFID has been a leader in legitimising and raising the profile of the politics of development generally,[14] and in particular efforts to identify effective and supportable strategies for enhancing the 'quality of governance'. In many respects this work is in its infancy, and the empirical and policy problems it raises, by their very nature, sit awkwardly with the technocratic and bureaucratic imperatives of orthodox development decision-making (see further discussion on this below), but the UK government is to be commended for championing an issue too long neglected. With sufficient patience and long-term commitment, it is reasonable to expect, in the medium term, a step-change in the quality and quantity of evidence (and theory) available to inform governance issues.

Fifth, the UK government has been instrumental in encouraging an expanded understanding of the scope of poverty: its multi-dimensional approach both reflects and reinforces an increasing awareness among scholars and practitioners that 'poverty' encompasses more than just inadequate income. Indeed, both the characteristics and experience of being poor entails not only a struggle to meet basic needs but, in all likelihood, social exclusion, inadequate opportunities to access schools, health clinics, and stable employment, political marginalisation, vulnerability to crime and violence, and weakened aspirational capacities, all of which can conspire to create, reinforce and perpetuate 'poverty traps', as well as wasting human potential and being offensive in humanitarian terms (Chronic Poverty Report, 2008). Eleven years ago, the presence of the UN's Human Development Index notwithstanding, the theory and measurement of poverty were for the most part construed in much narrower (i.e. almost exclusively economic) ways, giving rise to correspondingly narrow policy responses; today, there is widespread recognition that poverty comprises diverse factors. The range of disciplinary and theoretical perspectives on which this diversity rests provides a challenge for those more comfortable with a one-dimensional approach; a challenge is to recognise poverty's multi-dimensionality while forging a more integrated and coherent basis for measuring and addressing it.[15]

Sixth, arguably the most important policy achievement in recent years has been the emergence of a genuine left/right consensus regarding the importance of global poverty reduction. Though clearly a product of much effective agitation by civil society groups (e.g., Jubilee 2000 on debt relief, the Make Poverty History campaign), this consensus now spans the OECD nations, with even the US government, under Republican leadership and which came to power on an explicit policy of disengagement from international issues, now actively embracing global poverty reduction. In the UK, the Conservative party has made clear that if elected it would continue with policies promoting development and poverty reduction. Clearly the UK government cannot claim sole credit for this new consensus, but it has certainly been one of its global champions.

A brief critique

The many commendable aspects of the changes in development policy adopted and championed by the UK government in the past decade, and the significant increase in resources devoted to it, face their biggest tests in the coming years. If the most significant development of all is the apparent transformation in attitude to foreign aid by conservative parties (in the US as well as the UK and elsewhere), one crucial test of course will be whether promises made by the UK Conservative party in opposition materialise if it comes to power.[16]

For now, however, I think it is safe to assume that, barring some domestic economic meltdown, absolute levels of funding will be roughly the same no matter which party is in the majority; the greater challenges, and they are already looming with Labour still in office, are conceptual and political, namely (a) maintaining the commitment to multi-dimensional understandings of poverty (its causes, nature and consequences) and encouraging corresponding diverse policy responses, and (b) taking seriously the recognition that effectively addressing 'governance' issues requires a long time horizon, new theoretical frameworks and different skill sets from those that currently prevail within most development organisations. Faced with such challenges, the imperatives of orthodoxy—that is, of just expanding and replicating interventions believed to produce 'results' quickly, such as infrastructure—will weigh especially heavily; as such, those committed to governance issues will need to redouble their efforts if the initial gains achieved under a sympathetic progressive government are to be sustained under a more conservative government. Let me elaborate, since this critique may initially appear somewhat counterintuitive.

Development agencies of all stripes have a strong bureaucratic imperative to 'see' (Scott, 1998) problems in terms of the solutions they are able to offer. Though many academic commentators invariably regard such agencies, especially the large multilateral agencies such as the IMF and World Bank, as forceful advocates for 'neo-liberal' (read: harmful, exploitative, 'de-politicised', pro-capitalist) development policies (e.g., Ferguson, 2006; Li, 2007), a less insidious interpretation is that large agencies are primarily following a strong internal logic to render a diverse assortment of problems responsive to the instruments, models, assumptions and discourses over which they preside, which in turn are predisposed to generating policy/project responses readily amenable to being implemented, administered and assessed by bureaucratic means (Pritchett and Woolcock, 2004). 'Technical' problems that happen to fall safely within the bounds of this logic—building roads, administering inoculations, reducing hyperinflation—will be strongly promoted; those that do not (call them 'adaptive' problems[17])—engaging with customary legal systems, negotiating peace settlements, encouraging more effective local government—will face a constant uphill battle for resources and legitimacy. Why? Because careers are sustained, extensive (and expensive) educations are justified, and political needs are satisfied when problems can be persuasively explained by the experts, readily managed by the technocrats and safely administered by the bureaucrats.

We have no good development theory to tell us about the relative prevalence or seriousness of technical and adaptive problems, or that even provide a sophisticated basis for distinguishing between them (and/or other types of problems),[18] but in any case the upshot is that, within development agencies of all kinds, technical problems are strongly favoured (by both design and default), and ambiguous problems embedded in context-specific (often idiosyncratic) realities are reframed as variants on technical problems (Scott, 1998). Enlightened leadership may for a period create more political space and a higher intellectual profile for identifying and responding to adaptive problems,[19] but the default mode is always stacked in favour of 'seeing' all problems through a technical lens. During a crisis or even a period of uncertainty, orthodoxy relentlessly reasserts itself. In development, this means the policy pendulum tends to swing inevitably back towards economic growth and more particularly to the search for the technical macroeconomic policy instruments likely to bring it about. Rather than starting with the idiosyncratic array of development problems (some technical, some adaptive) and trying to identify context-specific responses, the organisational imperative is to begin with its 'products', which may or may not map onto the prevailing problems a country has.

Essential as economic growth clearly is for poverty reduction (Kraay, 2006), it is important to recognise that it is an outcome of complex and interdependent forces, not all of which are amenable to 'policy' control. Indeed, even getting some of these 'forces' and their institutional underpinnings to the point where they might plausibly be amenable to policy control is itself a key development challenge. In an age, however, where the development business is increasingly dominated by a combination of large private philanthropic organisations (e.g. the Gates and Google Foundations) deploying corporate performance models, governments impatient to show restive citizens that aid (especially in its expanded form) can 'work', and development agencies seeking to legitimise their very existence, the combined effect is to only enhance the power of bureaucratic orthodoxy outlined above: time horizons are shortened, 'proven' approaches (conditional cash transfers, micro-credit) in one context are expanded and replicated elsewhere (cf. Rosenberg, 2006), and pressures mount for clear metrics of 'success' (because 'what gets measured is what gets done').[20] Lost in the mix are those problems that take years (decades) to resolve, that inherently have no known solution ex ante, and that entail protracted negotiations, contests and experimentation (as did the formation of most institutions in the now-rich countries).

In this new corporate aid environment, the quest for solutions is itself the problem, because it fundamentally cannot yield the healthy *mix* of responses (known and unknown, knowable and unknowable) that complex development problems necessarily require. New Labour's hard-won gains in raising interest in, awareness of and resources for development, in promoting an expanded understanding of the causes and responses to poverty, and in encouraging greater dialogue between scholars and practitioners—all of which are to be commended—risk being compromised, it seems to me, if the end result is a heightened concentration of time, energy and resources on 'fixing' short-run, technical concerns, the attainment of which is verified through readily measurable indicators. Important as these responses may be in their particular place, the overriding objective should be to create and sustain the intellectual space and political patience needed to craft a mix of context-specific solutions to context-specific problems. Some of these problems will be short term, technical, measurable and predictable; many will not, however, and a preponderance of attention on the former will not only undermine the probability of resolving the latter, but, in the long run, even the probability of attaining the former.

Going forward: some modest and immodest proposals

The preceding analysis suggests that the development community currently faces something of a paradox: important battles to raise the profile, status and resources for poverty reduction appear to have been won, but at the cost of ushering in procedures for prioritising problems and measuring 'progress' that threaten to distort which issues are addressed, how they are addressed, and how decisions will be made regarding the extent to which success or failure has been achieved. For some this may appear a petty or second-order concern; after all, the issues are pressing (30,000 people die every day from poverty), time is short, patience is thin, and development professionals are gradually getting a better empirical sense of 'what works'. In these circumstances, why 'reinvent the wheel'? Why not just expand and replicate those interventions that have passed the scrutiny of rigorous assessment?

This would be inadequate because certain key issues of the type I have identified simply cannot be solved this way. The current (and appropriate) concern with 'governance' issues perfectly reflects this conundrum: there is now a broad consensus that 'institutions matter' for poverty reduction, that 'building the rule of law' is essential, but there is only a long and unhappy history of actually trying to act on this (Carothers, 2006). This is largely because the effectiveness of 'institutions' depends crucially on their legitimacy in the eyes of those living under them, and their content on knowledge that is in large part inherently local, discerned only through a (usually long) process of deliberation and contestation. Moreover, there must be mechanisms in place for addressing the fact that even the most carefully designed and faithfully implemented development project is likely to generate both conflict (even if it succeeds[21]) and other unintended outcomes. In short, building effective institutions actively requires 'reinventing the wheel' in every country context in which it is being undertaken.

What to do? In a perfect world, we would have development strategies in general and poverty reduction strategies in particular able both to discern how to identify and prioritise different *kinds* of problems according to local needs, aspirations and available resources, and to make reasonable predictions regarding what kinds and levels of impacts to expect from particular interventions over a given timeframe. Unfortunately no individual, organisation or discipline really knows how to do either of these core tasks. Absent such frameworks, development professionals must make a good faith effort to respond as best they can. At present, the vacuum in overarching strategy for addressing these core issues is being filled by organisational and political imperatives (fuelled by urgent pleas from high-profile charismatic advocates) that preclude the very space needed to begin articulating such strategies. For both intrinsic and instrumental reasons—that is, because it is important in its own right and because the effective deployment of finite resources to pressing humanitarian issues demands it—reducing global poverty must be seen as the truly complex problem it is.

One way to respond to the challenge is to give renewed attention to the prevalence and salience of 'adaptive' problems in development and practical mechanisms for solving them. An example is the Kecamatan Development Project (KDP) in Indonesia (Guggenheim, 2006), a nationwide poverty-reduction programme which also seeks to enhance the civic skills of participating villagers and in turn the responsiveness of local government. Built on social (in addition to economic) theory, KDP began as a study of village institutions in Indonesia and through the knowledge thereby gained, was able to design mechanisms for allocating development resources in ways that both reflected villagers' priorities and knowledge *and* provided channels for effectively mediating conflicts ensuing from the project (Gibson and Woolcock, 2008). If 'orthodoxy' had its way, such successes would immediately give rise, as they have, to calls to rapidly replicate KDP elsewhere, but it is the 'spirit' of KDP—its rich grounding in local knowledge discerned through extensive research conducted by Indonesians themselves—rather than the 'letter' of KDP—its formal structure and documentation—that should be the model for poverty reduction and 'governance' projects elsewhere. It is a time-consuming and 'messy' process, but it is the right *type* of decision-making process for this *type* of problem.

Conclusion

As a result of global imperatives, enlightened leadership and strident civic campaigning, the UK government's response to development issues generally, and poverty/inequality issues in particular, has advanced considerably over the last decade or so. Whether assessed in terms of administrative innovations, supportive rhetoric, committed intellectual leadership or enhanced financial contributions, the UK government has increasingly been leading international efforts to reduce global poverty. Crucially, it has succeeded in helping to build what—at least for the moment—appears to be a genuine left/right, transatlantic consensus for these issues; even opposition politicians in the UK now openly support active policies to promote development and poverty reduction.

Welcome for these important accomplishments must be tempered by concerns that stem, somewhat paradoxically, from success. The vast infusion of new resources, the rise of ambitious philanthropic foundations, the imperatives of target-driven strategies and yet a demand for immediate results and an increasing impatience with inherently long-term issues have the potential to direct attention away from those development problems—and they are legion—that have no clear metric of success, have solutions that are often not knowable ex ante, and that even when 'solved' in a technical sense may not map onto a clear policy instrument (actually or even potentially). A comprehensive and effective poverty reduction strategy will strive to support effective responses to both technical and adaptive development problems, cognisant that concentrating on technical problems alone will not (indeed cannot) make poverty history.

Acknowledgements

The views expressed in this paper are those of the author alone, and should not be attributed to the University of Manchester or other organisations with which he is affiliated. I am grateful to Adam Coutts and Graham Hacche for helpful comments and suggestions.

Notes

1 Recent historical scholarship has sought to date and place more precisely the origins of the industrial revolution, with some (e.g. Smith, 2008) arguing that it can be plausibly seen as the outworking of a centuries-long process in the UK, beginning in the 1600s, of investing in basic social protection (the so-called Poor Law) and identity registration.

2 Pritchett (2006) provides a good overview of these issues, stressing that it is as important to ask who is *not* poor as who is.

3 The most recent data from Chen and Ravallion (2008) at the World Bank suggests that the absolute poverty numbers at the global level are higher than previously estimated, but the rate of decline in the poverty rate is largely unchanged from previous estimates. These measures are based on a singular money-metric indicator of poverty. The UN's Human Development Index has sought, since 1990, to provide a broader assessment of human welfare based not only on income, but literacy and life expectancy.

4 In 2000, the international community set the goal of reducing by half, between 1990 and 2015, the number of people (a) living on less than a dollar a day (more precisely, $1.08 in 1993 prices), and (b) suffering from hunger. Progress towards the attainment of all the Millennium Development Goals can be tracked at http://www.undp.org/mdg/tracking_home.shtml

5 There are currently 192 member countries of the UN, 185 member countries of the IMF and World Bank.

6 Recent work (e.g. Milanovic, 2005) suggests that, in the last ten years, inequality levels within countries have begun to show more movement. This may just be because researchers now have measurement tools sensitive enough to capture such movement, but it is also likely that 'globalisation' and increasing returns to human capital—combined perhaps with changing norms of what is considered a 'just' distribution of wealth within firms (i.e., what is considered a 'fair' difference between the income of the janitor and the CEO), and the increasing political influence of financial elites—are also having an unprecedented impact.

7 A formal assessment of the efficacy of DFID's component strategies under New Labour, while desirable, is beyond the scope of this short chapter. For present purposes, I assume that the expanded budget, domestic profile and global presence of DFID is a positive outcome in and of itself, though of course for planning and impact discernment purposes it would be necessary to conduct a comprehensive evaluation.

8 This is not for the first time. The Labour governments of the 1960s and 1970s had, for parts of their periods in office, a Cabinet minister responsible solely for overseas development (during 1964–7 and 1975–6). I am grateful to Graham Hacche for stressing this point.

9 As Figure 1 indicates, the UK's current commitment to development, while impressive compared to most other wealthy countries, is merely returning it, in relative terms, to levels enjoyed in the late 1970s. Only when expenditure on development rises and remains above 0.55 per cent of GNI will it have truly entered new territory.

10 The UK does least well on its support for technology.

11 See Clemens (2007) for an excellent review of these volumes.

12 'Development' is certainly not unique in this regard, and (as I argue below) funding only programmes that have been 'proven' to work creates its own problems, but it remains widely recognised that millions of dollars are allocated to development efforts on rather slim empirical and/or theoretical foundations.

13 To be sure, the World Bank and IMF had begun to produce major reports on governance in the early and mid-1990s, but it was only later that governance issues, especially at the sub-national level, became part of everyday policy dialogue with countries, and institutionalised through the creation of comprehensive global datasets, dedicated trust funds and specific organisational units.

14 In this instance, DFID's stance reflects a keen sensibility amongst British academics (e.g. Leftwich, 2007; Burnell and Randall, 2008) that politics is central to understanding development processes and outcomes.

15 Capability theory, as pioneered by Amartya Sen and his followers, aspires to such a status.

16 See Slater and Bell (2002) for an early critique of New Labour's development policies. The approach I take here is rather different.

17 The distinction between 'technical' and 'adaptive' problems comes from Heifetz (1994). A more detailed analytical discussion of this general set of issues is provided in Pritchett and Woolcock (2004).

18 We also lack a solid theory, in any realm of development practice, for making reasonable inferences about the 'shape' of the likely trajectory of impacts over time—that is, whether impacts are likely to be monotonically increasing and linear, a 'J' curve (things get worse before they get better), a 'step function' etc.—but that is a subject for another paper (see Woolcock, 2009; King and Behrman, 2009).

19 Some would argue this happened at the World Bank during the ten-year presidency of James Wolfensohn (1995–2005), which overlapped conspicuously with the rise of New Labour in the UK. A notable feature of Wolfensohn's presidency was the creation of the Social Development Department, which was an explicit attempt to institutionalise both a substantive set of issues (e.g. resettlement, conflict, diversity) and an alternative perspective on development processes, policies and practices.

20 These comments on metrics should not be interpreted, of course, to mean that I am hostile or indifferent to measurement concerns; in the right place, as argued at the outset of the paper, measurement is a vital part of building a much-needed and rigorous evidence base for making informed decisions. The empirical challenge, however, is to build an evidence base as diverse as the problems and 'solutions' it is addressing, not to rely (as is too often the case) on single forms of evidence, or to only recognise the validity of data forms and sources that comport with what agencies recognise ('see').

21 This is so because successfully raising the incomes of the poor and empowering marginalised groups is likely to alter prevailing power structures, social relations and rules systems (Barron et al., 2007).

References

Barron, P., R. Diprose and M. Woolcock, 'Local conflict and development projects in Indonesia: part of the problem or part of a solution?', Policy Research Working Paper No. 4212, Washington, DC, World Bank, 2007.

Bourguignon, F. and C. Morrisson, 'Inequality among world citizens: 1820–1990', *American Economic Review*, vol. 92, no. 4, 2002, pp. 727–44.

Burnell, P. and V. Randall, eds., *Politics in the Developing World*, 2nd edn, Oxford, Oxford University Press, 2008.

Carothers, T., ed., *Promoting the Rule of Law Abroad: In Search of Knowledge*, Washington, DC, Carnegie Endowment for International Peace, 2006.

Chen, S. and M. Ravallion, 'The developing world is poorer than we thought, but no less successful in the fight against poverty', Policy Research Working Paper No. 4703, Washington, DC, World Bank, 2008.

Chronic Poverty Report, 'Breaking Poverty Traps', University of Manchester and Overseas Development Institute, Chronic Poverty Research Centre, 2008.

Clemens, M., 'Smart samaritans', *Foreign Affairs*, September/October, 2007.

Collier, P., *The Bottom Billion*, Oxford, Oxford University Press, 2007.

Ferguson, J., *Global Shadows: Africa in the Neoliberal World Order*, Durham, NC, Duke University Press, 2006.

Fogel, R., *The Escape from Hunger and Premature Death, 1700–2100: Europe, America, and the Third World*, New York, Cambridge University Press, 2004.

Gibson, C. and M. Woolcock, 'Empowerment, deliberative development and local level politics in Indonesia: participatory projects as a source of countervailing power', *Studies in Comparative International Development*, vol. 43, no. 2, 2008, pp. 151–80.

Guggenheim, S. E., 'Crises and contradictions: explaining a community development project in Indonesia', in A. Bebbington, S. E. Guggenheim, E. Olson and M. Woolcock, eds., *The Search for Empowerment: Social Capital as Idea and Practice at the World Bank*, Bloomfield, CT, Kumarian Press, 2006, pp. 111–44.

Heifetz, R., *Leadership without Easy Answers*, Cambridge, MA, Harvard University Press, 1994.

Kanbur, R., 'Economic policy, distribution and poverty: the nature of disagreements', *World Development*, vol. 29, no. 6, 2001, pp. 1083–94.

King, E. and J. Behrman, 'Timing and duration of exposure in evaluation of social programs', *World Bank Research Observer*, vol. 24, no. 1, 2009, pp. 29–53.

Kraay, A., 'When is growth pro-poor? Evidence from a panel of countries', *Journal of Development Economics*, vol. 80, no. 1, 2006, pp. 198–227.

Leftwich, A., 'The political approach to institutional formation, maintenance and control: a literature review essay', Working Paper No. 15, Research Programme on Institutions for Pro-Poor Growth (IPPG), 2007.

Li, T. M., *The Will to Improve: Governmentality, Development, and the Practice of Politics*, Durham, NC, Duke University Press, 2007.

Milanovic, B., *Worlds Apart: Measuring International and Global Inequality*, Princeton, NJ, Princeton University Press, 2005.

Palmer, G., T. MacInnes and P. Kenway, *Monitoring Poverty and Social Exclusion 2007*, York, Joseph Rowntree Foundation, 2007.

Pritchett, L., 'Who is *not* poor? Dreaming of a world truly free of poverty', *World Bank Research Observer*, vol. 21, no. 1, 2006, pp. 1–23.

Pritchett, L. and M. Woolcock, 'Solutions when *the* solution is the problem: arraying the disarray in development', *World Development*, vol. 32, no. 2, 2004, pp. 191–212.

Ravallion, M., 'Inequality convergence', *Economics Letters*, vol. 80, no. 3, 2003, pp. 351–6.

Ravallion, M. and S. Chen, 'Absolute poverty measures for the developing world, 1981–2004', *Proceedings of the National Academy of Sciences*, vol. 104, no. 43, 2007, pp. 16757–62.

Roodman, D., 'The commitment to development index for Africa: how much do the richest countries help the poorest continent?', Center for Global Development Briefing Paper, May 2008.

Rosenberg, T., 'How to fight poverty: eight programs that work', *New York Times*, 16 November 2006.

Scott, J., *Seeing Like a State: How Well-Intentioned Efforts to Improve the Human Condition Have Failed*, New Haven, CT, Yale University Press, 1998.

Slater, D. and M. Bell, 'Aid and the geopolitics of the postcolonial: critical reflections on New Labour's overseas development strategy', *Development and Change*, vol. 33, no. 2, 2002, pp. 335–60.

Smith, R., 'Social security as a developmental institution? Extending the Solar case for the relative efficacy of Poor Relief Provisions under the English Old Poor Law', BWPI Working Paper No. 56, University of Manchester, 2008.

Woolcock, M., 'Toward a plurality of methods in project evaluation: a contextualized approach to understanding impact trajectories and efficacy', *Journal of Development Effectiveness*, vol. 1, no. 1, 2009, pp. 1–14.

World Bank, *World Development Report 2006: Equity and Development*, New York, Oxford University Press, 2005.

Index

Note: page numbers in italics refer to tables and diagrams; alphabetical arrangement is word-by-word.

Editorial organisation © 2008 The Political Quarterly Publishing Co. Ltd